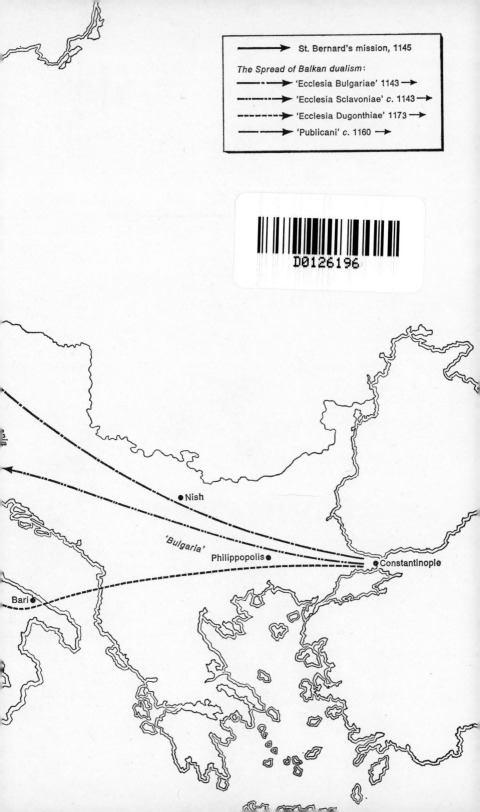

St. Bernard's mission, 1145

The Spread of Balkan dualism:

'Ecclesia Bulgariae' 1143 →
'Ecclesia Sclavoniae' *c.* 1143 →
'Ecclesia Dugonthiae' 1173 →
'Publicani' *c.* 1160 →

D0126196

• Nish

'Bulgaria'

Philippopolis •

• Constantinople

Bari •

Chapter I | Introductory

*The worst disease one can have
is to hate arguments.* – Socrates

The founder of Christianity said that his father's house had many mansions, but his followers have persisted in the conviction that they should all live in the same one. The divergences of practice and of belief which had already appeared among them in the writings of the apostles were accompanied by a ready assumption that they were to be deplored and avoided, and the early Christians rapidly developed an insistence that righteousness required a scrupulous adherence to the correct interpretation of the writings upon which the true faith was based. It was easier to agree on the necessity of orthodoxy than on its content. The fascinating processes by which uniformity of doctrine and discipline were achieved in the last centuries of antiquity do not concern us here; it is enough that the church entered the Middle Ages armed by its fathers not only with a coherent and comprehensive body of teachings, but with an organization to propagate them, and a theory of coercive discipline to maintain them. The very lively ghost of the Roman Empire which established its ascendancy over the world which the Emperors had lost to the barbarian peoples did so in the confident certainty that one faith and one church would ensure the salvation of all men. In the early middle ages that certainty was seldom and erratically challenged. The church was preoccupied with the enormous task of converting the new peoples of Europe, and the still greater one, having converted them, of providing the organization and education which would enable them to remain steadfast in the faith for ever.

Once the appeal which Arianism, the last of the ancient heresies, had made to some of the new peoples, most notably the Goths and the Lombards, had been eradicated, the enemies were not new heresiarchs but old Gods. Not until the eleventh century, when the present story begins, could they confidently be said to have been vanquished for ever from most of western Europe. Even so wherever Christianity was strong the possibility of dispute and its importance to those who participated in it were rapidly seen. In seventh-century Northumbria it was a matter of eternal life and death whether the tonsure should surround the whole skull, and the date of Easter be calculated by the Roman or the Celtic method, and important enough to bring kings to puzzle themselves in theological debate and to embitter the judgements of so charitable and balanced an historian as Bede. In the reign of Louis the Pious Amalarius of Metz endeavoured, with some success, to meet what many of his ecclesiastical contemporaries regarded as an urgent need by producing the first systematic attempt to interpret the liturgy as a whole, and by doing so laid himself open to a charge of heresy, was condemned after bitter attack by a synod at Quierzy in 838, and dismissed from his office in the diocese of Lyons.[1] He was only one of the Carolingian prelates who showed that the advance of Christianity in any of its aspects was inevitably attended by the possibility of debate and the danger of disagreement.

With few and trivial exceptions these early disputes took place among the higher clergy. Amalarius was the forerunner not of the heroes of this book, but of such men as Abelard, Aquinas and Teilhard de Chardin, who in attempting to bring Christian thought into line with the new intellectual developments of their day went beyond the conventional wisdom, and shocked more timid contemporaries who found it easier to comprehend the novelty of their conclusions than the value of their goals. Learned heresy of this kind had little in common with the doubts and certainties of ordinary, uneducated men and women. It was moved, in general, not by dissatisfaction with society, or even with the church and its activity, but by the internal dynamic of scholarship and speculation, where one proposition impels its victim ineluctably to the next. The common assumption that popular heresy derived either its impetus or its content from a debased awareness of the arguments of the schoolmen has, as we shall see, little to support it in fact.[2] Even the more sophisticated assertion that the increasing precision with which scholastic advance defined orthodoxy correspondingly increased the likelihood that any particular statement would be seen to be heretical has little relevance here: its victims were the schoolmen themselves, since they had the learning and the technique to advance new and subtle propositions. The cruder beliefs of popular heretics included few or none whose inconsistency with central tenets of Catholic teaching had not been obvious since patristic times. The early appearance of learned heresy has for us only one point to make, that the growth and advancement of Christianity, its continued ability to be adapted to new peoples and new times, involved as a necessary corollary the possibility of divergence of belief and practice within it.

Orthodox Christians, and orthodox historians, have always assumed and frequently asserted that heresy is unnatural, and therefore requires not only correction but explanation. Whether that is so in the moral sense, that it is contrary to the nature of good men, is a theological question, but historically it is evidently false: in the west orthodoxy – any orthodoxy – has reigned unchallenged only in exceptional periods and circumstances. Hence in exploring the appearance of unorthodox beliefs and practices in the eleventh and twelfth centuries which became a regular feature of European life ever since, we must approach it not in the spirit of alienists (whether charitable or severe) patiently accounting for irrational deviations from normality, but as historians observing the emergence of a natural, and even an essential ingredient of human development, at least as we have known it in Europe. This is only one, though one in the past insufficiently acknowledged, of the many traditions and institutions whose appearance we recognize in those centuries (without denying the antiquity of their roots) as the seedlings whose fitful and tangled growth has created the world we live in, and whose continuity with our own civilization we habitually acknowledge by giving our accounts of that period such titles as 'the making' or 'the awakening' or 'the birth' of Europe.

If this is true we cannot avoid asking why it was that this dissent, contained as it were in the womb of Christianity, failed to make its appearance for so long; why, although the classical heresies of Pelagius and Arius lingered until the end of the seventh century, medieval society gave birth to none of its own, at the popular level, until the eleventh.[3] The answer is limited both by our knowledge and our use of it. We know a good deal of the spread of Christianity, of the trials and martyrdoms of the missionaries who carried it from one barbarian court to another, and persuaded kings, who in turn commanded their people, of the superior potency of the Christian God and the superior elegance and plausibility of his cult. Their lives and achievements were diligently and sometimes brilliantly chronicled by the earliest European historians, of whom the greatest was Bede. We know how the bishops who succeeded the missionaries made themselves useful in the councils of their patrons, offering to peoples in the course of transition from the lives of nomad warriors to those of settlers, farmers and occasionally merchants, the techniques for the organization and government of stable societies which they had inherited from Rome and were able to adapt to simpler needs. But beyond that the deepest reasons for the rise of Christianity are obscure. Who were the priests, and how many, and how they were organized, who carried the message to the peasant, we can guess. At what times they reached what corners of the great forests, we can guess. Why the peasant listened to them, and what their message meant; when he disentangled his reverence for the new God from his obedience to the old; when, how, and even whether Christianity became the consolation of the simple in their misery, the source and frame of all their thoughts as the familiar picture of the age of faith would have us believe – these are questions which we scarcely dare ask, to which there is not a fragment of first-hand evidence that permits the attempt to answer.[4] The impenetrable silence of the forests was shared by their inhabitants.

Since history is impossible we must resort to generalization. Early medieval society was extremely simple in its structure and organization. The famous saying that there were three sorts of men, those who worked, those who fought and those who prayed, was near enough the truth. Goods circulated in sufficient quantity to allow historians to argue for the existence of 'revivals of trade' in the seventh, the ninth, and the tenth centuries. There were merchants, but there were not enough of them, and they were not deeply enough rooted in particular places for their presence to make any deep or permanent impression on the routine of everyday life. The professional functions of government, law, learning and medicine, as far as they existed at all, were roughly divided between the church and the secular aristocracy, and even among churchmen the higher were not always clearly differentiated from the nobility, or the lower from the peasantry. Among these orders there was superficially a bewildering variety of ranks, distinguishing multitudinous degrees of personal freedom between the serf who was tied to his land and wholly subject to its master, and the yeoman who held his allod by personal right, and could take it to whatever lord he chose, and between the king who gave gold or land for the loyalty of his followers, and owed service to none, and the knight who held a small fief of some local magnate at whose disposal he placed his armour and his strength. But at bottom the cliché was accurate: the great mass of mankind tilled the soil, with little to do with their lives except produce enough to keep their families alive if they could, and pass on the surplus, whether they would or not, in return for the protection of the knights against others of their kind, and of the priests and monks against eternal damnation. The religious requirements of such a world were equally simple. The higher must be assured of the propriety of their privilege, and the lower promised eternal happiness in return for the submissive acceptance of temporal misery. The more desirable what lay on the other side of the eye of the needle the more cheerfully might poverty be accepted and glorified on this; the more certain the wrath of a just God (his mercy was not much emphasized in this period) against any tendency to question the fairness of his dispensation on earth, or any attempt to abandon the station which his wisdom had ordained, the more securely the divine order would remain undisturbed by the sin of pride.

Since, in any case, opportunity for betterment rarely presented itself, there was no temptation to dispute such tenets. This was a society which barely managed to sustain itself at the level of subsistence. The seed which was sown might yield treble in a good year, but famine, disaster and disorder made sure that good years did not succeed one another with any regularity. From time to time, and especially in the reigns of Charlemagne and his son, the coincidence of good weather and comparative security from disruption allowed the surplus of wealth to reach a point where the conspicuous consumption of the nobility might include the patronage of building and learning. The increase of trade brought with it a greater circulation of coinage, and the possibility of seeking new forms of wealth, which in turn held out the promise that the means for the permanent increase of prosperity might be created, and what we know as 'economic take-off' begin.

The conditions of such an achievement are not only economic. There were until the eleventh century always new barbarians, Lombards, Arabs, Vikings and Magyars, to be attracted by manifestations of prosperity, and destroy them. The enemy within was even more dangerous and harder to control. The only means of government that was effective was the direct exercise of force. If a few dreamed that authority might be asserted through the medium of written directives there was neither the level of education required to erect nor the sanctions to enforce such a system. In what was almost entirely a natural economy there was no means of rewarding service except by gift of land, and power delegated therefore became within a generation or two power lost. Charlemagne appeared briefly to have solved the problem by generalizing the association of gifts of land with pledges of direct personal loyalty – homage – which had assisted his ancestors' rise to power, but even by the end of his reign it had become clear that it was easier to grant the land than to enforce the pledge. In consequence, although the Emperors claimed universal dominion the effective political units in Europe by the middle of the tenth century, or sooner, were of such a size as could be controlled by the entourage of one man, who proclaimed his power by promoting himself from *vicecomes* to Count. Private warfare, conducted chiefly by destroying the fields of the enemy, was endemic, regarded by contemporaries as a natural disaster, like flood, famine and disease, visited on them by the wrath of a just God, or the malevolence of the demons who infested the atmosphere. Even where any surplus of wealth could be produced in such conditions it could not be circulated. The obstacle to economic development in the early middle ages is graphically implied by the conventional tribute to a good and mighty king (especially associated with Henry I of England), that while he was on his throne a virgin could go unmolested from one end of his kingdom to the other with a purse of gold in her bosom. In the Dark Ages such a venture could seldom be undertaken by the most dissolute.

For these crudely sketched reasons the basic structure of western society remained broadly unchanged for several centuries. The procession of great events, the rise and fall of dynasties, the painful but ultimately successful defence of western Europe from external invasion, the emergence of papacy and empire as the twin pillars of its political order, concealed the slow advance of the forces that would make the medieval world. Between the seventh and tenth centuries the extension of vassalage, the elaboration of the seigneurie, the articulation of the monastic ideal and the salvaging of literacy provided the framework for the great expansion of the high middle ages. But while those potent forces gathered themselves so hesitantly the conditions which governed the daily routine and fortunes of most christians remained much the same. The church, therefore, was not required to provide accommodation for new religious needs. It maintained the machinery for intercession with the forces of destiny, the monasteries which prayed for the souls of all the faithful, the relics of saints which offered contact with the supernatural, the routine of feasts and fasts which marked the seasons of country life. Its commendation of doctrines which advocated the unquestioning acceptance of the order of things as they were was not confronted by any disposition on the part of that order to change, or by anything which suggested to men that it was in their power to change it themselves. The conservative virtues of humility, loyalty and obedience were those calculated to yield the best results in a world which had no gifts to offer more precious than order and security.

When, in the eleventh and twelfth centuries, the church began to find that it no longer commanded universal and unquestioning obedience, that there were some men who were not true followers of the faith not because they were heathens who had never been told about it, or Jews whose uncomfortable place as unbelievers in a Christian world had been traditionally, if grudgingly, accepted, but because they had deliberately rejected its teaching and authority, it was uncertain what to make of them. Needless to say the sources upon which this study is based were produced, almost without exception, by faithful and orthodox Christians. Their reports are those of men confronted by new monstrosities. They attributed them at first to the work of demons, or of the devil himself, or of simple insanity. But they soon remembered that such things had happened before. In every case of doubt it was natural to turn to the scriptures, and to the fathers of the church, which unfailingly offered precept and explanation to resolve every difficulty. Heresy was no exception, and the keys to its comprehension were provided by the greatest of Christian writers, St Paul and St Augustine.

St Paul's prophecy of the last days had a startling aptness for those who would understand the heresies which now began to appear. 'Now the Spirit manifestly saith that in the last times some shall depart from the faith, giving heed to spirits of error and doctrines of devils, speaking lies in their conscience, and having their conscience seared, forbidding to marry, to abstain from meats, which God hath created to be received with thanksgiving by the faithful and by them that have known the truth.' His warning turned out to specify the most notorious teachings of the greatest of all heretics, Mani, whose disciples renounced matrimony, and would eat no meat. Among Mani's followers the best remembered was Augustine of Hippo, who devoted much of his maturity to denouncing the most seductive of the many temptations of his youth. Within a few years of the first appearance of popular heresy in the west Adhemar of Chabannes, one of the best chroniclers of his time, had made the necessary connection. 'Manichaeans appeared in Aquitaine, leading the people astray. . . . They did not eat meat, as though they were monks, and pretended to be celibate, but among themselves they enjoyed every indulgence.'[5] The points which he thought it appropriate to note about his 'Manichees' were just those for which any reader of Paul and Augustine would look out, and established the assumptions which would dominate the explication of popular heresy not only in his own period but of its historians until the middle of the twentieth century: one of the best and most widely read modern accounts of early medieval heresy is entitled *The Medieval Manichee.*[6]

The attempts of Adhemar and others like him to reach an understanding of popular heresy and how to deal with it by assimilating it to Manicheeism will be treated in a later chapter. One consequence of their doing so, however, is inescapable from the outset. Because the sources are not only derived almost entirely from one side of the conflict, but substantially coloured by the assumption of those who compiled them that they already knew what they were dealing with, and could safely interpret what they heard from the heretics in the light of the infinitely more authoritative and more trustworthy testimony of Paul and Augustine, no history of this subject can save itself from a niggling and tedious preoccupation at every turn with the nature, significance and reliability of the information upon which it is based. The problems which arise may be illustrated and some future repetition avoided by a detailed examination of the surviving account of a single incident.

Bishop Gerard of Cambrai spent Christmas and twelfth night of 1024/5 at his palace in Arras, where news reached him that heretics were active in his diocese. 'He immediately ordered them to be found and brought before him. When they heard that they were to be questioned they prepared to escape, but were discovered by the bishop's officers and dragged back into his presence. He was very busy listening to other cases, and inquired briefly about their faith. He formed the impression that they avowed false doctrine, and ordered them to be kept in custody for three days. . .' The investigation which followed was conducted in an impressive setting. The third day was a Sunday, and the bishop, 'in full regalia, accompanied by his archdeacons bearing crosses and copies of the Gospels, processed to St Mary's church with a great crowd of clerks and of the populace to hold a synod. The whole of the appointed psalm, "Let God arise and let his enemies be scattered" was sung. Then when the bishop was seated in his court with the abbots, religious and archdeacons placed around him according to their ranks the men were taken from their place of confinement and brought before him.'[7]

The information which was exacted by this magnificent tribunal is presented to us in four forms, in addition to the rumours which preceded it, and it is noteworthy that the more remote the report becomes from the heretics themselves, the more elaborate and comprehensive become the doctrines which they are alleged to have held. At the expense of a little tedium a systematic assessment of these layers of allegation may help to show how evidence of heretical beliefs is built up. The guises in which the information is presented – each time by Gerard – are:

1. The rumours which had reached him about the heretics;
2. Their answers to his questions;
3. The confession of faith which they made and signed before he released them;
4. The sermon which he preached at the synod in rebuttal of their opinions;
5. The summary of the whole affair which he made in a letter to Bishop R. of a neighbouring diocese.[8]

1. The rumours which had reached the bishop before he met and examined the heretics add up to a comprehensive rejection of orthodox Christianity, but there is no indication how he obtained them. They were that 'they abhorred the ceremony of holy baptism, rejected the sacrament of the body and blood of Christ, denied that penance profited the sinner after confession, denied the authority of the church, condemned legitimate matrimony, saw no virtue in holy confession, and held that nobody after the time of the apostles and martyrs ought to be venerated'. It will be noted that apart from the condemnation of matrimony the consistent tendency of these

points is to set aside the role of the church as the mediator between man and God, and with it the paraphernalia of saints and sacraments through which the layman officially approached his maker. The objection to baptism, for example, is one which will become familiar. The orthodox sacrament became obnoxious to many now and during the next century or so on two grounds in particular, that it involved the assumption of assent by the infant to a series of propositions which he was not old enough to comprehend, and that it provided insurance in advance against sins whose omission or commission would be a matter of free will. In using such phrases there is some danger of imposing upon the men of Arras, or those who gossiped about them, an anachronistic awareness of what they implied, but this was the tendency of the position which Gerard was told they had adopted, and which dictated the questions he put to them.

2. The examination itself was relatively brief. The bishop, after some inaugural remarks, asked the accused,

'What is your doctrine, your discipline and your way of life, and from whom have you learnt it?'
They replied that they were followers of an Italian named Gundolfo. They had learned from him the precepts of the Gospels and the apostles, and would accept no other scripture but this, to which they would adhere in word and deed.
'How do you reconcile your belief in the Gospels with preaching against them?' [The bishop accompanied this question, notably, with a brief explanation of the authority of the Gospels for baptism, without mentioning the other sacraments which the accused were said to reject.]
'Nobody who is prepared to examine with care the teaching and rule which we have learned from our master will think that they contravene either the precepts of the Gospels or those of the apostles. This is its tenor: to abandon the world, to restrain the appetites of the flesh, to earn our food by the labour of our own hands, to do injury to nobody, to extend charity to everybody of our own faith. If these rules are followed baptism is unnecessary; if they are not it will not lead to salvation. This is the height of righteousness, to which there is nothing that baptism can add if every rule of the Gospels and apostles is observed in this way. If anyone says that baptism is a sacrament we would deny it on three grounds: first that the evil life of the minister cannot be the

vehicle for the salvation of him who is baptised; second that the
vices which are renounced at the font may be resumed later in life;
third, that the child who neither wills it nor concurs with it
knows nothing of the faith and is ignorant of his need for salvation,
does not beg for rebirth in any sense, and can make no confession
of faith: clearly he has neither free will nor faith, and cannot
confess it.'

This statement confirms the leading impression gathered from
the rumours. The central position of these men was that their
salvation was their own responsibility, and would be gained or lost
by their own efforts. The rules by which they would do it were also
clear to them, and there is no denying that they had grasped firmly
some of the important parts of the teaching both of the Gospels and
of St Paul. It also appears not only that they denied the necessity of
the intermediary role of the priesthood in principle, but that they
doubted the suitability and with it the ability of the priests of their
own day to perform it in practice. The theological point at issue is
clear and had been familiar since patristic times. Since the Donatist
controversy at least the church had found it hard to convince the
most zealous of the faithful that the efficacy of the sacraments did
not depend in any way upon the worthiness of the vehicle through
whom they were administered. This became a constant theme in our
period. One important point remains in doubt, whether in affirming
their reliance on the Gospels and the apostles the heretics intended
to abjure the rest of the Bible, or only in general terms to say that
they did not recognize other authority.[9] Finally it will be noted that
their confession contains no mention of their views on marriage, of
which the rumours had made so much, so that we cannot determine
whether it was they or the gossips who had made the step from the
restraint of the appetites of the flesh to the outright denial of matrimony. Gundolfo's views as they were understood by his followers,
therefore, represented a fairly pronounced form of what is known
nowadays as 'Bible Christianity'. It is possible that they may have
held opinions of a more extremely heterodox nature, but there is no
reason to insist that they did.

3. When the heretics had concluded their statement Bishop
Gerard embarked on a rebuttal which in its printed form runs to

forty columns of Migne's *Patrologia*, not far short of twenty thousand words. Indeed there would be a temptation to believe that in preparing his written account Gerard took the opportunity to enlarge upon what he had said, if the description of the occasion did not possess a certain air of weary authenticity.

> The day was now wearing to a close, and the lord bishop said to those who had come to listen to the proceedings, 'There are other things, brothers, which I ought to say to strengthen you in your faith, but in case I oppress you with a great burden of words let that suffice. Keep your faith unstained, and remember the words of the apostle Paul: "In the last times some shall depart from the faith . . ." '

Gerard's conclusion reveals one of the authorities which had helped to guide him in his questioning of the heretics. It may also explain why the determination expressed by the accused to 'restrain the appetites of the flesh' (in which they also followed St Paul) was persistently understood by the accusers to be tantamount to a denial of the legitimacy of matrimony, although their recorded words justify no such interpretation of it.

The recipients of this admonition were left 'stupified by the weight of the bishop's discourse', and said that 'they believed that the sum of Christian salvation could consist in nothing but what he had set out'; doubtless their untutored imaginations had difficulty in supposing that anything might have been omitted from so extensive a discourse. They were then called upon to join the bishop and the others present in a confession of faith, which was read out. They did not understand it at first because it was in Latin, but when it had been translated into the vernacular 'they confessed with a solemn oath that they abjured what had been condemned and believed what is believed by the faithful', and each of them attached a sign of the cross to the statement, as a mark of his adherence to it.

The affirmation which was required would, if it were accepted as a simple list of the errors which the accused had committed, certainly add to their number. They were, naturally, made to confess the necessity of baptism for salvation, and the possibility of sin committed after baptism being mitigated either by penance or by grace. They had to agree, what their words might reasonably have been taken to deny, that membership of the church was a requisite of salvation, which unless it simply reaffirmed the necessity of baptism must be taken as a condemnation of apostasy. Finally they were required to confirm their belief in the real presence at the mass, the necessity of communion to salvation, the virgin birth, the suffering of Christ on the cross, the ascension, and the legitimacy of matrimony. If it were supposed that all these affirmations were really necessary it would follow that the accused had denied the eucharist, and that docetism – the denial of the humanity of Christ – was probably to be added to their first statement of belief. Some have read the evidence in that way. It is, however, not only possible but probable that the affirmation was drawn up in accordance with some pre-determined formula, possibly suggested by the words of St Paul which the bishop had quoted, and that it would cover not only what the accused said they believed, but what the accusers assumed would be associated with those beliefs.[10] It is therefore a surer guide to the expectations of the bishop than the views of the accused. The suspicion that the oath was not directly based upon the confession is reinforced, though only negatively, by the absence from it of any denial that the efficacy of the sacraments depended on the virtue of the ministers, which was both one of the clearest and one of the most serious errors in the original statement. If they were not required to deny everything that they asserted it is the more probable that they had not asserted everything that they were asked to deny.

4. It is scarcely surprising that in the course of the hours which he permitted himself for the rebuttal of the heretics the bishop found time to cover all these points and a number of others. They included the condemnation of the practice which Celtic monks had followed,[11] but which is nowhere else mentioned in association with popular heresy, of washing one another's feet in sacramental fashion, of the denial that a church is a house of God, of the altar and of the use of incense; the refutation of objection to the use of bells in churches, and to insistence on burial in holy ground because it was only for the financial benefit of priests; the defence of ordination, and of prayers for the dead. He asserted the necessity of

confession, defended the use of psalmody in church services, insisted upon veneration of the cross, held that images of Christ and the saints should not be spurned because they were the work of human hands, and defended the hierarchy of the church.

Among these points which Gerard's oration covered are many which would be voiced in the future by heretics, particularly in the region of his diocese,[12] and it is quite possible that some of them at least had been heard in his time. Beyond its reference to St Paul his exposition did not draw consistently on patristic sources. There is no explicit suggestion of Manicheeism, and some of the most notoriously 'Manichaean' practices, such as the avoidance of meat, are not mentioned; it is therefore reasonable to suppose that some of his fears at least were founded on reality. Nevertheless it is clear that this is not a list of the errors of Gundolfo and his followers, who had neither professed nor been asked to abjure them. Its presence in the account of their trial, however, does not require any elaborate explanation.[13] It was a standard device of rhetoric to use some real occasion as the purported reason for the expression of views which an author wished to place in circulation, as St Augustine had presented his long-nourished theory of the two cities as a response to the sack of Rome by the Visigoths,[14] so that Gundolfo's followers may be regarded as the immediate excuse rather than the only reason for the presentation of their bishop's defence of his faith. Alternatively, those who prefer the prosaic to the rhetorical mode of explanation will recall that bishops and others in positions of authority do not always think it necessary to wait for a misdemeanour to be committed before they denounce it. In either case Gerard's remarks may encourage the suspicion that these were not the only critics whom the church of his region had encountered at this time, but they do not justify the attribution of so exotic a variety of convictions to the followers of Gundolfo.

5. That Gerard had been worried about heresy before this incident is confirmed by his own final account of it, contained in the prefatory letter which is attached to the account of the synod. It is addressed to Bishop R. of a neighbouring diocese, either Roger I of Châlons or Reginard of Liège.[15] Gerard claimed that he had previously warned his colleague that there were heretics in his diocese,

and that the infection of his own by their 'missionaries' was the consequence of R's having been successfully deceived by those whom he had himself interrogated, and whom he had released without condemnation or punishment. In the diocese of Cambrai 'they could not be made to confess by any manner of persuasion until some of those whom they had imbued with the evil of their heresy were taken, and partially explained their teaching to us'; the 'partial explanation' was characterized, the letter concludes, by the denial of mass, the rejection of penance, and the condemnation of matrimony.

Gerard's letter is not wholly consistent either in itself or with the document which it accompanied. It is clear that those who were questioned at the synod were from the diocese of Cambrai, not the 'missionaries' from outside; but if these missionaries were not captured, what is the point of claiming that they could not be made to divulge their beliefs? Had some of them been taken on an earlier occasion, but refused to speak? Or were Gerard and his clerks convinced, as authorities sometimes are, of the presence of a sinister antagonist which they cannot identify? The latter suspicion may be reinforced by the comment that those who were caught only 'partially' confessed. That is to say that Gerard knew before he started, or thought he did, what the right answers to his questions would be. He therefore felt it proper to summarize the heresy to his fellow bishop by specifying three errors to none of which the accused had in fact confessed. It was true that their assertion that salvation followed from a scrupulous observance of the precepts of the Gospels, and from nothing else, might be held to involve the denial of penance, but we will remember, if Gerard did not, that simple people do not always recognize or endorse what the sophisticated regard as the logical corollaries of their stated convictions. On the same grounds yet more scepticism must be attached to the assertions that they denied both the mass and matrimony, for their recorded words – recorded under the aegis of Gerard himself – say no such thing.

It is not, of course, to be expected that an eleventh-century bishop should hold himself bound by the rules of evidence which would be applied in a modern court, or by a modern historian. That is why his assertions, honest and zealous as they undoubtedly were, must be treated with scepticism. The temporal circumstances, the particular beliefs of particular heretics who may or may not have understood the implications of everything they said, were little to him, for he was concerned with the security of the faith against its eternal enemies; nevertheless, they are everything to us. The point is of some importance in the light of the attitude of the accused men to the whole proceeding. No doubt they were frightened by their three days in prison,[16] awed by the magnificence of the occasion, and exhausted by the eloquence of the bishop, and no doubt all these things contributed to their submissiveness. Nevertheless an unsympathetic account leaves a clear impression that they were surprised to be told that what they believed was heretical. When they were first challenged they replied, with something of the sense of being misunderstood which enthusiasts often have, that 'nobody who is prepared to examine with care the teaching and rule which we have learnt from our master will think that they contravene either the precepts of the Gospels or those of the apostles'. When the bishop had finished his address they could only reply that they believed that 'the sum of Christian salvation could consist in nothing but what the bishop had set out'. When they had subscribed their confession, to which they made no demur, they departed happily enough, having shown themselves free of the pertinacity which was the true mark of the heretic.

It is possible, of course, to see dissimulation in all this, as Gerard apparently did; like all inquisitors we can see it everywhere if we look for it. Two considerations weigh powerfully against it. The theory of dissimulation requires that the dissimulators should have been able to distinguish between what was orthodox and what was not in their beliefs: why then did they confess unhesitatingly to beliefs about baptism which were plainly heretical? Secondly, one of the most remarkable episodes in this whole affair is the reluctance of the accused to sign a confession of faith simply because they could not understand the language in which it was written; they had after all the assurance of the bishop that it was fully orthodox. In that they showed themselves indeed the stuff of which heretics were made, by insisting that they could only affirm on their own knowledge, and not on the assertion of authority. But by signing it with their crosses they equally proclaimed their adherence to the doctrines it specified, for if they had been doing so insincerely, just to get away, they would scarcely have made such a fuss, or deprived themselves of a splendid excuse for disowning their confession of orthodoxy once they had regained their freedom.

Bishop Gerard's heretics emerge from this scrutiny as much less radical theologians, but perhaps as rather more interesting men, than he supposed them to be. They appear as simple men, who through Gundolfo heard the message of the New Testament, and were moved by it. From it they drew some conclusions about the nature of righteous living and the role of the church which were natural enough in the context of the fervent conviction which they evidently entertained, that salvation required devoted and vigorous personal effort. A man who is really frightened of hell fire tends to lose his confidence in the efficacy of other people's efforts to save him from it. As for the mysterious Gundolfo, he must be left to fancy. He had presumably departed from Arras and its region before this date, and nothing else is known of him. He has been a convenient figure, as an Italian, as perhaps a merchant, as possibly a fugitive, to sustain a variety of interpretations of this episode, but strictly there is no alternative but to judge his disciples, as they would certainly have preferred, by their own account of themselves.

The account of the synod of Arras is unusual in containing within itself so many distinguishable versions of the story which it tells, but in many ways Bishop Gerard, or the clerk who composed it at his behest, is typical of the writers to whom we owe the sources upon which this book is based. Most of them were perfectly honest, but they looked for what they expected to find. When they had the opportunity to question heretics, or men accused of heresy, the questions which they put were prompted less by their experience than by their reading of the Bible, and of the fathers of the church. When they did not get the answers which they expected they were less inclined to attribute it to their having been misled by their own preconceptions than to the mendacity, or lack of frankness, of their witnesses. When they had to pick out the salient points in some story or rumour which had reached them, or in what they had seen and heard for themselves, they were naturally disposed to choose the ones which were consistent with, or suggestive of, the threats which they had already identified. In this they did not differ greatly from most historians or reporters of any period, for it is always necessary to make sense of the scattered pickings of observation and chance report by placing them in the context of a broader frame of reference. In short, there is no such thing as a complete or wholly objective historical account, and the sources for early medieval heresy are no exception.

Two consequences of this particular frame of reference are especially important. In the first place it produced a strong tendency to concentrate on what various groups of heretics had in common, rather than to distinguish the differences between them. Hence there was an increasing probability as time passed that each manifestation of religious dissent would be assimilated by those who encountered it into the general pattern which already existed in the minds of the observers. This tendency has been carried very much further by modern historians with the results that, until recently, the appearance of the dualist heresies of the Byzantine world in the west was believed to have taken place a century or more before – as it now seems to most historians – it really did, and that popular heresy in this period has appeared to be more uniform than it really was. Secondly, as those who asked the questions became increasingly confident that they knew the answers already the character of investigation was replaced by that of confession. That process was concluded when the inquisition began to use torture to make sure of getting the right answers, which it was authorized to do by Innocent IV in 1252. From this point onwards, as observers of modern totalitarian states know too well, the statements of heretics are a rich source of information on the fears of the inquisitors, but not on the beliefs of the heretics. But the introduction of torture, while it finally discredits the evidence of the inquisition in the eye of the modern writer, was only the culmination of a long process which made the predictions of the interrogators self-fulfilling. The imprisonment of the men of Arras before the synod, the setting of the synod itself, and the questions which Gerard put, all increased the likelihood that they would seek their release by complying with the expectations of the tribunal, and the inclusion in Gerard's oration, the confession of faith and the letter to Bishop R. of important tenets which had not appeared in their voluntary statement gave it a coherence which, from the bishop's point of view, it greatly needed. In general such factors as these gain in weight as the church's experience and nervousness of heresy increased, and I have therefore leaned most heavily in the pages which follow on the earliest evidence, and used as sparingly as possible what comes from much after the middle of the twelfth century – though for the Cathars there is no other – when the stereotypes were becoming fully formed and widely known.

There remains one more effect of the contemporary analysis which has had great importance. The identification of the history of popular heresy in the medieval west with that of 'the medieval manichee' succeeded until very recently in distracting attention from consideration of its real causes. It makes no difference to the sources: even if their authors had not thought that they were dealing with Manichees – and sometimes, like Gerard, they did not – they would have continued to attribute the appearance of heresy either to corruption from some external source, whether supernatural or simply foreign, or to native wickedness. They were concerned, quite properly from their own point of view, not to account for heresy, but to correct it and prevent it from spreading. But if bishops and chroniclers may be excused the discussion of causes, historians may not. Even at the risk of being wrong – and happily it is, on the whole, a less serious risk for us than it was for our heretics – we are bound to ask whether the first popular rejection of the authority of the western church did not imply some changes in the nature of the society which that church had done so much to form. And in contemplating the pioneers of dissent, who with all their naïvetés, absurdities and excesses have received short shrift from chroniclers and historians alike, we will do well to remember the advice of Spinoza: *humanas actiones non ridere, non lugere, neque detestari, sed intellegere*. They are greatly in need of understanding.

Part One: | *Wolves in Sheep's Clothing*

Chapter II | The Awakening of Europe

The cities of northern Italy preserved their
ancient character for longer, and began their medieval recovery
sooner, than those of other parts of Europe. In a world where
advance was so often achieved through the recovery of the past it is not
always easy to distinguish between freakish survival and precocious
revival, so it is fitting that Ravenna should have been the home
of the first convicted heretic of the central middle ages. It had been
the seat of Byzantine government in Italy until the beginning of the
eighth century, and a brief Lombard occupation did not destroy its
pre-eminence. The bishopric remained one of the richest as well as
one of the most prestigious in the west, and the habit of maritime
trade persisted sufficiently in the ninth and tenth centuries to preserve a merchant community there, and an artisan class vigorous
enough to support a guild organization.[1] It even appears that the
city had retained the tradition of public and secular education which
had disappeared from northern Europe, for the heretic it produced
is described as a grammarian.[2] His name was Vilgard, and his heresy

appropriate to his profession. He was visited in a dream by Virgil, Horace and Juvenal, who promised that his devotion to their works would soon be rewarded by fame the equal of their own. Thus inspired Vilgard 'began to preach many things contrary to the faith', and in particular that 'the words of the poets ought to be believed in all cases'; after a time he was convicted of heresy by the Archbishop, but his punishment is not recorded.

The Cluniac chronicler Ralph Glaber, who tells the story of Vilgard as part of his demonstration of the prophecy of the apostle John that 'Satan would be released when a thousand years had passed' (although Archbishop Peter died in 971), attributes his fall to the characteristic preference of the Italians for secular to religious learning. The guiding genius of his order, Saint Odo of Cluny, had himself once dreamed of Virgil, whose works were shown to him as a beautiful vase filled with writhing serpents,[3] and as admiration for pagan literature increased the tension which his dream expressed was often echoed again. Vilgard's most learned contemporary, Gerbert of Aurillac, was whispered to be a magician, and in the middle of the eleventh century another Italian grammarian, Anselm of Besate, complained that he was 'shunned as a demoniac, almost as a heretic' because of his scholarship. Anselm also was troubled in his dreams, and once thought himself in heaven, the object of contention for his loyalty between the spirits of his saved ancestors and three beautiful virgins who represented Grammar, Logic and Rhetoric, and who won the day.[4]

It is possible, as some have thought, that Vilgard advocated a humanist rejection of Christian belief, if perhaps more likely that he was unclear, or misunderstood, in attempting what would be one of the great intellectual tasks of the next century, to harmonize Catholic faith with a love of classical learning. In either case he belongs to the context of that debate, rather than to the tradition of popular heresy, to which intellectual advance made little direct contribution. There is, however, another incident which shows, more emphatically than Vilgard's, how the early stages of educational advance might be associated with religious deviance more easily, or in a different manner, than would be the case later, when education began to shed the aura of suspicion and mystery which attended the first stirrings of its revival. The schools of Orléans reached the height of their fame as a centre of literary studies in the middle of the twelfth century, but it was when he went there to study 'true authors' that a Norman clerk named Heribert made the discovery which led to the first burning of heretics in the medieval west, in 1022.[5] He met two clerks, Stephen and Lisois, 'widely famed for their wisdom, outstanding in holiness, generous with alms', who introduced him to doctrines to which he was unwise enough, when he returned home, to try to convert his master Aréfast. Aréfast, a relation of the Counts of Normandy and high in their counsels, was shocked by Heribert's tale, and thought it his duty to report it to Robert the Pious, and to urge the king to do everything he could to uproot the heresy from his realm. He was promptly commissioned to go to Orléans himself in the guise of a student, and to infiltrate the seditious gathering; the evidence which he would give was as sensational in its nature, and received as uncritically, as is generally the case of information obtained in that way.

The clerks at Orléans received Aréfast with caution, and taught him at first by discussing texts of the scriptures in an unexceptionable way, though 'employing certain figures of speech'. As they became more confident of his attentiveness their language became more unusual, until they addressed him in the tones of religious illuminism:

> We regard you as a tree in a wood, which is transplanted to a garden, and watered regularly until it takes root in the earth. Then it is stripped of thorns and other excess matter, and pruned down to the ground with a hoe, so that a better branch can be inserted into it, which will later bear sweet fruit. In the same way you will be carried out of this world into our holy company. You will soak in the waters of wisdom until you have taken shape, and armed with the sword of the Lord are able to avoid the thorns of vice. Foolish teachings will be shut out from your heart and you will be able with a pure heart to receive our teaching, which is handed down from the Holy Spirit.

By this metaphor Stephen and Lisois laid claim to a *gnosis*, a special knowledge of the holy which might be shared only by those who would undergo, as they had, a process of personal transformation.

When Aréfast expressed his eagerness to go further, he was offered his transformation:

> There is no doubt brother that until now you have lain with the ignorant in the Charybdis of false belief. Now you have been raised to the summit of all truth. With unimpeded mind you may begin to open your eyes to the light of the true faith. We will open the door of salvation to you. Through the laying of our hands upon you you will be cleansed of every spot of sin. You will be replenished with the gift of the Holy Spirit, which will teach you unreservedly the underlying meaning of the scriptures, and true righteousness. When you have fed on the heavenly food, and have achieved inner satisfaction you will often see angelic visions with us, and sustained by that solace you will be able to go where you will without let or hindrance whenever you want to. You will want for nothing, for God in whom are all treasures of wealth and wisdom, will never fail to be your companion in all things.

Aréfast was assured, in short, that by his initiation he would be freed of the ordinary restraints of the human condition, and insulated against the mistaken and distorted convictions of ordinary Christians, would enter a world in which he would share with his brother initiates a special intimacy with the divine, an understanding of the *real* meaning of the scriptures, which was denied to the lump of orthodox humanity. This process to which he was subjected, of preparation and initiation, has been regarded as an indication that Stephen and Lisois were neo-manichees, and the laying-on of hands which they promised as the *teleiosis* of the Bulgarian Bogomils which, as the *consolamentum*, would be the central sacrament of the western Cathars by the end of the twelfth century.[6] On the contrary, this transposition of reality, the insistence that language, experience and truth would all assume an entirely new aspect as a result of the initiation, confirms that they were nothing of the sort. Bogomilism, like Christianity, had of course its instruction and its ceremony of confirmation in the faith, but it was not, any more than Christianity, a gnostic religion in this sense, of having a special knowledge, a special perception of divinity and reality which were reserved to initiates, and wholly remote from what was believed by outsiders. To the Bogomil who received the *teleiosis* and the Cathar who was consoled, as to the Christian when he was

baptized, the faith to which he now finally committed himself was
the same as that in which he had been trained and prepared; there
were no new or secret doctrines, no relearning of familiar language,
and the change thus marked in his spiritual condition did not
transport him into a world distinct from that which was inhabited
by those who had made less progress on the same road.

Gnostic sects had proliferated among the early Christians, and
there is nothing to deny, or support, a suspicion that by obscure
survival or chance reading Stephen and Lisois had picked up their
ideas from some such source. But caution will reflect that such
groups as these have always been common enough, and still are,
at the fringes of intellectual circles in particular.[7] The language
which assures the security of the initiates by excluding all contrary
opinion as, by definition, not simply uninformed or mistaken, but
the product of delusion, which is founded on the premise that only
those who have accepted the teachings of the sect in full are capable
of commenting on it, which confines reality itself to the circle of the
transformed, is familiar in our own restless times. Such coteries
habitually reinforce their solidarity by meeting if not in secret, at
least with discretion, and by evolving ritual and ceremony which
will, whether justly or not, arouse the direst suspicions of outsiders.
So it was with the heretics of Orléans. They met by night, it was
alleged, in a cellar to which they summoned the devil, that they
might enjoy with him and each other – heedless of sex, blood
relationship, or religious vows – an intercourse which 'they regarded as holy and religious work'. The infants born of these
unions were burned, and their ashes turned into a dust which was
used in sacrament, and which had the power of fixing whoever
consumed it irrevocably in his adherence to the sect.

The lurid orgies attributed to the clerks of Orléans are described,
in fact, in words taken from Justin Martyr's indignant account of
the slanders which were directed against early Christians, and from
the end of the twelfth century would be repeated with increasing
elaboration to form eventually the basis of the medieval witch craze.
They must be interpreted, therefore, not as a description of what
Stephen, Lisois, and their fellows actually did, but as the way in
which the Catholic chronicler – a monk of the house which Aréfast

later joined – found himself able to express the orthodox understanding of it. In that light the suspicions which he expressed have
a certain universality, resembling as they do familiar stereotypes
not only of antiquity and the middle ages, but of modern times.[8]
By propelling themselves, as it were, into another world the heretics
almost compelled the orthodox to suppose that it was the world
ruled by the Devil; by proclaiming divine law, as it was commonly
understood, to be empty and meaningless, they inevitably engendered the belief that they must flout it in the most outrageous, and
tempting, fashion that could be imagined.

The theology of Stephen and Lisois was consistent with their
gnostic spirit. The ceremonies and sacraments of the church were
condemned as illusory; 'Christ was not born of the Virgin Mary;
he did not suffer for men; he was not really buried in the sepulchre,
and did not rise from the dead; there is no cleansing of sin in
baptism, nor in the sacrament of the body and blood of Christ
administered by a priest. Nothing is to be gained from praying to
the holy martyrs and confessors.' On the face of it these are denials
that would become familiar, of the humanity of Christ and the
legitimacy of the doctrines and disciplines which the church had
evolved since his time. But the demeanour of Stephen and Lisois
at the public interrogation which followed their arrest, shows that
their teachings had a still more radical basis than that. When the
bishop of Beauvais proclaimed his belief in the birth, humanity,
suffering and resurrection of Christ, they replied 'We were not
there, so we cannot believe that these things are true.' They denied
the virgin birth because 'What nature denies is always out of harmony with creation,' and revealed their fundamental conviction
quite starkly when it was put to them that divine creation necessarily
preceded the operations of nature:

> You may tell all this to those who are learned in earthly things,
> who believe the fabrications which men have written on the skin
> of animals. We believe in the law written within us by the Holy
> Spirit, and hold everything else, except what we have learnt from
> God, the maker of all things, empty, unnecessary, and remote
> from divinity. Therefore bring an end to your speeches and do
> with us what you will. Now we see our king reigning in heaven. He
> will raise us to his right hand in triumph and give us eternal joy.

The canonical definition of heresy includes the condition that it is 'an opinion founded on scripture, contrary to the teaching of the church. . . .' The stipulation is not an empty one. Although in the negative aspects of their beliefs, in what they denied of Catholic teaching, Stephen and Lisois seemed to have much in common with other heretics among their contemporaries and later, the ground which they stated for it placed them in a wholly different category. The men of Arras who were questioned by Gerard of Cambrai had read the New Testament, and been led by it to doubt some of the teachings of the church. Mani and Bogomil, and the western Cathars of the next century, were all led by the same process to question Catholic belief (in different degrees) still more radically and comprehensively. But all of them, whatever place they gave to their own capacity to interpret the scriptures, held, rightly, that their beliefs were ultimately founded on them, or on parts of them. They could, in fact, engage with Catholics in a debate which had some common ground, which started at least from the same place. Stephen and Lisois were in a wholly different case. 'The fabrications which men had written on the skins of animals' were nothing to them but part of the great delusion in which all who had not shared their own transforming experience conducted a meaningless existence. They had removed themselves so completely from the world of other men's reality that they were not, according to the strict letter of the canonical definition, heretics at all. Their *gnosis* carried them beyond heresy, 'out of this world, into our holy company'.

If the sect of Stephen and Lisois was not heresy, neither was it popular. Canons of Orléans belonged to the aristocracy of the church, and among them these two were not humble; they may have owed their benefices to royal provision, for Lisois had once been 'beloved by the king for his apparent holiness', and Stephen was formerly the confessor of Queen Constance, who avenged his treachery by striking out his eye with a stick as he left the church in which they had been tried. According to Adhemar of Chabannes nine other canons were burned with them, and the body of a tenth, named Theodatus, who had died three years earlier, was exhumed when he was found to have been of their number. John of Fleury reported that the total burned was fourteen 'of the higher clergy and more respectable laity of the city', and the two of their disciples whose repentance is noted were, respectively, a clerk and a nun.[9] What Aréfast had uncovered, in short, was a cult of spiritual élitism composed of members of the social and (in that as clerks they were *literati*) intellectual élite, in a city which, backward as it was, was itself a centre of royal favour, spiritual prestige, and educational progress. Their history is told here largely out of respect for tradition, for they were perfectly right to suppose themselves a world away from most of those with whom these pages are concerned.

Adhemar of Chabannes created this confusion by assuming that the clerks of Orléans were 'Manichees', and it is worth noting that Paul of St Père de Chartres, upon whose chronicle this account is chiefly based, did not apply that label to them, even though his recourse to Justin Martyr for details of what happened at their meetings makes it plain that he was as ready as any of his contemporaries to seek the aid of the fathers in the identification of present ills. Adhémar wrote of them in the context of another, slightly earlier, appearance of heresy which he reports with regrettable brevity. About 1018 'Manichaeans appeared in Aquitaine, leading the people astray. They denied baptism, the cross, and all sound doctrine. They did not eat meat, and pretended to be celibate, but among themselves they enjoyed every indulgence. They were messengers of Anti-Christ, and caused many to wander from the faith.'[10] Some of them, he said, were discovered and destroyed at Toulouse, and others appeared in various parts of the western Languedoc, 'concealing themselves in hideouts and corrupting men and women wherever they could'.

In spite of Adhémar's natural assumption that these Manichees were like those of Orléans – especially in the quality of their sexual lives – his account makes it plain that they were not. He describes an evangelistic movement, quite distinct from that which Aréfast had to seek out surreptitiously and join in secret, and one directed, if any precision at all can be attached to the language of so short a report, to the populace in general. He knew from St Augustine that the ideals they proclaimed were those of the Manichees, but also, as his words betray, that for celibacy and the avoidance of meat the monastic order offered a far closer and more familiar model.

A return across the Alps will present the same dilemma. In 1028 Archbishop Aribert of Milan undertook a visitation of his suffragan dioceses.[11] At Turin word reached him that 'a new heresy had recently been established in the castle above a place called Monforte'. He immediately ordered that one of the heretics should be brought before him, 'so that he could have a trustworthy account of it'. He heard a strange story. He was confronted by an educated man – *ingenuus et acutissimus*, – named Gerard, who welcomed the opportunity to expound his beliefs, although he was sophisticated enough to tread carefully at the points where he verged on heresy.

Gerard represented a love of virginity as the foundation of his convictions. He and his brothers had wives indeed, but instead of sleeping with them, they 'loved them as we would mothers or sisters'. They would not eat meat, and held all their possessions in common. The community recognized elders, *majores*, whose particular duty it was to maintain a continuous chain of prayer, never pausing by day or night. Most strikingly of all, 'none of our number ends his life except in torment, the better to avoid eternal tortures . . . if any of us is dying a natural death his neighbour among us kills him in some way before he gives up the ghost'. Remarkable though they were, none of these points was heretical except the last, which emerged not in Gerard's initial statement, but during the examination which followed it. This eccentricity apart he might have been describing a voluntary religious community of a kind common enough in early eleventh-century Italy, which under more orthodox direction would give birth to new religious orders at Camaldoli, Vallombrosa and Fonte Avellana. It may indeed be suspected that Gerard's community shared part of its inspiration as well as of its aspirations with the new monasticism, one of whose stimulants was the wide admiration aroused by the Greek monks whose communities had flourished in Byzantine Italy during the tenth century, and many of whom wandered farther afield to spread their reputation and the ascetic tradition which they practised, to universal regard, so much more assiduously than their counterparts in the Latin traditions.[12] Byzantine monasticism was itself divided in the tenth century by a debate similar to that which would arise in the west in the eleventh, as to how far it befitted a monk to press his humiliation of the flesh. Among the most extreme were those who had been affected by the 'Messalian' tradition, which advocated universal celibacy, for laity as well as religious, and which was characterized in its religious observances by the endless chain of prayer.[13] Cosmas the Priest, who wrote of the Bogomil heresy in tenth-century Bulgaria, was forthright in expressing his conviction that the expression of such extreme hostility to the flesh engendered heresy among the laity, and it seems possible that Gerard and his fellows were a case in point. That view would certainly be consistent with the neo-platonist influence which became apparent, on questioning, in their theology, and which was also associated with the Messalian stream of Byzantine monasticism in general, though not necessarily in relation to the particular points discussed by Aribert and Gerard.

Aribert began by asking for an account of Gerard's doctrines, and particularly of his views on the Trinity.

'I mean by the Father eternal God, who created all things, and in whom all things come to rest. I mean by the Son the soul of man beloved by God. I mean by the Holy Ghost the understanding of divine wisdom, by which all things are separately ruled.' [This was less than exact.]

'What have you to say of our Lord Jesus Christ, born of the Virgin Mary by the word of the Father?'

'Jesus Christ of whom you speak is a soul sensually born of the Virgin Mary; born, that is to say of the Holy Scriptures. The Holy Spirit is the spiritual understanding of the Scriptures.'

At this point Aribert changed his line of questioning, perhaps hoping to detect other areas of weakness before he returned to what had been if not a heterodox certainly an unusual account of the Trinity.

'Why do you marry if it is not to have children? How are men to be born?'

'If all men married without corruption the human race would increase without coition, as the bees do.'

'Where do we find absolution from our sins? From the Pope, or from a bishop, or from any priest?'

This was the crucial question, the issue not only of doctrine but of authority, and Gerard was forced for the first time unambiguously to concede his heterodoxy.

'We do not have the Roman Pontiff, but another one, who daily visits our brothers scattered across the world. When God gives him to us spiritually we are given complete absolution from our sins.'

Now, after establishing how the heretics ended their lives in torment, Aribert returned to the central issue, and asked Gerard 'whether he believed in the Catholic faith held by the Roman church, in baptism and in the Son of God born of the flesh of the Virgin Mary, and that his true flesh and blood are sanctified by the word of God through the Catholic priest, even if he is a sinner'.

'There is no Pope but our pope, even though his head is not tonsured, and he is not ordained.'

The heretical nature of Gerard's beliefs was no longer in doubt, but the source of the heresy has been in dispute ever since. The insistence on chastity, and on abstention from meat have been taken as evidence, here as with Adhémar's 'Manichees', of the presence of Bulgarian Bogomils or their influence, and the practice of putting each other to death has been likened to the ritual suicide, the *endura*, which was attributed to some Cathars late in the thirteenth century.[14] The *endura*, however, was a suicidal, not a homicidal practice, and one which was taken up by the Cathars, if it was at all, very late in their history, when disorganization and persecution had brought the Cathar religion beyond the point where it can reasonably be compared with these earlier heresies. The treatises which detail the beliefs of the Cathars at the height of their prosperity explain rather that the myth of the *endura* grew up because the inflexibility of their insistence that no food must be taken without a prefatory prayer was such that those too weak to say their prayers sometimes preferred to starve to death rather than break the rule.[15] This is very different from the practice expounded by Gerard. Moreover Gerard's discussion of the problem of coition presents a position which neither Cathar nor Bogomil would have endorsed. His assertion that ideally the human race would increase without coition is directly contrary to the view of the true dualist that human bodies imprisoned fragments of light, or the souls of angels stolen from heaven by Satan, and hence that their liberation by ending the human race was precisely what was to be desired; Gerard presented chastity as an end in itself, whereas for Bogomil or Cathar it was a means to an end.

The same response points to the alternative. The classical image of the bees, whose supposed capacity to increase their numbers without coition had provided St Ambrose, Isidore of Seville and Alcuin with an image of true purity, would express admirably the exaltation of chastity that was nourished by the neo-platonist strain which late Carolingian theology developed under the leadership of Eriugena. The same neo-platonist impulse to remove divinity from the language of the flesh is exhibited by Gerard's description of God 'in whom all things come to rest', of the Son as 'the soul of man beloved by God', and of the Holy Spirit as 'the understanding of divine wisdom', which corresponds closely to Eriugena's description of the Trinity. Eriugena's tradition was maintained in the schools of northern Gaul in the tenth century by men like Hericius of Auxerre and his pupil Remigius, and at places like Lobbes, Laon and Liège, at all of which Ratherius of Verona, in whose writings it was widely reflected, spent prolonged periods after he attained his bishopric. Whether or not Gerard of Monforte had actually been educated in Gaul, the vocabulary and orientation of the discourse which he conducted with Aribert undoubtedly displays that influence.[16] It was an intellectual background which harmonized easily with the ascetic and spiritual traditions of the Greek monasticism to whose presence in Italy the ethical aspirations and Messalian rituals of the followers of Gerard seem to be attributable: both, after all, were derived ultimately from the writings and spiritual heritage of the Greek fathers. This is not at all the same thing as to suggest the presence at Monforte of any influence from the Bulgarian Bogomils; it is possible that they too, at some stage in their evolution, may have owed something to the promptings of orthodox neo-platonism, but there is nothing to indicate that there was any link between them and Gerard, whose teachings and religious practices are readily explicable without recourse to them.

There is no indication of the size or composition of most of

Gerard's following. The castle of Monforte was a natural centre of influence, and possibly of local resistance to Archbishop Aribert's consolidation of the domination of Milan over its region which carried with it an increased subjection of the peasantry to the aggrandisement of their lords.[17] Nevertheless that Gerard was an educated man, and that the countess of the Monforte was one of his disciples suggest strongly that this is another case of heterodoxy among the privileged rather than of 'popular' heresy in the social sense. On the other hand this was not a gnostic group. Despite the apparent eccentricity of its rituals, its leader neither laid claim to any peculiarly esoteric familiarity with the divine will, nor displayed any reluctance to conduct his discussion with Aribert on the basis that as reasonable men they could exchange views on the interpretation of the scriptures in a reasonable way.

Aribert himself indulged no further speculation. He sent a body of soldiers to the castle to arrest the heretics, the countess among them. They were taken to Milan, but instead of accepting the Catholic faith they took advantage of the interest which they aroused – and showed, again, a different temper from the clerks at Orléans – to seek converts to their faith, and 'as though they were good priests daily spread false teachings wrenched from the scriptures among the peasants who came to town to see them'. Such activity was too much for the city fathers, who insisted on burning those who refused, as many did, to be converted to orthodoxy. It was against Aribert's wish, as the chronicler does his memory the justice of recording, that a large number of them went to their deaths.

Among the ill omens of the millennium which were so carefully collected by Ralph Glaber was the story of another heretic, very different from Vilgard of Ravenna. He was a peasant named Leutard, of Vertus in the diocese of Châlons-sur-Marne, and his heresy, regarded by Ralph as a *vesania*, was attributed, once again, to a dream.[18] Leutard, asleep in the fields after an exhausting day's work, dreamed that he was visited not by classical poets, but by a swarm of bees which entered his body through his genitals, and made their way through it stinging him and buzzing loudly as they left his mouth. They seemed to speak to him, 'bidding him to do things impossible to men', and when he awoke, more tired than he had been before, he set out to obey their commands. He cast off his wife, 'as though he effected the separation by command of the Gospel', and then went to the church and broke up the cross, and the image of Jesus. To the onlookers he explained that he did so in obedience to divine revelation, and quickly attracted a considerable following among the common people; after a time Bishop Gebuin of Châlons succeeded in convincing them that Leutard should be condemned as a heretic, and he, deprived of his influence, drowned himself in a well.

The pathetic history of Leutard of Vertus may lend itself too easily to speculation. The sensation of burning in the genitals was one symptom of ergotism, or St Antony's fire, the disease contracted by eating flour made from weather-damaged corn, which numbered insanity among its consequences; coupled with the parting from his wife it is also an obvious target for those who would count sexual guilt among the roots of religious enthusiasm. Ralph Glaber records only two of his doctrines, that the payment of tithe was needless and foolish, and that some parts of the scriptures were of value, while others should not be believed. Whatever may be hazarded about the nature of Leutard's personal motivation, it is more significant that this message brought him a following which persisted for some ten years after his death, when Gebuin's successor Roger found it necessary to call a synod to combat it in 1015, and that he inspired the first of a series of incidents which connected heresy with the diocese of Châlons in the first half of the eleventh century. Bishop Roger was probably the recipient of the letter which Gerard of Cambrai attached to the account of the synod of Arras in 1025, which accused him of having questioned heretics in his diocese but failing to unmask and punish them, with the result that their message spread to Arras. His successor, also named Roger, himself wrote to Wazo, Bishop of Liège between 1043 and 1048, to ask his advice on how to deal with 'some peasants who followed the perverse teaching of the Manichees [and] were holding secret meetings' in his diocese.[19] The three incidents are widely separated in time, but there is no other diocese of which it can be said that three consecutive bishops had to deal with popular heresy before the middle of the twelfth century.

It is difficult, nevertheless, to decide how closely the heretics associated with Châlons resembled each other. Roger II told Wazo that the 'Manichees' of whom he complained 'make anyone they can join their sect, abhor marriage, shun the eating of meat, and believe it profane to kill animals, presuming to assimilate to their heresy the words of the Lord in the commandment which prohibits killing'. His summary is very similar to that which Gerard of Cambrai may have sent his predecessor, Roger I, and that fact, coupled with the use of the term 'Manichee', will give us pause, when it is recalled that Gerard's summary had been, in point of fact, not an accurate statement of the information which he obtained from the men of Arras whom he questioned, but his own view of the central tenets of the heresy with which he had believed himself to be confronted. The preconceptions of the bishops led them to assume rather than to establish that each of these threats to the faith proceeded from the same source.

The men of Arras had of their own volition professed a faith which laid particular emphasis on the precepts of the Gospels and the apostles, which led them to stress neighbourly charity, to avoid living at the expense of injuring others, and to doubt (although they did not persist in denying) the necessity of the sacraments to supplement these virtues, and their capacity to compensate for their absence. They apparently agreed with Leutard that not all parts of the scriptures were necessary, and both with him and with the later heretics of Châlons that 'the restraint of the appetites of the flesh' was appropriate to the pursuit of a life dedicated to religion. That was natural in a world where the monasteries set the highest spiritual and ethical ideals; when it was stated by the men of Arras it was universally held to imply a denial of matrimony, but that they had not said so is a caution against accepting the judgement of Roger II of Châlons that the heretics whom he reported to Wazo regarded their 'abhorrence of matrimony' and 'shunning of meat' as anything more than a disciplining of the flesh.

The three heresies associated with Châlons, then, had much in common. All were vigorously evangelist, and based their precepts on rigorous personal purity. All derived their convictions from the New Testament; it will hardly be imagined that it was the Old which Leutard regarded as the binding part of scripture, and the assertion of Roger II that 'if uncouth and ignorant men become members of the sect they immediately become more eloquent than the most learned Catholics' suggests very strongly that they had some means of instructing their followers in the scriptures, rather as the men of Arras said that they had been taught to study them by Gundolfo.[20] Gundolfo is also a reminder that these similarities should not necessarily be assumed to imply direct connections between the heretics, and there are differences suggested between them even by these short and ambiguous accounts, such as that Leutard's opposition to tithes (a point particularly likely to be noted by those to whom they were paid) was not shared by the others, and that if Roger II's assertion that the heretics of Châlons believed that the Holy Spirit descended on them through an imposition of hands is to be believed it distinguishes them from both their predecessors.

These are the heretics of the early eleventh century or just before. They have been described as the known constituents of a 'vast heretical movement',[21] and no assessment of them can help but found itself on some presumption about the extent to which they are to be regarded as representative of others now unrecorded. The records themselves are not quite exhausted. If Ralph Glaber's assertion that 'many others' holding the esoteric convictions of Vilgard of Ravenna were put to death by sword and fire in Italy, and that some even carried them from Sardinia to Spain, lacks plausibility it must nevertheless be accepted as a pointer to some manifestation of religious dissent; the unfortunate Greek monk who had been set on in Rome some years earlier because his unfamiliar gestures made people think him a heretic may support the same suspicion.[22] In his interrogation of Gerard of Montforte Aribert of Milan did not share the reliance of his northern colleagues on the 'Manichaean' stereotype, and the way in which he turned his questioning away from the Trinity when he saw the direction in which it was going, and pursued other evidence of heresy before he returned to clinch it, may suggest that he had seen something of the sort before. All of these cases, perhaps, may imply that the presence in Italy not only of Greek but of Irish monks, of various degrees of enthusiasm, sometimes inspired imitators who wavered on the verges of orthodoxy. To the north also there are a few signs of the incompleteness of surviving knowledge. Wazo's biographer Anselm, to whom we owe the preservation of the letter of Roger II of Châlons compared that case to an incident at Goslar in 1052 when the Emperor Henry III had some men hanged as heretics because they refused to kill a chicken. Anselm regarded the episode with disapproval, and was confident that if Wazo had been there he would have opposed it, on the grounds that the evidence was insufficient. He saw Wazo, when he counselled Roger of Châlons to act with caution, and not to resort to coercion by the secular power, as 'restraining the usual frenzy of the Franks from stirring up any kind of physical cruelty', and while he cited the historical precedent of the hunting of the Priscillianists in fourth-century Spain it is possible that he had in mind some other episode nearer his own time, for an anonymous poet from Liège said at about this time that false doctrine flourished in France.[23] The oration of Bishop Gerard at Arras also prompted the suspicion that among the variety of heresies which he thought it proper to rebut may have been some which he had actually encountered, and his letter to Bishop R. seemed to imply that he had heard of heretics in his diocese whom he could not capture, as well as those whom he did.[24]

Other such hints and hypotheses might, no doubt, be garnered from an exhaustive search of eleventh-century literature, but whatever allowance is made for its deficiencies it is difficult to believe that the handful of heretics who are more amply reported were the tip of a very considerable iceberg. They seem to have been regarded as oddities, and to have aroused less general alarm and despondency than their successors in the next century. Among the chroniclers Ralph Glaber, Adhemar of Chabannes and Anselm of Liège each reported more than one incident because they thought it appropriate, as historians do, to complete their patterns of information when they could, while Landulf Senior, who is our informant about the group at Monforte, is also the major source on the Patarenes of Milan, whom he regarded as heretics.[25] These are not random reports, but serious attempts by four skilful and important writers to tell what they knew. In sum it was not very much.

The six incidents which it has been possible to examine in some detail divide themselves readily into two groups. Vilgard of Ravenna, Stephen and Lisois, and Gerard of Monforte were all *literati*. They agreed in giving their private visions and convictions priority over the authority of the church, and each of them, to some degree, drew some part of his inspiration from the religious and intellectual currents of his time. Beyond that they had little in common. Their teachings differed from one another in fundamental respects, both in the content and in the manner of their belief. The classicism of Vilgard, the gnosticism of Stephen and Lisois and the neo-platonic asceticism of Gerard may well have had some common ancestry, in the sense that they all reflect in their ways revivals of ancient habits of thought, but as they were actually held by these men, in the eleventh century, they are quite distinct one from another, and the evidence does not justify any attempt to draw them into a common pattern.

In clear contrast with these, Leutard of Vertus, the men of Arras interrogated by Gerard of Cambrai, and the heretics reported to Wazo by Roger II of Châlons, were all, in the phrase used of the last, *rustici, idiotae et infacundi*,[26] uneducated men who depended for their knowledge of the church and the scriptures on what they were told by others, either orthodox or unorthodox, but their beliefs have a certain coherence with one another. The differences between them were sufficient to bar the natural suspicion, indulged both by their religious superiors and many of their historians, that they were members of the same sect, but they resembled one another much more closely than their more sophisticated counterparts to the south. The resemblance is not difficult to account for; it had its origin, very clearly, in a literal understanding of the simplest ethical precepts of the New Testament. In their case the simple conviction of the virtues of personal austerity, coupled with the suspicion which it naturally encouraged of the elaboration of the church's sacraments and the incapacity of its priests to support their claims to spiritual prestige by the holiness of their lives, was not overlaid or variegated by the influence of other intellectual traditions to which education might have exposed them. The circumstances of their own lives, the environment which formed their mentalities, were much the same, and therefore when they heard the news of the Gospels or the sayings of St Paul they reacted to them in much the same way, and sought their salvation along the same path. How they heard of them must remain unknown. When Adhemar of Chabannes remarked that his 'Manichees' of 1018, who seem to have preached the same message of austerity, obedience to the Gospels and rejection of a church which appeared to have deserted them 'pretended to be like monks' he offers the best judgement that can be made. It was in the reformed monasteries of Cluny, Gorze and Brogne – the last particularly associated with the western low countries – that realization of the extent to which the church had departed from its mission was gaining ground most rapidly in the tenth and early part of the eleventh centuries, and the monks were beginning increasingly to assume the duties of popular preaching, and even the service of parishes, which the secular clergy were still ill-equipped to undertake. Evidence of a direct connection between their activity and these earliest heresies is lacking, but the ideals which they disseminated were close to those which the heretics expressed, and were fully capable of arousing greater enthusiasm than could always be successfully contained within the bounds of Catholic obedience.

The appearance of popular heresy in eleventh-century Europe has been attributed by many scholars to the influence of the Bogomil church of Bulgaria,[27] which was beginning at the same time to preach its message of personal austerity, hostility to the flesh, and denial of the sacraments and authority of the orthodox church, beyond the boundaries of the province in which it originated. That interpretation is plainly inconsistent with the analysis offered here. Not only is evidence wholly lacking of any direct contact between the Bogomils and any of the western heretics, and of any direct expression in the west of the dualist theology upon which Bogomilism was founded, but the differences between the heresies of the west themselves destroy the assumption that they are to be accounted for by reference to any single origin. The assertion that if none of these groups individually shows many signs of Bogomilism they may be held to do so if they are taken as a group collapses before the conclusion that they cannot be taken as a group. Stephen and Lisois denied the humanity of Christ, Gerard and his associates stressed chastity above all things (though not, as we have seen, on dualist grounds), the men of Arras denied the necessity of baptism, and those of Roger II of Châlons' letter believed that the Holy Ghost came to them through the laying-on of hands; but these cannot be regarded as pieces of a Bogomil jig-saw puzzle when they are themselves fragments of four different pictures.[28] What the heresies of the west had in common – and it is very little – was disobedience to the church, and the readiness to interpret the scriptures in their own way; the conclusions which they reached were too various to reflect the dissemination of any external influence.

The heretics were not alone in feeling a conflict between the prompting of conscience and the precepts of the church. The spiritual heroes of their day were also sustained in their struggle with evil by the inner light of the soul. An Abbo of Fleury or a Gerbert of Aurillac could appeal to his private conviction of righteousness against those who accused him of attacking the church when he argued for its reform. A William of Volpiano renounced the world and the flesh to seek his inspiration directly from the spirit by meditation upon the divine, perceived by what Ratherius of Verona had called the *interiores oculi*, or the eye of the heart.[29] The church of the Carolingian age which promised salvation to those who obeyed, who were instructed by lesson and symbol and were content to entrust their salvation to diligent attendance and conscientious observance of its prescribed disciplines, had plainly failed in the eyes of such men as these to transform the lives of the faithful with the message with which it was charged and to demonstrate in its government and the conduct of its ministers the rejection of the world and the embrace of the spirit. The monks who retired to the mountain sides of Camaldoli and Vallombrosa to wage war with the devil in private spiritual combat thereby devalued the

daily communal ritual as a weapon in their struggle. In this generation as in others, the fuel for the renewal and regeneration of
Christian life was looked for, by those most anxious to achieve it,
not in the institutions or observances of the church which they
sought to reform, but in the inner fires of their own souls.

The tension thus engendered between the urge to spiritual progress and the authority and discipline of the church was expressed
by Gerard of Cambrai in the sermon which he preached at the
synod of Arras in 1025. Beyond the rebuttal of individual heretical
propositions he was concerned to maintain that the mere spiritual
illumination to which the accused laid claim was not enough for
salvation. It must be pursued also through a series of specific and
concrete acts of devotion, submission and contrition; the function
of relics, miracles, reverence for the cross, prayers for the dead,
incense and ritual, as well as of the sacraments themselves, was to
make salvation available in tangible form to all who sought it sin-
cerely, to show the faithful an accessible faith. In this he identified
the danger which enthusiasm held for the church universal, that it
threatened to create a spiritual élite to whose members alone was
reserved the knowledge of God, perceptible only by their inner eye.
This was the tendency which the clerks of Orléans had carried to its
furthest point, when they proclaimed their indifference to what
'men have written on the skins of animals'. On his way to Orléans
to infiltrate the sect Aréfast had stopped at Chartres to seek the
advice of Bishop Fulbert, 'the Socrates of Gaul', only to find that
he was away from the city. But Fulbert had given his answer some
twenty years earlier, when he wrote to Adeodatus about the proper
relation of inspiration to faith. Knowledge of the divine, he said,
was unattainable to unaided human wisdom; it was by turning out-
wards to the disciplined study of the scriptures, of the law of the
church and the writings of its fathers, that the will of God might
best be discovered; reliance on the guesswork of the inturned spirit
had given birth to all the great heresies of the patristic age. Nobody
might dismiss the services and requirements of the church as
elaborations and superfluities, for the *via legis divine* was a single
road, the same for all Christians; there was not one law for the
perfect, and another for the imperfect.[30]

The heretics of the eleventh century, then, were part of the religious world in which they appeared. Both in the bodily austerity of their ethics and in their readiness to turn to the inner world of the spirit they reflected the ideals and aspirations which were shared and often preached by the leaders of the spiritual, and especially of the monastic life. Even this banal conclusion, however, must be qualified, for it will not have escaped notice that the argument which Gerard of Cambrai directed against the men of Arras was better adapted to what he mistrusted in the general tendency than what was avowed by the particular men before him; once again he had seen more in their confession than they had confessed. It was true, of course, that their teaching arose from a readiness to grant what appealed to their own conscience priority over what was urged upon them by the church, but what they had avowed was not obedience to an inner light remotely comparable to that proclaimed by Stephen and Lisois, but the conviction that salvation would be attained by adherence to a simple programme of ethical conduct. A heretic by definition is a man of conscience, one who chooses his beliefs instead of embracing those commended by the church, and all these heretics were guided by the beacon of their souls. But the nature of the guidance which they received thereby was so varied that it cannot be held that their spirituality, the nature of their religious impulses, points any more clearly to a comprehensive explanation of their appearance than either the doctrines which they preached or their social or intellectual backgrounds.

To deny that the sudden appearance of popular heresy in eleventh-century Europe is to be accounted for by any single explanation which applies to all these cases of it may be to seem to shrink from the duty of explanation itself. It is not so. There remains one thing that all these heretics have in common, and which also accounts for the profound differences between them. The eleventh century saw the beginning of one of the formative periods of European development, a time whose transformations left nothing untouched. The heretics were isolated from each other, and formed nothing which can properly be described as a 'heretical movement', of whatever size or importance. They were not isolated from the world in which they lived. Most of them were touched, in one way or another, by

the gathering dissatisfaction with the capacity of the church to perform its spiritual duties, although they did not, for the most part,
attack it directly. At Ravenna and at Monforte the influence is also
perceptible, in different ways, of the revival of classical learning
which would be Italy's first contribution to the renaissance of the
twelfth century, while at Orléans the first growth of patronage and
activity around a cathedral chapter and its school had one of its
more bizarre side-effects. As the activity of the church increased it
not only advertised in proclaiming its ideals the extent to which it
fell short of them, but increased the burden which attendance at
services and sacraments and payment of tithes placed upon the
faithful, some of whom doubted the justice of the demands; thus
Leutard of Vertus, a poor man himself, not only smashed the cross
in his parish church but denounced the exaction of tithes, and the
men of Arras were sceptical of the claim of a sinful priest to be able
to wash away for ever the sins of their patently less sinful children.
Behind these manifestations of cultural and ecclesiastical progress
lay the momentum of increasing wealth, with the social change and
strain which it brought with it. Arras was one of the first cities of the
north to feel the pulse, and some of its natives informed their bishop
that they wanted to live by the labour of their own hands, and to do
no harm to others, only a few years before the first signs of the
emergence of a privileged bourgeoisie in their city reached a surviving record.[31] Gerard of Monforte likewise, in insisting that he
and his brothers held their goods in common, expressed not only
an ancient monastic ideal, but a criticism of the increasing preoccupation with the accumulation of wealth, and the social divisions
which it created, which was already apparent in Lombardy. Among
the heretics, as among the monks and hermits, a growing insistence
on abjuration of worldly comforts and pleasures is a visible measure
of the increase of consumption around them,[32] and is therefore,
in the early eleventh century, spasmodically and tentatively expressed, but undeniably present. There was no part of medieval life
that religion did not touch, and none therefore that did not touch
religion; the heretics of the eleventh century were few, incoherent
and isolated from each other, but they signalled the changes that
were on the way.

Chapter III | *The Crisis of Reform*

By the middle of the eleventh century the demand which the heretics had voiced with others for a way of life more consonant with that commended in the Gospels and exemplified by the apostles had become a powerful engine of reform. It was expressed soonest and most clearly among the monks, and especially in Italy, where the presence of the Greek tradition in widely diffused though incoherently organized forms offered an alternative model of the spiritual life to the closely structured fabric of the elaborated Benedictine monasticism which the authority of the Carolingians and the prestige of the abbots of Cluny had made universal in the north. The business of the Cluniac monk was to pray for the souls of the innumerable benefactors of his house, and to play his part in the construction of a replica of heaven where the passer-by might have his soul uplifted by the beauty of the house and the sound of angels singing. When he died St Benedict would recognize him by the neatness of his habit and the sobriety of his demeanour, and intercede to ensure that he obtained the place in the heavenly choir for which he had passed his life on earth rehearsing. It was a gracious, but scarcely a heroic ideal, formed in the tenth century when peace and order seemed unattainable enough without the additional luxury of struggling for personal spiritual ecstasy. At Camaldoli and Vallombrosa the conception of monastic life as pre-eminently a communal enterprise was jettisoned. Their inmates, freed from the exhaustive demands of a litany that consumed the day and half the night, cultivated their souls by individual prayer and contemplation, and symbolized their progress in the abandonment of the world by retreating further and further up the sides of the mountains at whose feet their houses were situated.

The return to contemplation exerted growing pressure on monastic institutions. It is to be expected that the two most familiar expressions of the view that the demands of Cluny's choir service were excessive, already becoming widespread by 1080, should have come from Italians; in 1056 Anselm of Aosta thought of making his vows there but rejected it in favour of Bec because it would not leave him enough time for reading and private meditation, and at about the same time Peter Damiani, biographer of Romuald, prior of Fonte Avellana, and prophet of the new monasticism, complained that even in summer the monks of Cluny had no more than two hours a day outside the choir and refectory.[1] This spirit soon spread beyond the Alps. The first radical departure from the Cluniac tradition in the north was the foundation of the Carthusian order by Bruno of Cologne, in 1083. The Carthusians lived, ate and prayed in their cells, and performed their manual labour in their individual gardens, emerging only once a day (except on feast days) to join in common worship. Like the Italians too, they linked the pursuit of introspective spirituality to that of extreme poverty, rejecting all gifts except books for their library: the splendid chalices and vestments which portrayed the magnificence of heaven to the Cluniacs represented to them only thraldom to worldly things. The most successful of the other new orders, Cîteaux, Tiron or Savigny, departed less radically from the old ideal. They preserved the Benedictine Rule as the basis of their lives, and with it the identification of virtue with subjection to a common discipline. Nevertheless their interpretation of it was new. A Cistercian, like a Cluniac, prepared himself for heaven, but it was not in the greatly reduced choir service that the important work was done. 'He must spend the short time which remains of his life on earth with us' said St Bernard, 'in order to scrape off the filth of secular life and shake off the dust of the world so as to be fit to enter the heavenly mansion.'[2] Whether he devoted himself to the humility of manual labour or to the private spiritual and ascetic exercises which were encouraged in accordance with that view, therefore, the Cistercian though he lived a communal life had his salvation very much more in his own hands than his Cluniac cousin: he was expected to do more to eradicate his own sins than to pray for the forgiveness of those of others. That spirit was clearly reflected in the criticism of the Cluniacs for failing to exact a full year's novitiate, and for accepting the vows of oblates too young to understand them. These practices had always been breaches of the Rule of St Benedict, but they seemed far more serious in the context of enhanced individual responsibility for worthiness in fulfilling the monastic vocation than in the older tradition, which attached less emphasis to the state of the inner spirituality, and more to orderly and regular contribution to the tasks of the community. In this respect, though it carried none of the same theological implications, the Cistercian attitude was akin to that of heretics who denounced the practice of infant baptism on the ground that the individual could not claim merit in a faith which he was too young to understand.

The pursuit of holiness by the path of personal perfection was naturally accompanied by a change of personal values. Renunciation of the world had several aspects. To live outside it required spiritual even more than physical separation. Hence the humiliation of the flesh, the adoption of less comfortable clothing and living quarters, of a more rigorous diet. Chastity was exalted to a still higher place among the virtues than it had formerly occupied because it proclaimed not merely sexual abstinence but the conquest, in all these ways, of the bonds of bodily desire. The difference between the old code and the new was best expressed in a changed conception of poverty. In the Rule of St Benedict, as to the Cluniacs, poverty meant the renunciation of personal ownership. It did not demand that the community itself should be without wealth. On the contrary, Cluniac ideals required the monastery to be rich, so that its buildings might make a fitting frame for the heavenly choir, its services be decently conducted in imposing garments, amid clouds of incense and from finely prepared hymn books, while its abbots sustained their obligations to the poor by carrying a chest of gold for alms on their frequent journeys, to the world by sustaining themselves with dignity in the company of the secular princes through whom they disseminated their code of peace, order and decency in human affairs, and to their guests and patrons by dispensing the most generous hospitality. As William the Monk said to the heretic Henry of Lausanne, in response to his criticism of the wealth of prelates, 'If one ought to be hospitable one must be permitted to have a place to put a guest and the means of looking after him'.[3] If he were a Cluniac he might have had to offer the same defence to St Bernard.[4] For the new communities poverty was more starkly defined. It was not enough for the monk to lack possessions if the wealth of his house assured him of worldly comfort, and tied him to the sources of worldly corruption. The monks of Grandmont were forbidden to accept gifts, and even to beg for alms for food until their storehouse was empty, and then only with their bishop's permission; the Cistercians would not accept cultivated land and the servile dues that went with it, and held their lay benefactors at a cold distance, refusing to entertain them at the monastic table. Dissociation from the stain of earthly riches was the hall-mark of the new spirit.

The proliferation of monastic foundations and the grouping of the secular clergy into communities of canons regular did not exhaust the possibilities for the pursuit of the spiritual life. The natural condition of contemplation for many was solitude, and the semi-eremitical quality of the most advanced of the new institutions remained less than a complete fulfilment of it. Early medieval society, a world of forest-clearing communities in the wilderness, was accustomed to solitaries outside civilization, and yet not at a great distance from it. Among the hunters, outlaws, bandits, innkeepers who lived in the forests and along the river banks, and who found the world moving nearer to them in the eleventh century, were, no doubt, always some who devoted themselves wholly to religious lives, naturally at home with these 'rebels against every culture'.[5] In the age of reform they came to represent an eloquent model of perfection, the growth of their prestige (perhaps more than of their numbers) attested not only by the biographies which some of them earned, but by the witness of almost every chronicle and monastic cartulary that there was scarcely a community which did not have hermits living at its edge. Many pursued their vocation for life, but their example also created, in effect, a new stage in spiritual education, for almost every prominent reformer served his time in the desert. For those who changed from an old life to a new a spell of solitude was a *sine qua non*. A famous example is that of the forest of Craon, on the borders of Maine and Brittany, where in the early 1090s there was gathered a brilliant constellation of spiritual heroes. Robert of Arbrissel had been archpriest of his diocese, and retired in disgust at his failure to persuade the priests to give up their concubines; Vitalis of Mortain had been chaplain to his count, whose household he found a poor place for the improvement of his soul; Bernard of Tiron had been prior of the great house of St Savin, and fled from the worldly cares of the abbacy to which he was threatened with election.[6] For such men as these all roads led to the desert, and like half a dozen others they emerged again from Craon to become famous preachers of repentance and reform, and to found the orders of Fontevrault, Savigny and Tiron.

All of these were educated men, and had a design for their retreat. The life that they lived in the forest was deliberately modelled on that of the desert fathers, the *antiquiores patres* whose biographies provided vivid instruction in the pursuit of spiritual exaltation through the humiliation of the flesh. But the hermits included in their number a far wider range of devotees, from disgruntled abbots to the repentant thieves and harlots who followed Robert and Vitalis, and the reformed bandits who became the first community of Affligem in the same decade.[7] Nor was there a simple antithesis between the eremitical and the monastic life. Many of the hermits had spiritual directors among the monks or secular clergy, and others, like Roger of St Alban's and many at Cluny, actually retained their monastic vow of obedience while being permitted to live in solitude in the grounds or outlying possessions of their abbey.[8] For those who wished, it even became possible to follow the spiritual life without abandoning their place in the world. Bernold of Constance placed under the year 1091 in his chronicle this description of the religious condition of his time:

> The common life flourished in many parts of Germany, not only among monks and clerks living together under religious vows, but even among lay people, who devoutly give up themselves and their goods to the common life, so that if they have not the monastic or clerical habit they are not inferior to them in merit. As servants (of monks or clerks) . . . they imitate Him who came not to be served but to serve and who taught His followers to attain their salvation through service. Renouncing the world . . . they set themselves to live the common life after the manner of the primitive church. . . Innumerable men and women have devoted themselves to this way of life in these times, living in common under obedience to clerks or monks, and give themselves wholly, like serving maids, to the performance of their daily duties. In these villages the daughters of humble people give up marriage and the world, and apply themselves to live under the direction of a priest. Even the married set themselves to live religiously, and to obey with as much devotion as the religious. This way of life prospers to a tremendous extent in Germany, where sometimes whole villages hand themselves over as communities to religion, so that they may compete ceaselessly to attain holiness in their lives.[9]

Since the quest of most of the heretics of the early eleventh century had been for a way of life which seemed appropriate to the ideals of the Gospels as they understood them, the immense extension of opportunity which these innovations provided went far to meet it. For the men of Arras, or even of Monforte, the desire to cultivate austerity and simplicity of life might, if they had been seized by it a generation or so later, have been readily satisfied within the framework of some legitimate, Catholic, community. The erroneous doctrines which their interrogators discovered them to hold had been the consequence, not the cause, of their disillusionment with the patterns of life that were open to them, and if that disillusionment had been answered, and their spiritual aspirations catered for in a form which retained the possibility of direction and guidance from orthodox priests, they need not have become heretics at all. This is the explanation of the apparent paradox, that although the second half of the eleventh century saw a universal and vigorous variety of religious conflicts, it also saw the virtual disappearance of popular heresy. The 'heretical' currents which had flowed until that time had been in reality little more than some of the manifestations of the very widely felt ambition for a humbler, harder and more exacting spiritual life that was met with brilliant success (for a time) by what is usually referred to as the movement for monastic reform, but in fact represented a great expansion of spiritual opportunity in a rich variety of forms. The path of righteousness was no longer reserved to those whose temporal condition and spiritual ambition permitted them to be content with the Rule of St Benedict as it had traditionally been interpreted by the Black monks.

Anxiety for holy living was not the only dynamic of religious change, nor by the mid-century the most important. The movement for spiritual reform was a diffuse one, finding expression in most parts of Europe and in many ways which proceeded, more or less, independently of one another. The movement for the reform of the church, and specifically of the papacy, was sharply focussed both in its temporal circumstances and in its spiritual goals. The Synods of Sutri and of Rome in 1046, when the Emperor Henry III secured the condemnation of three rival claimants to the papal throne and replaced them with his own nominee, are traditionally accepted as the beginning of the papal reform. Like all revolutionary occasions it had many aspects, but from the present point of view one is of overwhelming importance. The central preoccupation of the debate which now reverberated through Europe for half a century was not with how those who wished to devote their lives to God should do so, but with the fitness and ability of the priests of the church to perform their task. In directing controversy to the priests the reformers made it one which was of direct, immediate and daily concern to all Christians. In asking not simply whether the priests led good lives, or how if not they might be made to do so, but how the quality of their lives and the circumstances of their ordination affected their position as channels of divine grace to the laity, they deepened the debate to make it, in the most literal sense, a radical investigation of the nature of the church itself and of its claim to the succession of the apostles and the vicariate of Christ. To the bishops who had examined the heretics of the earlier decades, Gerard of Cambrai or Aribert of Milan, the doubt which their zeal for austerity seemed to imply for the efficacy of the sacraments was the most serious reason for concern. Historically, as we have seen, they were wrong, for these questions were secondary to the heretics themselves, but theologically they were right, for it was on the power of conferring the sacraments that the authority and position of the church depended. But because the heretics did not perceive that this was so, their activities did not constitute, for the most part, a vigorous or deliberate attack on the church: they would have been content, if it had been allowed to them, to go quietly on their own ways. The papal reform changed all that. Thenceforth the central issues in which the heresies of the twelfth century would have their roots related to the necessity of the Catholic sacraments to salvation, and the right of Catholic priests to administer them and to claim the spiritual authority which flowed from their doing so.

In one sense at least the papal reform can be said to mark the birth of Europe, for it was the first public event that everybody knew about. Popes had been deposed and thrones had been shaken often enough, but there had never been a conflict, sustained over many years, in which people of every rank of society felt directly involved. It was discussed in the streets of Paris, Cologne and Florence, it was the occasion of risings in Milan, Worms and Cambrai, and those who lived after it remembered it as a cataclysmic event. 'What else', asked Sigebert of Gembloux, 'is talked about even in the women's spinning-rooms and the artisans' work-shops than the confusion of all human laws . . . sudden unrest among the populace, new treacheries of servants against their masters and masters' mistrust of their servants . . . all this backed by authority, by those who are called the leaders of Christendom.'[10] Sigebert identified two qualities which would threaten the ability of priests and bishops to command the allegiance of their spiritual subjects. In the first place, that it was attended at every stage by rumour and inaccuracy, sustained and inflamed by the propagandists of both parties, meant that what the reformers said might easily become less important than what they were believed to have said, and what they did readily confused with what was done in their name. Secondly, this in turn magnified and exaggerated the conviction, which was not without foundation in the decrees and pronouncements of the reforming popes, that traditional authority had been overthrown by papal command, and that the faithful of Christ had the duty of exposing and undoing the wrongs of those who claimed the authority of his mantle.

From the outset the reform was centred on the nature and validity of clerical office. The family conflicts which preceded it in Rome proclaimed that the Tusculan Benedict IX was dissolute, the anti-Pope Silvester III a schismatic, and Gregory VI, though of blameless life and welcomed by the reformers, a simoniac who had bought his office from Benedict. The new era was firmly inaugurated at the synod of Rheims in 1048, when Leo IX invoked the relics of St Remigius to obtain the confessions of the assembled prelates that most of them had obtained the spiritual offices which their personal lives rendered them unfit to hold by purchase or other improper means, from lay proprietors and patrons who ought not to have been able to dispose of them; many resigned, to be shriven and re-appointed by the Pope. The driving ideology of the reform, though it was not fully endorsed by all its proponents, was that of the *Adversus Simoniacos* of Cardinal Humbert, whose third book, written about 1058, maintained that the evils of the church flowed from the fact that the right to exercise its spiritual powers had been usurped by secular princes, and thence implied that many of the church's priests were improperly ordained and incapable of transmitting its sacraments.[11] The climax of the campaign was the adoption by Alexander II and Gregory VII of the decree of the Council of Rheims that the faithful should not attend the masses of uncelibate or simoniac priests as a universal and vigorously publicized weapon against their recalcitrant subordinates. Thus, in true revolutionary fashion, they called upon the people to judge and discipline the hierarchy over which they themselves presided. The letters of Gregory VII, a propagandist of immense histrionic talent, reverberate with the motif of his pontificate:

> to clergy and laymen, high and low, who love the law of Christ. . .
> Your bishop has openly tolerated in his clergy things altogether
> repugnant to our command, or rather St Peter's – that those who

had women might keep them, and that those who did not have them might commit the unlawful brazenness of taking them. . . Accordingly, by apostolic authority we charge all of you, both greater and lesser, who stand by God and St Peter, that if he is determined to continue in his obduracy you should show him neither respect nor obedience

Those who obtain churches by the gift of money must utterly forfeit them, so that no one for the future may be allowed to sell or buy them. Nor may those who are guilty of the crime of fornication celebrate masses or minister at the altar in lesser orders. We have further appointed that if they disregard our rulings, or rather those of the holy father, the people may in no wise receive their ministration. . .

servants of the sacred altar persisting in fornication must not celebrate the office of mass, but are to be driven from the choir until they show themselves worthy by penance

we have been placed in a position where whether we will or not we are bound to proclaim to all the peoples, and especially to Christians, truth and righteousness according to the word of the Lord: 'Cry aloud, spare not, lift up thy voice like a trumpet and declare unto my people their transgressions.' And the prophet says, 'Cursed be he that keepeth back his sword from blood' – who fails, that is, to rebuke the carnal. We make this prelude because among the many evils which beset the world certain ministers of Satan and precursors of Antichrist in Lombardy are trying to overthrow the Christian faith and calling the wrath of God upon them.[12]

The ministers of Satan there referred to were the Archbishop of Milan and his clergy. The passions, the techniques and the implications of the conflict which gripped the west for half a century were displayed in vivid miniature in that city, which from 1056 to 1075 was deeply shaken by a vigorous and explosive alliance between religious enthusiasm and social tension in the movement of the Patarenes.[13] The church of Milan was among the proudest in Europe. At a moment when the cult of the urban patron was at its height Milan had in St Ambrose one unrivalled in prestige. To its ancient eminence it had added the triumphs which made it 'another Rome', when Archbishop Aribert outmanoeuvred Pavia to crown Conrad II king of the Lombards there in 1025, and ousted

Ravenna to have his representative join the Pope, as an equal, at the imperial coronation two years later. The archbishop's command over the society of the city and its region matched his spiritual authority. He was chosen traditionally not only by, but from among the cathedral chapter, whose members were drawn mostly from the *capitanei*, the leading families of aristocratic society; the *capitanei* were in turn tied to the archbishop as his vassals, and owed most of their wealth and status to the enfeoffment of their ancestors with cathedral lands in 983. Among the citizens, who were now acquiring riches at a growing pace as the geographical position of Milan made it one of the first regions to benefit from the great economic advance of the eleventh century, the merchants owed their establishment of a market in the city to his privileges and protection, and the judges, notaries and advocates thrived on the business of his courts. The wealth of the church, therefore, was the cement of Milanese society, and its control the principal concern of its leaders and guarantee of its stability. The 'Ambrosian tradition' which permitted marriage to Milanese clerks was an essential part of this pattern, and the existence of standard tariffs for entry to every office of the church, including ordination itself, and every benefice which accompanied them, was not simply an 'abuse' to be reviled by the idealistic, but the expression of a carefully articulated system for the amicable distribution of land and wealth among the members of the established order.

When the current of reform turned towards Milan, therefore, it would find the twin monsters of iniquity, simony and clerical marriage, deeply entrenched and stubbornly defended. The danger was compounded by two things. In the first place, Milan had none of the reformed monasteries which in other places, notably at Florence, offered a starting point for the gradual dissemination of the new spirit: when it came it would be forced in from outside.[14] And secondly, if Archbishop Aribert (1018–45) had brought the power and prestige of the city to a new height, he had also, in doing so, exacerbated its social divisions. The vavassours, the second rank of the feudal nobility, had suffered from his policy of consolidating land in the hands of the church just at the moment when they were gathering enough awareness of their common strength to seek the amelioration of their position, and had joined Conrad II in his wars with Aribert to gain, in the *constitutio de feodis* of 1038, an imperial guarantee of the heritability of their fiefs. Aribert mobilized the citizens in response, and taught them by example the power of 'the people under arms'; he paid the price by spending most of his last years in exile, and leaving when he died in 1045 a tradition of violent hostility between citizens and knights as his political legacy, dangerously complementary to the edifice of ecclesiastical abuse which must invite attack in the years after his death.

The message of reform was brought to Milan by the son of a vavassour named Ariald, who began to preach it in the neighbouring countryside and was told by his hearers to go to the city, where some might know how to answer his arguments. Ariald's life exemplified his teaching; he lived in chastity, in poverty and in prayer, and he launched his campaign by bringing together a group of clerks to renounce the style of their fellows and live a common life at the church of the Trinity, observing the ideals which he taught them. Their inspiration was well described by Arno of Reichersberg, who called them '*filii ordinis canonici*',[15] imitators of those who combined the regular lives and penitential exercises of monks with the preaching and sacramental duties of the secular clergy whose office they now undertook to perform, in effect, for the people of Milan.

Although the tradition that the word 'Patarenes' by which the followers of Ariald became known was derived from that for 'ragpickers' seems to be mistaken,[16] it represents a continued insistence by the defenders of the old order that he drew his support from among the most disreputable and unstable elements of the community. That was certainly not true of the leadership. His first associates, Landolf Cotta and his brother Erlembald, were from a family of the *capitanei*, and the priest Anselm of Baggio, who became Bishop of Lucca in 1057 and Alexander II in 1062, was also of wealthy origins. According to Ariald's biographer, Andrew of Sturmi, the movement was vertically rather than horizontally divisive: 'one household was entirely faithful [i.e. pro-Patarene], the next entirely faithless; in a third the mother believed with one son while the father disbelieved with another. The whole city was thrown into disorder by this confusion and strife.'[17] Some of the most influential members of the city community were the moneyers, who secured their position by family succession from minting-rights granted by the Carolingians, and extended their interests, naturally enough, into money-lending and land speculation. The church of the Trinity in which Ariald established his base had been founded by a member of one of the most prominent of these families, Benedetto Rozzo, and was still under the patronage of his successors, and another moneyer named Nazarius supported the community and provided them with the necessities of life; nevertheless Andrew of Sturmi's judgement was right, for most of that class remained loyal to the clergy and aristocracy with whom their interests had lain. Similarly, when Erlembald became leader of the movement after Ariald's assassination in 1066 he surrounded himself with a bodyguard 'of young men of the city, of both orders, the people and the nobles', but some of them were paid for their services, and their activities did not prevent the archbishop from regarding the *maiores nobilium* as his chief defence against the Patarenes: it may be recalled that it was the *maiores* of the city who had insisted on burning the heretics of Monforte in 1025. On the whole it seems that the strength of the Patarenes was to be found among the *cives*, assisted by a few of the more privileged who had repented the sins of their class, a common enough situation. But the *cives* were no rabble; they were the merchants, the notaries, the lawyers and judges who would be the mainstays of the urban community of the future. The rabble existed, and fickle as its reputation turned eagerly against whatever enemy appeared, first on one side and then on the other.[18]

The Patarenes conceived themselves, of course, in different terms. To their supporters, Andrew of Sturmi, Bonizo of Sutri, or Alexander II, they were above all the *fideles*, the *Dei famulus* and *Dei athlete*, Ariald the *vir Dei* and *martir Christi*.[19] Their struggle was against the heresies, as they were now designated by reformers, of simony and nicolaitism (clerical marriage), and against the corruption of a clergy which, according to Ariald, had relapsed into the darkness of the pre-Christian age, into idolatry and the worship of false gods. His preaching assailed the clerks with sustained ferocity, representing them as the blind leading the blind, their churches as stables, their sacraments as the ordure of dogs: the old and corrupt church which supported them must now be replaced by a regenerated clerical order whose life and discipline, like that of Ariald and his companions, would demonstrate its adherence to the true spirit of the Gospels. Those who heard the masters of the city castigated with such violence of language and such force of sentiment did not confine their response to a mere boycott of the delinquents' services. The period of Patarene strength was marked by regular turbulence. Priests were assailed in their houses and dragged from their altars, and made to sign pledges of celibacy and dismiss their wives on pain of losing their benefices, and when the layman Erlembald assumed the leadership after Ariald's death the rule of force was open. He conducted himself like a general, surrounded by his bodyguard, magnificently dressed though he wore a hermit's shirt beneath, flying from his lance the banner of St Peter which Alexander II had given him: 'He now subdued the city by the sword and by gold and by many and diverse oaths; none of the nobles could withstand him.'[20]

The challenge of the Patarenes raised questions about the nature of spiritual authority which carried far beyond Milan. In defending their traditions the Milanese clergy did not simply rationalize abuse. They believed, rightly or wrongly, that in insisting not only upon their right to marry, but on maintaining their liturgy, their patterns of worship, their observance of Christian feasts, they observed the injunctions of their patron, no less venerable and no less authoritative than those which Rome wished to impose upon them. When Alexander II presented Erlembald with the *vexillum Sancti Petri* which became his standard he proclaimed in effect, as he had when he presented such banners to the Normans when they prepared to invade Sicily and England,[21] that there was here a territory to be brought within the sphere of Petrine authority, and it was perhaps the most lasting consequence of the Patarene upheavals that by the end of the century the Ambrosian church had largely abandoned its claim to walk its idiosyncratic way. Yet however that may have been it was not the purpose of the Patarenes simply to champion one source of human authority against another. Theirs was a movement of enthusiasm, driven by the confidence that they possessed an understanding of the truth of the Gospels which elevated their judgement above human contention, and it harboured all the dangers for the exercise of spiritual authority in general which that conviction implied.[22] The open break between the Archbishop and Ariald and Landolf had come in 1057, when the clergy appealed to Victor II to assist them against the disrupters who acted in his name. He commanded the two leaders to appear at a provincial synod at Fontanetto, and when they refused they were excommunicated. It seems that only the lifting of the ban shortly afterwards by his successor Stephen IX, a greater zealot for reform, prevented the Patarenes from becoming openly schismatic: the authority of St Peter would be no greater than that of St Ambrose if his vicar failed to adopt the position which the truth required of him.

Two years later the most fundamental of all questions for the nature of the church became inescapable. Ariald's denunciation not only of the Milanese clergy, but of the sacrament which they administered approached if it did not embrace the Donatist heresy, that the validity of the sacrament depended on the worthiness of the priest. It was a short but a crucial step from the disciplinary recommendation that the services of the vicious should be avoided, and it echoed the implication of Cardinal Humbert that if the ordination of simoniacs was invalid their sacraments must be so as well. Such a conclusion would have posed insurmountable difficulties for the church, for it would have left not only Milan but Christendom bereft of true priests to a point where the apostolic succession itself must be called in doubt. In the long run the very possibility that a church might be sustained by men depended on the impossibility of its foundations being undermined by their sins: as Augustine, whose writings against the Donatists provided the definitive discussion of these questions had put it, if the merits of the giver and the receiver were to be relevant to the efficacy of the sacrament, 'let it be God's merit in giving and my faith in receiving: for me two things in this are certain, God's goodness and my own faith. But if you intervene how can I know anything for certain?'[23]

The papal legate who appeared in 1059 to pronounce upon the charges against Archbishop Guido and his clergy was not Cardinal Humbert, but Peter Damiani, who had already insisted upon the

Augustinian position in his *Liber gratissimus*. He found the tensions of the city compounded by resentment of Roman intervention, but he gave his judgement in unambiguous terms. He demanded the obedience of Milan to Rome, and therefore to reform; he called upon its priests to confess their simony and renounce it for the future; and he imposed severe penances upon them for their wrong-doings, including the pilgrimage to Compostella for the Archbishop himself. But he refused to allow that either their simony or their subsequent sins had negated their priestly orders, and his decision was confirmed by a general decree of the Easter synod at Rome in the same year. This was the turning point, though not the con-clusion, of a crucial debate. In 1067 Damiani faced the same issue again when Florentine monks accused their bishop of simony, and suffered the accusation of being a simonist himself when he refused to accept the contention of the impassioned community that Bishop Nicholas' orders were invalid. Alexander II and Gregory VII both steered close, in practice, to the position of Humbert when they held that bishops who failed to act against simoniacs and nicolaites ceased thereby to claim the obedience of their flocks; Gregory came closer still when he held that priests who had been ordained, in ignorance, by an excommunicate bishop, must be ordained again.[24] They did not pronounce the orders or the sacraments of such priests invalid, but they left the church's position as the vehicle of divine grace dangerously vulnerable, nevertheless, to the consequences of human infirmity. During these two pontificates papal policy was perilously close to the Donatist position. The judgement which Damiani gave at Milan and its subsequent confirmation are there-fore of momentous importance, for it affirmed, at the critical moment, that the apostolic succession was incorruptible by the vices of the successors, and that the church's capacity to assure the salvation of the faithful was not compromised however great the imperfections of those by whom it was transmitted. In consequence, although the Patarenes still had several years of quasi-legitimate subversion before them, their most radical challenge had failed, and those who raised it again in the future would be clearly designated as enemies of the church.

.   .   .

If the Patarenes did not get the answer they wanted, the questions which they had raised continued to be asked, and to be trumpeted across Europe in the pontificate of Gregory VII. The passions and ambiguities which they stirred were clearly illustrated by the death of a priest of Cambrai named Ramihrdus, who was found in 1076 to be preaching against the vices of the clergy of that city.[25] He was examined by an episcopal synod, which found his answers impeccable on every point of doctrine, and asked him, conventionally enough, to confirm his sincerity by taking communion. This Ramihrdus refused to do. He said that every priest present, bishops, abbots and all, was up to his neck in simony and other vices, and that he was forbidden by papal decree to accept the sacrament from their polluted hands. His position was correct, but it was not to the liking of the assembled prelates, and the servants of the bishop, acting (no doubt) at the prompting of outraged loyalty, dragged Ramihrdus to a wooden hut and set it alight.

The martyrdom of Ramihrdus, for so it was, attracted the hostility of a significant combination of forces to the clergy under whose auspices it was accomplished. The people of Cambrai and of the villages where he had preached preserved his ashes and cherished his memory for many years, and Gregory VII wrote to his legate Hugh of Die to demand punishment of the outrage and vindication of his policies: a year later Bishop Gerard of Cambrai visited Rome, confessed that he had obtained his see simoniacally, resigned it and was restored by the Pope.[26]

The story of Ramihrdus demonstrates the narrowness of the precipice upon which papal policy was balanced. Neither he nor Gregory maintained that the mass which he had been ordered to take at the hands of one of the simoniacs would have been invalid: it was a question of propriety and discipline, not of doctrine. But to Ramihrdus' followers, as to the faithful of the other dioceses where Gregory called for boycotts of the unchaste, the distinction was too fine to be successfully maintained amid the wars, the riots, the distortions of propaganda and counter-propaganda which his policies generated. The Pope was not a Donatist, but he often seemed to behave like one, and in consequence his reign saw the culmination of a train of events which left the parish clergy and their superiors open thenceforward to the contention that if they lapsed from perfection in their lives they abdicated the authority of their office. For ordinary men, generally untrained and uneducated, who pursued their duties in the intimate curiosity of small and introspective communities it would be a heavy burden to bear.

The first spectacular manifestation of the change which the Gregorian epoch brought both to the temper and the preoccupation of popular religious debate was the career of Tanchelm, who preached in the Low Countries for some five years before his death c. 1115.[27] Through the hysterical accusations which the clergy of Utrecht addressed to the Archbishop of Cologne to beg that this monster, once imprisoned, should not be released to terrify them again, and through the smugness with which the biographers of St Norbert emphasized the extraordinary wickedness of the man whose work in Antwerp their hero had set out to undo, it is not easy to reach a clear assessment of Tanchelm, but two things are plain: he hated priests, and he frightened them.

It seems likely that Tanchelm had been a priest himself, for the prelude to his preaching had been a diplomatic mission which he undertook to Rome on behalf of Robert II of Flanders, to secure the transference of part of the diocese of Utrecht to that of Thérouanne, where the Count's influence was greater.[28] It was exactly such a task as would reveal the papal curia at its venial and worldly worst, and it appears that Tanchelm was one of those who found his faith in the Holy Church shattered by a visit to the Holy City. When he returned he consigned the whole caboodle, Pope, cardinals, archbishops and bishops, to damnation as corrupt and avaricious men, and urged his followers to avoid their sacraments and refuse their tithes.

Beyond insisting that he held that the sins of the priesthood invalidated their orders and their sacraments, the sources on Tanchelm are more concerned to depict the quality of his life and preaching than its content. He had a powerful dramatic talent which transfixed his supporters with devotion, and his enemies with horror. It was said that he had secured his first devotees by seducing the wives of fishermen who then enlisted their husbands to his cause, that he lived like a prince, and that he was followed wherever he went by a band of three thousand armed men; if the figure reflects only the gossip of an unstatistical age the length of his career supports the assertion which accompanies it that he was too popular for any secular magnate to bring force against him. He dressed himself as a people's king, with gilded clothes and gold twisted through his hair, and preached in the open fields 'as though he were a king summoning his people, as his followers crowded around him carrying swords and flags like royal insignia'. The message that he delivered – 'down with the priests' – was accompanied by a demonstration of sweeping contempt for their powers. He distributed his bath water to his followers to be used as a sacrament, and to compare with the consecrated wine that the clergy offered. As the crowds milled around him he would summon to his presence a wooden statue of the Virgin, with which to join hands as he pronounced the words of the marriage service, as a prelude to demanding wedding-gifts for himself and his bride; even in that he showed a flair for mass psychology, by offering one purse to the men and another to the women, and inviting them to compete in generosity.

Beneath the scandal which Tanchelm aroused in the orthodox it is possible to understand something of his appeal. His talent for manipulation is obvious, but it still needed material to work on. He began his mission in the bleak and primitive coastal region at the mouth of the Scheldt, and finished it in the populous town of Antwerp. In both places he spoke to people who received little from the church beyond demands for money and the spectacle of corruption which was exemplified by Antwerp's only priest, who lived in sin with his niece.[29] The alternative which Tanchelm offered contained more than blasphemy. His parodies of the Catholic sacraments not only created excitement and unity in his audience, but demonstrated his reliance upon the common reception of the word of God which he preached with spectacular fervour; his claims that he possessed the Holy Spirit and that he and his followers constituted the true church not only implied the rejection of the old but offered a path by which all men of good faith might seek salvation by their own merits, without reliance upon the ministrations of a manifestly unsanctified priesthood. Two incidents which the canons of Utrecht recorded in their letter to show how Tanchelm's followers imitated the pattern of his mission emphasize its salient points. Eberwacher, a country priest who had accompanied his master to Rome, seized the tithes of the church of St Peter in Utrecht and drove out the priest by force. A blacksmith called Manasses 'Following the example of his wicked master, founded a sort of fraternity commonly called a guild. It was composed of twelve men, representing the apostles, and a woman as St Mary.'[30] The canons naturally assumed that the purposes of the guild were obscene, and the function of 'Mary' far from virginal, but its object was far more probably devotional, and the number is reminiscent of the monastic principle that a new community should consist – for the same reason – of at least twelve monks and their abbot. Eberwacher's exploit confirms the violent anti-clericalism of Tanchelm's movement, but it also implies that he wanted the church for some purpose of his own, and like Manasses sought a way to sustain the exaltation which was aroused at Tanchelm's public gatherings by more regular communal devotion among his adherents.

The sensational nature of the sources leaves it far from certain how far, if indeed at all, Tanchelm departed from orthodox Christian teaching in relation to morals and the sacraments themselves[31] though it is hard to doubt that he was indeed heretical in the view that the corruption of the church had destroyed its apostolic mandate and the sacramental powers of its priests. It is very clear, on the other hand, that he aroused much enthusiasm, and most of it among the rural and urban poor. The blacksmith Manasses, like the weavers who still venerated the memory of Ramihrdus in the region of Cambrai, and perhaps like the citizens of Arras whom Bishop Gerard had interrogated in 1025, represented those who received the worst deal from both church and society. They were mobile, many of them detached from family and countryside to seek their future in crowded and precarious townships, and as members of growing communities poorly served by the church and wholly at the mercy of chance employment and ambitious employers, the victims of the process which was creating new wealth and new privilege for a minority of the many who pursued them. Tanchelm brought them an articulate assault on their enemies, a demonstration of the impotence of both natural and supernatural powers against him, and a degree of unity with one another. It was, at least to the extent that the bare outline of his career can be reconstructed, a pattern that would be repeated in the future, just as St Norbert and his companions, when they took over the church in Antwerp and sought to recover the lost ground by the example of humility in their common life and devoted preaching to their parishoners, anticipated the response of St Francis to the same conditions a century later.

About 1120 two priests, Frederick and Dominic William, and two laymen, Amalric and Durand, from the parish of Ivois near Trier, were accused of denying infant baptism and transubstantiation.[32] Amalric escaped, Durand confessed and abjured his heresy, and Frederick proved the substantial accuracy of the charges against the four by defending the propositions which had been attributed to them. His defence does not survive; the chronicler is content to note the two texts from St Augustine which the Archbishop quoted in refutation, insisting on the efficacy of the mass and the irrelevance to that of baptism of the infant's capacity to understand it. There is no hint of either the origin of the heresy or the mode or extent of its propagation, and the chief interest of the story lies in the fate of the fourth defendant, Dominic William. He denied that he had ever held the heresies in question, and when witnesses appeared who said that they had heard him do so in public, offered to clear himself by ordeal. He was told to say a mass, and at the consecration, the moment when he would be irrevocably damned if he were lying, the Archbishop interrupted him: 'If you have dared to say impiously that the life-giving sacrament which you hold in your hand is not the true body and blood of Christ I forbid you, in its presence, to receive it. If your belief is not that but the true one, take it.' He took it, went on his way vindicated, and resumed the preaching of his heresy.

Dominic William was a brave man. It is easy to say that if he really did not believe in Catholic teaching he had no reason for fear, but he lived in a world which was charged with the universal conviction of the nearness of supernatural power and the magic of holy things. Nevertheless he defied them, and nothing happened. Like Tanchelm he deliberately challenged the awful fate which awaited the blasphemer and survived, and like Tanchelm, though no other details of his beliefs remain, he represents a further manifestation of the extent to which the unquestioning acceptance of the power of the Catholic sacraments had been sapped in the generation after the papal reform reached its climax. It was with considerable relief that the chronicler was able to record that shortly after these events Dominic William was taken in adultery, and 'met a death worthy of his wickedness' after all.

Guibert of Nogent's account of his interrogation of Clementius of Bucy and his brother Everard, at the end of 1114, is a classic example of how St Augustine's descriptions of the Manichees were relied upon for the elucidation of contemporary events.[33] His assertion that the heretics met by night for sexual delight and used the ashes of the children of these unions as a sacrament is an exact echo, like the same tale told of the clerks of Orléans, of the stories which the fathers of the church had retailed as slanders levelled at the earliest Christians, and later turned against their own heretical opponents,[34] and he cited Augustine's statement that the Priscillianists would say anything to avoid conviction as the ground of his advice to the interrogating bishop to ignore Clement's assertion that he believed all the statements of orthodox teaching which were put to him. Like the inquisitors Guibert knew the answer to his question before he asked it, and would give no credence to any other.

Whether Clement's acceptance of orthodoxy was in fact dissimulation is difficult to decide. He was *rusticus*, an illiterate who said that he had embarked upon the path of error because he thought that the words of the Gospel, *beati eritis*, meant 'blessed are the heretics', and his protestation to Guibert and the bishop when they took him through the articles of faith that on each of them 'we believe everything that you say' is reminiscent of the reaction of the men of Arras in 1025 to Bishop Gerard's sermon. Nor, in the circumstances of the examination, can much weight be attached to the success of the authorities in producing a matron and a deacon who testified that they had heard him preach heretically; he might have done so unintentionally, as his defence implied, or the witnesses might have been led by their august examiners. On the other hand that his brother Everard not only confessed to heresy but declared himself impenitent must point to a deliberate rejection, on his part at least, of the authority of the church. In spite of Guibert's confidence, however, his account of how Lisiard of Soissons handled the case suggests a measure of doubt in the bishop's mind. In the first place Clement was subjected to the ordeal by water, a procedure which was not usually invoked unless there was thought to be a lack of decisive natural evidence,[35] and in the second when the water rejected him the bishop imprisoned him, together with his brother and 'two other proven heretics who had come from the village of Dormans to watch the spectacle', while he sought the advice of a forthcoming synod at Beauvais. The bishops assembled there decided to examine the heretics again at a special synod to be convened at Soissons, but it never met because 'the faithful people, fearing leniency on the part of the clergy, ran to the prison, seized them, placed them in a fire outside the city, and burned them to ashes'.

The circumstances of the case and the nature of the record alike deprive Guibert's assertion that Clement and his brother were members of a sect 'dispersed throughout the Latin world' of all credibility. The heresies which he attributes to them are that they denied the virgin birth, infant baptism, the mass, and the necessity of burial in holy ground, and condemned marriage and the eating of meat, but since his own account proclaims his certainty that he knew what they believed whether they admitted it or not there is no knowing how much of this list Guibert manufactured. There is, however, a hint of authenticity in the consequence that they drew from the denial of the mass, that 'they called the mouths of all priests the mouth of hell', while their mistranslation of *beati eritis* suggests that they believed their teaching to be that of the Gospels.

The rejection of infant baptism as unavailing to an uncomprehending child is a predictable consequence of that position, and though the denial of the necessity of burial in holy ground was something that the Bulgarian Bogomils had done in the tenth century it was also a comment on one of the many customs which, though now pressed by reforming churchmen for admirable reasons, nevertheless represented a source of expense and restriction to their flock. The abjuration of meat and the advocacy of chastity might, of course, have been part of a dualist cosmology, but it is far more likely that they simply elaborated the conception of the nature of holy living which had been so energetically propounded by the monks and hermits for a century past, of which Clement's endorsement is attested by Guibert's statement that he and his followers 'held that they followed the apostolic life'.

The histories of Clement and Everard, and of Frederick and Dominic William, are too scantily recorded to offer any basis for conjecture as to the inspiration, motives or following of their heresies, or to bear close comparison with Tanchelm's movement, which was nearest to them in time and place. They do, however, confirm the spread of a tendency to see salvation as a matter of individual responsibility, to distrust the authority and holiness of the church, and especially to doubt its capacity to perform its sacramental functions. To this limited extent they are consistent with the thesis that has been advanced of the relation between the quality of dissent and the upheavals of the papal reform, which had done so much to rob the church of its magic, the priests of their authority, and the sacraments of their position as the unquestioned repositories of holy power which was the ultimate sanction of orthodoxy.

The heresy of Eon de l'étoile lends itself less easily to systematic interpretation.[36] Eon was a Breton, probably a knight, since he was both *illiteratus* and of good family, who heard himself referred to at mass one day, in the words *per eundem Dominum nostrum*. Thus assured of his divinity he gathered a following among whom he lived like a king, surrounding himself with 'the magnificence, the trappings and the haughtiness of royalty', terrorizing churches and monasteries for two years or more before he was captured and brought before the Council of Rheims in 1148. There he showed Eugenius III and the other dignitaries present a forked stick which he always carried, and explained how when he held it with the fork pointed upwards God ruled two thirds of the universe and left the remaining third to him, and when he reversed it 'I keep two parts of the world for myself, and relinquish one to God'.

The Council dissolved in laughter, and concluded that Eon was plainly demented, and must be imprisoned to bring an end to his assaults on the faithful, but subjected to no other punishment. It was a level-headed reaction, and a unique one, for though heresy was commonly enough described as madness there is no other case in which the heresiarch himself was treated simply as insane. It was also obviously the right reaction, for even now the accounts of him read like text-book cases of paranoid schizophrenia, whose central characteristic is the determination of the sufferer to interpret what is said and done around him as referring exclusively to himself, as Eon did when he heard the words of the mass.[37] That, however, does not dispose of the case, for whether insane or not he wielded considerable influence over his followers, one of whom went to the stake still convinced that Eon's divine powers would save his disciple from the flames by causing the ground to open and swallow him before he was touched by them.

Their judgement of Eon made the chroniclers less interested in the doctrines that he preached than in the grandiose style of his leadership. The resemblance to Erlembald or Tanchelm in his princely trappings and the number and violence of his followers is revealed as superficial by his having celebrated his own mass, and ordained some of his followers archbishops and bishops, on whom he conferred titles like 'Wisdom', 'Judgement' and 'Knowledge'. Where Tanchelm had set out, with ferocious ingenuity, to strip ecclesiastical pomp and elaboration from what he conceived as the central simplicities of the Christian faith, Eon's dream was to supplant the grandeur of the church by a still more grandiose edifice of his own. To their followers, however, the difference was probably slight. Both preachers satisfied the yearning for charismatic authority and the unity which it could create, and both expressed it with the same dramatic defiance of the supernatural auxiliaries of the church which advertised their own claims to more than human authority. In Eon's case the tapping of anti-clerical sentiment which is inherent in the techniques which he used seems to have been reinforced by hunger. William of Newburgh heard from some of his disciples, who since his death had wandered the world in penance, 'that they always had bread, meat, fish and more delicate food to hand as often as they wanted it'. He concluded, understandably enough, that these were illusory banquets served by demons, but Eon's power over his devotees would be as readily explained if they were the contents of monastic barns and cellars, plundered in one of the poorest regions of France, and in years of particularly acute famine, as the 1140s were.

It seems that the 'heresy' of Eon lies near the boundary of that concept. Neither his own pathetic inspiration nor the needs which he satisfied and the sentiments which he aroused in his followers were essentially religious, though the age had no terms in which it was more natural to express them. Nevertheless they bear a clear affinity to the passions aroused in the more explicitly religious movement of Tanchelm, and they testify to a diminution in the popularity and influence of the Breton priests whose morals Robert of Arbrissel had tried in vain to reform, and once more to a decline in the church's capacity to sustain discipline in its flock by the conviction of its supernatural support. In its way the very absurdity of Eon – like that of many a more sinister demagogue – emphasizes the depth and ubiquity of the emotions which he stirred.

The change which took place in the pattern and tone of popular dissent during the generations of the reform was real and important, but it did not extirpate its most fundamental impulse. At Liège in 1135 there was discovered a group of people who 'while appearing to observe the Catholic faith and lead a holy life, denied legitimate matrimony, held that women ought to be shared in common, forbade infant baptism, and maintained that the prayers of the dead are of no use to the souls of the living'.[38] The resemblance of this catalogue of evils to those which the bishops of Cambrai, Châlons and Liège had exchanged about the heretics they discovered a century earlier is very striking. To those who see in the earlier cases evidence of the influence of the Balkan dualism which dominated western heresy by the end of the twelfth century this episode appears as an invaluable connection. It should be apparent by now, however, that quite apart from the absence of any unambiguous evidence of such an affiliation from this very short account, that interpretation is entirely superfluous. What was found at Liège in 1135 was a group of lay-people sharing a common life, pursuing the apostolic ideals of chastity and poverty, and rejecting what they saw as the elaborations which the church had imposed on the precepts of the Gospels. In this they indeed resembled their fore-runners of the eleventh century, as they did in the construction which gossip placed on their way of life. They resembled them also in a third respect: they were not aggressive, did not summon crowds to their aid to attack the church. 'When they could not deny these heresies the people wanted to stone them, but they were frightened and took flight during the night. Three of them were captured and imprisoned of whom one was burned at the stake, while the other two made a confession of faith and returned to the church.'

Martyrdom, no doubt, betokens a measure of obduracy, but it does not amount to the exuberant hostility to priests which was displayed by an Erlembald or a Tanchelm. Similarly, while Frederick and Dominic William at Ivois and Clementius and Everard of Bucy preached their faith and sought converts to it, and while their convictions were essentially anti-sacerdotal, their principal inspiration was the quest for the Christian life, and the desire to take responsibility for the salvation of their souls into their own hands. Ariald of Milan, Ramihrdus of Cambrai and Tanchelm were all moved by that same apostolic ideal, although in their cases temperament and circumstance imparted a very different flavour to the mode in which it was expressed. The crowds and the violence were exceptional, but the tradition of lay piety and the search for communal devotion, accompanied by self-denial and evangelical purity continued in much the same form as it had appeared at the beginning of the century, though it was now likely to be associated with a theology more distinctly marked by distrust or rejection of the Catholic sacraments.

This distrust was a natural concomitant of the ethos of spiritual self-reliance in which it appeared, and it was undoubtedly exacerbated by the scepticism of the priestly office and its holders which the Gregorians had disseminated in the heat of their revolution. As the church began to resettle after its moment of chaos, however, it was reinforced and sustained by the more durable successes and failures of the reform, which by elevating the priesthood separated it from the laity and by setting new ideals for its quality and conduct continued to underscore the infirmities of its human representatives.

The parish was one of the prominent beneficiaries of the great land clearing of the eleventh century. As tiny communities were, in effect, merged by the eradication of the desert between them the boundaries of the parish churches which had been arbitrarily deposited in the wilderness by Carolingian patrons were more sharply defined. As the holding of land increasingly became fragmented among numerous lords the parish, in some areas at least, supplanted the seigneurie as the natural framework of the peasant community, and expressed its function more regularly with the creation of confraternities, prayer groups and charitable associations which were the counterparts, and probably the models, of the brotherhoods which the heretics created.[39] This assertion of the parochial organization was assisted both by temporal and by spiritual institutions. The lords began, under persuasion, to grant the area around the church immunity from their jurisdiction, even sometimes in matters of blood, and the right of sanctuary whose maintenance and defence was constantly insisted upon by twelfth-century diocesan synods. The battle of the reformers to exclude laymen from the enjoyment of spiritual revenues was rewarded by a steady movement to hand over the rights to burial fees and seasonal offerings, and very often of tithes, not indeed to the parishes themselves, but to the bishops or monasteries in whose jurisdiction they lay. The church became the centre of peasant life, where 'parishioners went to mass at least once a week, where the principal family occasions of baptism, marriage and burial took place, in whose shadow the dead rested and alms were distributed to the poor'.[40] Yet especially in the rapidly growing urban communities, most numerous and most explosive in Flanders, this progress was very uneven. Where the responsibility was judiciously exercised parish services might keep place with growth; at Bruges a second parish church was founded at the end of the eleventh century, and three thirteenth-century foundations had been developed from sanctuaries active for many years before, and at Ghent the monks of St Pierre and St Bavo who shared the rights of the city at the beginning of the period had founded two more parishes there by the end of the eleventh century, three in the rapidly expanding *portus* by 1169, and another in the neighbouring countryside. Such industry was not universal. Brussels did not achieve a second parish until 1210, and at Antwerp although Tanchelm's activity forced the clerks of St Michel to hand over their church to the Premonstratensians they did not grant them full parochial rights, over which they successfully defended their monopoly until the end of the middle ages. The vigour of the towns stimulated the growth of population in the countryside as well, but its parochial provision was no better; in the fourteenth century there were still one hundred and twenty-five communities in the diocese of Cambrai which had no parish church.[41]

It is immediately noticeable that, at least in general terms, the areas most susceptible to popular heresy were precisely those in which parochial organization was most behind hand. Nevertheless the presence of the church did not invariably assure its immunity from criticism. The transference of dues from lay lords to ecclesiastical ones transferred also the hostility which they aroused. In the case of tithes it might be particularly pointed, not only because they were so often made over to monastic foundations rather than directly to the churches whose services they were, in principle, intended to maintain, but because they were the subject of a difference of opinion among the monasteries themselves. The older houses accepted them readily, but most of the reformed orders did not, at least in the years of their early apostolic vigour, and they criticized those who did with their customary frankness. St Robert of Molesme complained to his monks that 'we have an abundance of food and clothing from the tithes and oblations of churches, and by skill or violence we appropriate what belongs to the priests. Thus surely we feed upon the blood of men and share

in their sins'.⁴² The expression of such views, and the litigation to
which the possession of tithes so often gave rise, ensured that the
reformers were not alone in noticing that the effect of their surrender by the laity was often 'to bring out the secular character of
the monks rather than the religious character of the tithes'.⁴³ The
increasing determination of the church that the faithful should
avail themselves more punctiliously of its services was a source not
only of spiritual consolation, but of financial exaction: the regularity
with which the synods of the early twelfth century pronounced that
'no price may be exacted for holy oil, chrism and burial', or for 'the
sacraments and such services' attests their impotence to prevent
it.⁴⁴

The objections which laymen might feel to this extension of the
church's services were not, however, only financial. Historians have
been too ready to accept the view of twelfth-century bishops that all
heresies were novelties, and that those who resisted baptism, confession, marriage, the last rites and penance were departing from
the established customs of the faith. As a matter of theology this
may have been true, though it is not beyond contention. As a matter
of practice it is, at best, a distortion of the truth. The theologians
of the eleventh century had given much attention to the sacraments,
and had emphasized their place in the church with a new urgency
which stoked the passions that produced the attack on simoniacs
and married priests, and later shaped the evolution of church life
under the direction of the learned bishops whose emergence was
perhaps the greatest achievement of the reform. Enforcement of
attendance at mass on Sundays became more vigorous, if not always
more effective; the ancient tradition that baptism might be performed by a layman in emergency was more rigorously and more
narrowly enforced, and in the same way it was insisted that confession must be made to priests, and made regularly; the marriage
which had by tradition been, in effect, a civil contract, was moved
into the church, or at least to its door, and presided over by the
priest; the system of penance for the sins both of the living and
the dead was greatly elaborated and more universally applied.⁴⁵ In
all these ways the church was the innovator, pressing its attentions
more firmly into the everyday life of its people, and the protests of

the heretics were often conservative in relation to practice considerably more than to principle.

That all this ran directly counter to the spirit of enhanced individual responsibility, the notion that salvation lay in interior perfection rather than meticulous attention to ritual, which lay at the heart of all the great religious movements of this century, may not have been inescapable in logic, but it must often have appeared so to the *simplices* who followed the heretics. It was greatly emphasized by the process, which again represented one of the successes of the papal reform, of separating the clergy more clearly and more sharply from the laity. The assertion that they must follow a distinctive pattern of life, far more of them now in communities which observed their special rule and were to some degree secluded from the world, was complemented by this increased emphasis on the duties which they and they alone could perform in the Christian life, and dramatically symbolized by a change in the most solemn moment of worship. Until now communion in two kinds had been the rule, but henceforth, though the layman went to mass more often he found when he did so that the wine was reserved to the priest alone. It was a powerful reminder that the church was not of the world, and one calculated to encourage any tendency there might have been to question whether the mortal hands that held the chalice were worthy of the spiritual eminence which it proclaimed. At a more mundane level the enforcement of attendance at services whose language was incomprehensible helped to emphasize this growing separation of the priests from their congregation; the confusion which it inspired in Clement of Bucy and Eon de l'étoile was perhaps less important a manifestation of it than the request of the men of Arras in 1025 to have their declaration of faith translated so that they could understand it before they avowed it, and the indignation which a papal legate expressed at Toulouse in 1178 when he found it necessary to discuss the mysteries of the faith in the language of the people.[46]

The religious rebels of the late eleventh and early twelfth century were more similar in their convictions and more coherent in their objectives than those of the preceding fifty years. Socially too they seem to conform to a more regular pattern. Except for Clement of

Bucy and the demented Eon de l'étoile they were priests, most of them known to have been moved by disgust at the corruption of the church and despair of its capacity to reform itself. All of them began their work in the countryside,[47] but those who transferred their attention to the cities became the spokesmen of tumultuous and passionate mobs described by their critics as the dregs of society, the workless and rootless poor, who joined with vigour the attack upon those whom they saw as the sources of their misfortune.

These generalizations contribute to a plausible and familiar picture, but they do not tell the whole story. It is true that the growing towns attracted many more in the hope of work and wealth than were destined to find it, and that those who failed to strike gold were flung into an abject dependence on casual employment, vagabondage and beggary, uncushioned by the ancient structures of family, manor and village which gave their rural counterparts a defined, albeit a miserable, place in the world; the cloth workers who became the devotees of Ramihrdus are the classic example of this process.[48] But it was not only in the towns that such people might collect, for Robert of Arbrissel and Vitalis of Mortain when they preached in Maine and Brittany were also followed by what are described as hordes of beggars, thieves and harlots, whose origin remains obscure. A more substantial objection is that these descriptions themselves are not only brief and impressionistic, but entirely conventional in character. In only one case, that of the Patarenes, is it possible to compare them both with narratives more sympathetic to the objectives of the movement, and with a relatively precise knowledge of the social structure in which it appeared. The result, like those of studies of better documented crowds in later periods, is to show that whatever frightened observers might have said, those who became involved in the tumults of Patarene Milan were not the shiftless, the rootless and the despairing, but the solid citizens, artisans, merchants, lawyers, who already had a stake in the city, and would later form its commune.[49]

It has been apparent at many points in this narrative that although the movements with which it has been concerned do not lend themselves to a simple analysis in terms of class conflict they often involved those who either gained or suffered from a great

variety of social changes, and sometimes assisted in the resolution
of problems that arose from it. By forming their 'guild', for example,
Manasses and his associates, inspired by Tanchelm, found not only
a forum of common worship which compensated for the inadequate
provision that was made for them by the church, but, potentially at
least, a means of satisfying the social and human needs which a
parish church serves in addition to its religious functions. It is one
explanation of their appearance, therefore, that they constituted a
spontaneous response to the needs of changing situations which had
not been answered by existing institutions. The importance of this
aspect of the popular movements was enhanced by the fact that
medieval society conceived itself as being primarily divided not by
the horizontal distinctions of wealth and status, but by the vertical
one of function: a man might care a great deal, certainly, how rich
or respected he was, but he felt his place in society to be defined and
his loyalties to others to be dictated, by the *ordo* to which he belonged. The Gregorian redefinition of the proper relations between
the clerical and the lay orders had many repercussions. By 1090 it
had reached the point where Bonizo of Sutri, in his collection of
canons, made it more important than the old threefold division
between *laboratores*, *pugnatores* and *oratores*, lumping kings, nobles,
merchants and peasants together in a single *ordo laicalis*.[50] This
was the theory which found its ultimate expression in the disappearance of communion in two kinds for the laity.

From the claim of Gregory VII to have the right to depose
emperors to the gathering of priests into communities subject to a
common rule and a distinctive way of life, many of the conflicts and
debates of these years can be seen as expressions of the confusion
into which both social change and religious progress had thrown
the familiar pattern of orders. The great increase in the forms in
which the contemplative life might be led, and the tension between
its claims and those of the *vita apostolica*, amounted to a breaking
down of the *ordo* of the monks into a less monolithic, but also a
less cohesive structure. The confusion into which individuals of
dynamic spirit and high ideals were thrown by the tension which
they discovered between the life which their *ordo* imposed upon
them and that for which their spirits yearned was resolved by many

of them when they retired to the desert, detaching themselves from all order, and emerged again to found new institutions whose rule and habit would satisfy their fresh aspirations; in their ways, Ariald, Ramihrdus and Tanchelm were also men who found themselves at odds with the restraints which their orders placed upon their ideals, and rebelled accordingly. Among laymen too, the old pattern was breaking up; the *negotiatores* and *artifices* who founded guilds and led communal revolts had ambitions and requirements which differed from those of the *agricultores* who had formerly composed the whole of what was neither noble nor clerical. When the Gregorians changed the conception of the clerical order they also found that it was necessary to redefine the role of the laity in the church, and propagated the notion of the *miles Christi*, who as one of Gregory VII's 'vassals of St Peter', as a crusader, a Templar or a Hospitaller could take his place in the march of the church. Among those who availed themselves of the opportunity were many who had suffered from another change in the ordering of society, when the growth of primogeniture and the need to hold family lands together made the younger sons of noble families a class distinct from their elder or clerical brothers, who until they could find wives with estates of their own must follow their own fortunes and create their own pattern of existence; it is possible that the *iuvenes ordinis nobilis* who composed the bodyguard of Erlembald, and conceivably also Eon de l'étoile, belonged to that category.[51]

The society of Gregorian Europe was fluid in many dimensions; both vertically and horizontally, both conceptually and in fact, the familiar world was dissolving, and many men knew neither what their place was, nor what it ought to be. Such a climate is unpropitious to the maintenance of religion centred upon ritual,[52] and nourishes the urge of the disoriented to guard themselves against the corruptions of a disintegrating world, and seek by direct inspiration to prepare their own souls for the reception of their maker. In those conditions they clamour for a charismatic leader, who can demonstrate his independence of the discredited hierarchy by showing in his life the spectacular austerity of an Ariald, or the pomp and magnificence of a Tanchelm or an Eon, parodying that of worldly princes, and who can defy the forces that sustain established authority by marrying the Virgin, surviving the ordeal of the mass, or plundering monasteries to feed his followers. Such leaders found in the years around the turn of the century that wherever they might appear, in town or country, an enthusiastic reception awaited them. Whether it was to follow Robert of Arbrissel to the desert or Peter the Hermit to relieve the Holy Places, to massacre the Jews of Worms and Mainz, or assist Erlembald or Tanchelm to drive corrupt priests from their altars, the crowd was there to take its place, for the first time, in the great and small events of the age. In these cases, as in others, it had a single objective, to purify and cast out what was observed as a source of pollution which established authority had failed to extirpate.[53] That force did not always work in favour of heretics, as Clement of Bucy and his associates found when 'the faithful people, fearing weakness on the part of the clergy, ran to the prison, seized them, placed them in a fire outside the city, and burned them to ashes'. Guibert of Nogent was a thoroughly conservative man, who had written with celebrated disdain of popular initiative when he described the communal rising at Laon a few years earlier, but on this occasion he was more complacent. 'To prevent the spreading of the cancer,' he concluded, 'God's people showed a righteous zeal against them.' He failed to understand that the zeal of God's people might as easily be turned against whatever cancer appeared to them as the cause of their miseries. At Soissons it was the heretics, and at Laon it had been the bishop's officers whose venality and crimes had precipitated the revolt. In the long run the bishop's officers had more to lose.

To argue that popular heresy was the result both of the church's failure to reform itself, and of its success, may appear a spectacular indulgence in hindsight. On the whole the Gregorian reform was a success. It achieved a substantial transference of power and resources from lay to clerical hands, and if the process was noisy and even bloody in some of its aspects, as in the appointment and investiture of bishops, it was, by and large, remarkably peaceful in others, including the surrender by the laity of so many of their customary revenues, most notably tithes, which were derived from spiritual sources. The church was parted significantly if not wholly from the fabric of feudal incidents, and the identity of the clergy as a distinct order of society was re-established. A pattern of faith and worship began to be disseminated, albeit slowly, which commanded the assent and loyalty of most Christians and would be consolidated by the Lateran Council in 1215 into the enduring forms of Catholic life and spirituality. It would be foolish to maintain that if these developments had not taken place the growth of heresy would not have been much greater, or that the faith was not more effectively defended and the aspirations of the faithful more certainly satisfied by a better organized, better disciplined, and ultimately better educated priesthood.

Nevertheless success had its price. In the short run, the more loudly the ideals of the apostolic church were proclaimed the more vividly its shortcomings were advertised. In the long run, as the ideal approached realization it would become apparent that there were some, though perhaps a tiny minority, to whom it would be unacceptable.

Chapter IV | *The Religious Alternative :*
Henry of Lausanne
and Peter of Bruys

The dominant theme of the last two chapters has been the incoherence of religious dissent. A few common attributes have emerged. The reaction against the impersonal and institutional framework of Carolingian religious observance and towards the search for a personal link between creature and creator, away from the unquestioning acceptance of the revealed truth as it was expounded by the church and towards commitment to the inner light which might beckon a man from his own conscience, manifested itself widely both within and outside the church. It was accompanied by a steadily increasing concern for purity of life, and therefore by growing hostility to a priesthood whose claim to holiness was plainly unsupported by the virtue of its members. Certain doctrines became more frequently associated with rebellion: that sacraments administered by corrupt priests were worthless, that baptism availed nothing to infants too young to understand it; by implication, therefore, that the position of the church as the vehicle of salvation, the intermediary between man and his God, was inconsistent with both the nature of revelation and its own imperfection. But for each man and each group the translation of these sentiments into doctrine and action was a partial and haphazard affair. No comprehensive alternative to the teaching or claims of the church has survived from these years. The beliefs of individual dissenters can be made to seem either coherent in themselves or consistent with each other only by assuming that they held convictions that they did not avow, and by attributing to them adherence to ancient or eastern heresies with which no surviving evidence connects them. There is no justification for making that assumption. When a Leutard, a Lisois or a Tanchelm lost the faith that the church would provide for his salvation he did not turn to another religion conveniently left in a back cupboard from antiquity, or imported with a cargo of silks from Byzantium. He was cast on his own devices, and followed his inner beacon, employing certainly what thoughts might be suggested to him by the religious debates of his time, as far as they reached him, or by his observation of the workings of the church and the world, but lacking either the knowledge, the sophistication, or the human contact that would have enabled him to mould his instinctive conviction of what was good into an articulate faith. These were lonely and embattled men, unable to counter the overwhelming apparatus of Catholic authority except by clinging stubbornly to their private revelation, and none of them possessed, so far as we can see now, the power to fashion from it a connected statement of its meaning or a better answer to the abuse of their critics than abuse (however well deserved) in return. The seeds of heresy had been sown, and what would become characteristic heretical tenets had been expressed, but there had not yet appeared anything comparable with the great heresies of antiquity, a version of Christian life and teaching that could stand as a recognizable alternative to that which was proclaimed by the Catholic church. If we distinguish in that sense between the heresiarch, the formulator of a faith, and the mere rebel, Henry of Lausanne was the first heresiarch in modern European history.

Our knowledge of Henry's early life is confined to the assertions of St Bernard of Clairvaux that he had been a Black monk, and that he began his career as a preacher at Lausanne.[1] His first appearance, in the region of Le Mans in about 1116, is described in revealing terms.[2] His reputation had been growing in the area for some time before he approached the city. When he did so,

> he sent to the bishop two disciples who resembled him in his dress and way of life, just as our Saviour had sent his people ahead of him ... they reached the outskirts of the city on Ash Wednesday ... they carried a standard in the way that doctors bear staves, a cross with wrought iron fixed at the top, and their bearing and manner suggested some sort of penitent. The bishop, a man of great piety, received them gently and devoutly. Not anticipating the wiles of the Trojan horse he greeted them cheerfully and generously, and although he was about to set out for Rome ordered his archdeacons to allow the false hermit Henry to enter the city peacefully and preach to the people.

There was, as a matter of fact, no reason why Hildebert, without the hindsight betrayed by his chronicler, should have suspected the wiles of the Trojan horse. Preachers of this description had carried the message of reform far and wide, particularly in north-western France. The hermits were regarded as men especially fit to call the world to repentence. As one of them, Bernard of Tiron, put it 'A preacher of the church ought to be dead to the world . . . he earns the right to preach (*licentiam praedicandi*) by virtue of his mortification. Therefore the fact that I am a monk and dead to the world, far from depriving me of the right to preach confers it upon me the more.'[3] With his companions from the forest of Craon, Vitalis of Mortain and Robert of Arbrissel, Bernard preached widely in northern and western France. 'They wandered barefoot through the regions of Gaul, and preached the word of God in villages, castles and cities. They tore men away from the errors of their lives, and like strong and vigorous battering-rams, their force assisted by divine power, they assailed the ramparts of vice and infidelity.'[4] The penitential garb which advertised the nature of their mission did not commend itself to every observer; Marbod of Rennes described Robert of Arbrissel as 'marching barefoot through the crowds, having cast off the habit of a regular, his flesh covered by a hair-shirt, wearing a thin and torn cloak, bare-legged, beard tangled, offering a new spectacle to the onlookers since only a club was missing from the outfit of a lunatic', followed by a motley of disciples 'rushing through the district like a herd, wearing filthy clothes, famous for the thickness of their beards and, it is said, wearing shoes in the countryside, but going barefoot in the towns'.[5]

Marbod's comment, with its suggestion of hypocrisy and distrust of disorder, reflects once again the familiar tensions of the age of reform. The deployment of the wandering preachers against the resistance or apathy of local clergy was a device, inevitably, of Gregory VII, who had granted another such, Wederic of Ghent, *apostolicae auctoritatis licentia* to preach against the corruption of the Flemish clergy shortly before Ramihrdus was disciplined by his bishop for doing so at Cambrai.[6] Robert of Arbrissel and Vitalis of Mortain were entrusted with the mission of preaching by Urban II, as Bernard of Tiron was by his successor a little later, and their business was especially to denounce the two great enemies, simony and clerical unchastity. They did it vigorously, publicly, and with the usual ambivalent consequences. From such an enterprise hostility and unrest were inseparable, whether it came from the archdeacon of Coutances who had a wife and several children, and approached Bernard of Tiron, 'surrounded by a great crowd of priests and clerks' to challenge his right to address the people of that town, or from a man like Marbod who though personally irreproachable held that the result of Robert's revelation of the sins of churchmen to the common people would be 'not to preach but to undermine'.[7] Hildebert of Lavardin was a man of a different cast, an energetic administrator and a proponent of reform, the friend and patron of Robert of Arbrissel, unlikely to refuse permission to an eloquent preacher in the season of penance. It is ironic that in consequence he should be known to posterity not only as a fine classical scholar and the author of charming verse, but as the victim of the most spectacular success of popular anti-clericalism that had yet been recorded.

The effect of Henry's mission was catastrophic. He precipitated a popular rising against the clergy, they were boycotted by the shopkeepers, their houses sacked, and their lives saved – it is asserted – only by the forcible intervention of the count, who was nevertheless unable to prevent the heretic from controlling the city for some weeks. He left it only when Hildebert returned from Rome in the late spring, and even then the bishop did not recover his authority easily. He was greeted by a mob which expressed fury that his clergy had resisted the heretic, and asserted his leadership only by the combination of patience and a fire which did great damage in the suburbs, and chastened the ardour of their inhabitants sufficiently to enable Hildebert to expel Henry from the city. Even then his triumph was incomplete: he 'took every precaution to calm by reason and humility the popular fury which Henry had seditiously stirred up against the clergy, for the people had become so devoted to Henry that even now his memory can scarcely be expunged or their love for him drawn from their hearts'.

The account of Henry's sojourn in Le Mans, from the *Gesta Pontificum Cenomannensium*, is a *locus classicus* of heretical reporting. It is finely blended with all the elements most readily associated with popular attacks on the church. The tattered appearance of the heretic, the disreputable nature of his followers, his impassioned rhetoric and grotesque sexual exploits, and his final unmasking by the good bishop, returning from Rome in the nick of time, add up to a scenario which it would be hard to better. In short, the story is almost too good to be true. Henry is introduced in archetypal phrases, haggard, long-haired, wild-eyed, always ready to preach in his fearful voice, *sono tonitruo*, 'his home in the doorways, his bed in the gutters'. Almost at once the narrative becomes inconsistent. He had a reputation for unusual holiness and learning, but it did not rest on his morals or piety:

> women and young boys – for he used both sexes in his lechery – who associated with him openly flaunted their excesses and added to them by caressing the soles of his feet and his buttocks and groin with tender fingers. They became so excited by the lasciviousness of the man, and by the grossness of their own sins that they testified publicly to his extraordinary virility, and said [a surprising conclusion, it may be thought] that his eloquence could move a heart of stone to remorse, and that all monks, hermits and canons regular ought to imitate his pious and celibate life.

It seems, nevertheless, that Henry's instruction was not confined to caresses, for the passage concludes 'they claimed that God had blessed him with the ancient and authentic spirit of the prophets, and that he knew and told them many things which were unknown to others'.

This introduction to Henry offers a combination of assertions designed to discredit him as thoroughly as possible, to prepare the pious reader for shocks to come, and to fortify the weak against infection. It is plain that he criticized the lives of monks, hermits and canons regular effectively, and gained influence by doing so; it was therefore necessary to make it clear, without departing wholly from the truth, that he was not a man fit to offer such criticism, that he was unlikely to delineate a holier alternative, and that it was not primarily to his teaching that he owed his success. This does not mean that the *Gesta* is to be distrusted. The presence of some elements in the story which do not contribute to the impression that the chronicler would prefer to create is assurance of his honesty, and it is not surprising that some of the physical demonstrations that were stirred by the highly emotive and charismatic style of preaching in which Henry excelled should have seemed to those whom he attacked to justify the most lurid accusations against him. It is necessary also to remember that the distinction between the expression of wicked thoughts and the performance of wicked acts seemed less important to the chronicler than it may do to us. His purpose was not primarily to record what happened, but to show its place and meaning in the divine plan, 'so that the invisible things of God may be clearly seen by the things that are done, and men may by examples of reward or punishment be made more zealous in the fear of God and the pursuit of justice'.[8] He was concerned to extract from events the real truth which lay behind them and – especially important here in relation to Bishop Hildebert – to glorify the heroes of the church and expose its enemies. Hence if Henry's character was truthfully expressed by the assertion that he seduced women and young boys it did not matter greatly whether or not he actually did so: the crucial point was that he was a man of this degree of wickedness, as the extent of his heresy proved since heresy itself was a form of seduction far more serious and terrible in its consequences than mere bodily debauchery.

Through the lens of these notions the *Gesta* offers a reliable and conscientious account. Henry entered the city as a penitent, and the eagerness for his message extended even to some of the younger clerks, who helped to prepare a platform for him, and sat weeping at his feet while 'his speech resounded as though legions of demons spoke through his open mouth'. What he said is unrecorded, but it 'turned the people against the clergy with such fury that they refused to sell them anything that they wanted to buy, and treated them like gentiles or publicans. Not content with pulling down their houses and throwing away their belongings, they stoned and pilloried them.' Some fled the city, and when those who remained tried to negotiate with Henry they were beaten up by his followers. They addressed a long letter to him, accusing him of deceit and heresy, and threatening him with excommunication. William Musca bravely offered to deliver it personally, and to reproach the heretic in public: he does not seem to have disconcerted Henry, who 'nodded his head at each sentence of the letter, and replied in a clear voice "you are lying" '.

The burden of the charges which the letter contained was that Henry had been charitably received, and had responded by slandering the clerks and fomenting violence against them. No specific instance was offered of the 'slanderous and pernicious things' that he had said against the Catholic faith, 'which a faithful Christian would shudder to repeat'. His next move shocked the chronicler deeply, but a dispassionate examination of it reveals much of the character of his mission. He called a meeting at the church of St Germain and St Vincent, and

> pronounced a new dogma, that women who had not lived chastely must, naked before everyone, burn their clothes and their hair. No one should accept any gold or silver or goods or wedding presents with his wife, or receive any dowry with her: the naked should marry the naked, the sick marry the sick, and the poor marry the poor, without bothering about whether they married chastely or incestuously. While they followed his instructions he admired the beauty of the women, and discussed which ones had fairer skin or better figures than the others. In spite of this the people subjected their every wish and deed to his command.

In spite of the penultimate sentence, which may be mere embroidery or may anticipate the design which Henry was shortly to reveal, the penitential nature of this exercise is clear. Public confession, elaborate self-abasement, the destruction of the hair which symbolized lust and the clothes polluted by it, were of a piece with his brand of charismatic evangelism then, as they might be now. Henry did not stop there. When the fallen women had purged themselves before the assembly he called upon the young men present to marry them, taking up a collection from which he gave each of the women four *solidi* to replace the clothes that had been burned. The chronicler was appalled, and triumphantly recorded that the experiment was a failure, and that the women soon returned to their former trade, though he was not sure whether they were driven to it by lust or poverty. Nevertheless the interest which Henry showed in them as well as the penitential nature of his work, emphasizes again how close he was to more respectable reformers, for Vitalis of Mortain and Robert of Arbrissel both had special concern for the rehabilitation of prostitutes. Since he could find the resources for it Robert's solution, the foundation of the great abbey of Fontevrault, was no doubt a more practical one than Henry's, yet whatever the chronicler may have thought Innocent III would commend marriage to a fallen woman as a meritorious work.[9]

On this occasion Henry attacked three things that were changing the nature of marriage in his time. He resisted the Gregorian attempt to extend the church's control over marriage by making it a sacrament: twenty years later he would argue with a monk named William that 'the consent of the persons alone makes a marriage, without any ceremony, and a marriage thus contracted cannot be dissolved by the church for any reason except adultery'.[10] William had to concede to him that 'it is an institution of the modern fathers that marriage is consecrated', and it is noticeable that the Le Mans chronicler does not impugn the validity of the marriages contracted at Henry's advice, of which he disapproved so much. In addition the church was now interpreting the canonical insistence that marriage was incestuous if the parties were related in a new and more rigorous way, insisting that the degrees of consanguinity must be counted not from both partners simultaneously, but from either, so that they must have had no common ancestor not for three generations, as formerly, but for seven. The new regulations gave endless trouble, and would in the end be relaxed by Innocent III. Finally, the dowry was becoming a more widespread requirement and making marriage a mechanism not of human relations, but of financial management – and not only physical marriage, for it was thought a notable mark of the goodness of Vitalis of Mortain that he would be prepared to admit a novice to his nunnery at l'Abbaye Blanche without one.[11]

The effect of these changes among the poor in small communities can only have been to produce a drastic reduction in the number of marriages that could be contracted, and to frustrate a great many that were desired. Among the knightly class its dramatic consequences are well known. The young knights of northern France went far and wide in search of brides who could bring them good dowries, and to whom they were not even distantly related, and their efforts were the basis of a new literary culture which gave its name to the age of chivalry. Those who could not travel were less fortunate and less able to record their problems for posterity, but the famous peasants of Rosny-sous-Bois struggled for three generations to persuade the papacy that it was unfair to insist upon a regulation that forced them to choose between incest, if they married inside their village, and serfdom, if they sought legitimate brides among their unfree neighbours.[12] The 'new dogma' which Henry pronounced at his meeting, therefore, was to deny the authority of ecclesiastical innovations whose social consequences were disastrous for those who listened to him. That is why 'they subjected their every wish and deed to his command'.

Henry's career for the next twenty years is obscure. He is not referred to again until 1135, when he was brought before Pope Innocent II at the Council of Pisa by the Archbishop of Arles, in whose diocese he had presumably been active.[13] He was condemned, but there is no statement of the nature of the heresies of which he had been accused. According to Geoffrey of Auxerre he now renounced them, presumably to avoid severe punishment, and was handed over to the Abbot of Clairvaux to become a monk there.[14] It is not known whether he reached Clairvaux or not, for he disappeared from sight again, for almost another decade, before St Bernard was despatched to the Languedoc, in the company of a papal legate, Cardinal Alberic of Ostia, to undo the effects of his work. This was the first use of the institution which developed eventually into the papal inquisition, a macabre tribute to Henry's genius, and it may be that the involvement of St Bernard, whose order continued to be regularly concerned with these missions until the foundation of the Dominican Order, was the consequence not only of his fame as a preacher, but of the fact (if Geoffrey of Auxerre is right about what happened at Pisa) that Henry was now a renegade Cistercian novice.

It is plain from the letters of St Bernard, and of Geoffrey, who accompanied him, that Henry had had a considerable impact in the Midi. Bernard was a man of rhetoric, but his description of 'churches without people, people without priests, priests without the reverence due to them, and Christians without Christ' depicted an alarming situation.[15] Churches were no longer revered, he said, and the sacraments of baptism and extreme unction no longer accepted by the people. Henry had been driven from Poitiers and Bordeaux, and St Bernard followed his path through those cities to Cahors, Périgueux, and finally Toulouse, where the heretic was firmly entrenched with influential supporters. Henry did not wait to face his formidable antagonist, but fled to the countryside, where he had devotees in the villages, and his unwillingness to join battle lost him support. He was still at large when Bernard returned to Clairvaux, but his flight had been well advised, for he 'went into hiding and found the roads so well blocked and the footpaths so carefully watched that he was safe hardly anywhere, and was captured and brought to the bishop in chains'.[16] The implication is that St Bernard's mission was followed by an organized man-hunt, and its object was apparently not allowed to escape again. No more is heard of him and it must be presumed that he died in the bishop's cells, probably after a short interval since he was not, apparently, brought for trial before a council of the church, as ordinary practice would have dictated.

Even so bare an outline as this of the career of Henry of Lausanne leaves no doubt that he was a formidable enemy of the church. Wherever he went in France he had the ability to arouse popular enthusiasm against ecclesiastical authority, though it is worth noting that except at Le Mans, to whose special circumstances it will be necessary to return, there is no allegation that his activities were accompanied by violence. He brought into the arena against him two of the church's most distinguished leaders in Hildebert and St Bernard, he aroused the anxiety of a third in Peter the Venerable, and he provoked the papacy to depart from its habit of leaving such cases to the local authorities, and send a special mission against him. The chronicle of Le Mans and the letters of St Bernard testify vividly to the impact that Henry made on his contemporaries. What he actually said they indicate briefly and contemptuously, in the conventional manner, holding it no service to the faith to preserve such wickedness for posterity. A singular stroke of fortune has preserved in two manuscripts, both of southern French provenance, a full statement of his main teachings, in the form of a record made by a monk named William of a debate between the two. There is no indication of where or when it took place, or who William was, or to whom he addressed his narrative. Only his opening sentences offer any context for it:

> After I left your distinguished company I had a great argument with the heresiarch Henry. I have written a careful account of the dispute for you, so that if the brute should chance to descend upon your region you will know that he has been convicted of heresy by many good reasons and arguments, and will be sure to keep him away from the doors of your church.[17]

These words seem intended to protect some other bishop against the fate of Hildebert, the absence of any mention of Henry's conviction at Pisa suggests that it was written before 1135, and the provenance of the manuscripts points to the region where he spent most of his recorded career. As for William, there is no reason to associate him with any other known author, and his work reveals only that he was a competent theologian, well read in the standard works of the fathers, and, in his own time, of St Anselm of Canterbury. He did, however, possess one important quality; by contemporary standards he was remarkably fair-minded. At a number of points he refrains from presenting Henry's teaching in terms as extreme as his reader would have found plausible or even probable, as when he makes it quite clear that the heretic admitted the validity of the mass, though only when the priest who celebrated it was free from sin. His account is one-sided, in the sense that Henry's propositions are stated only briefly, and rebutted at great length, but he records one or two telling interjections, and the propositions themselves are given as direct quotations, clearly and concisely stated.

To the confidence which these qualities inspire William adds a hint that he may have been aided in his work by something more than the debate itself. 'In your first chapter,' he says, 'you say that churches should not be made of stone or wood,' and he speaks also of 'your chapter about penance' and 'your third proposition'. These references are clearly not to other sections of William's own manuscript, where the topics are treated in a different order from the one they imply, and they echo a remark which Peter the Venerable made a few years later that he had 'read a book which is said to stem from [Henry]'.[18] Henry's learning has been doubted because when Hildebert expelled him from Le Mans he tested and found wanting his knowledge of the daily offices, but whether that was because Henry had a poor memory, or was uncharacteristically nervous in public dispute with so eminent a figure, or unfairly represented by the chronicler, these passing remarks of William and Peter the Venerable clearly support the contrary judgement of St Bernard, that he was an educated man, and was capable of expounding his teaching with some precision.

It was clear to William, and Henry agreed with him, that the central questions in their debate were those of the authority of the church and the role of the priesthood, especially as it was affected by the unsatisfactory moral condition of both. The issue of authority was raised as soon as they met.[19] 'I approached him with the words "I would like to know under whose obedience you preach, and who has charged you with this mission." '

Henry's reply was familiar to all of his way of thinking: 'I profess obedience to God, not man; I was sent by him who said "Go therefore, teach ye all nations." '

William responded by advancing arguments for the divine authority of the priesthood, and the necessity (which was by now beginning to be insisted on more rigorously than formerly) of being properly licensed to preach. Immediately they were involved in the question how far the individual was free to interpret the precepts of the Gospels, which is crucial to the whole issue of ecclesiastical authority, and how far he was bound by the writings of the fathers of the church, which according to Henry 'contain some valid arguments, but do not lead to salvation'. Of course not, says William, only divine grace can do that, but 'if you refuse to listen to them you cut yourself off from the unity of the church and show that you are a schismatic . . . you will do great injury to the church in thus condemning so arrogantly her doctors and prelates'.[20] The ground therefore was clear. What was judgement to Henry was arrogance to William, and the essential difference between conformist and nonconformist, both in thought and in temperament, was defined.

It is notable that the account of Henry's doctrines which follows shows no trace of the horror of the flesh and the pursuit of holiness through extreme abstinence which had appealed to most of his predecessors. On the contrary, as we have already seen, he denied that marriage was a sacrament not because cohabitation in the flesh was wrong, but because the church was not entitled to interfere with it, and because he objected to the effect of its interference on people's lives. A similar concern lay behind his attack on the wealth of the church. 'Bishops and priests ought not to have money or benefices', he said, and 'churches should not be made of wood or stone', while William 'did not wish to discuss with him the appurtenances of priests, or the pastoral ring and staff, all of which are sanctioned by authority for the sanctification and regulation of the Christian life, or the significance of the array of vestments, the flashing jewels and glittering gold, or what their origins were'.[21] William's reticence was sound, for more respectable men than Henry were concerned by the ostentation of the reformed church, and we may doubt whether anything that he said about it was more scathing than, for instance, St Bernard's remarks on the subject. Nobody today can admire the glories of the renaissance of the twelfth century, the contents of the cathedral treasuries of Europe, and beyond all the cathedrals themselves, without wondering how they were paid for by a society which, expanding though its economy was, still struggled on the margin of survival. Henry of Lausanne knew.

The wealth of the twelfth-century church represented something more than conspicuous consumption. It was also a direct consequence, and a symbol, of the way in which the clergy, by reforming itself, had drawn away from, and above, the laity, and especially from the poor. To hold that churches should not be built of stone *or wood* was not simply to rebel against the emergence of Gothic, but to recall that 'Wherever two or three are gathered together, there shall I be', that as Peter of Bruys maintained, 'when God is called, he hears, whether in a tavern or a church, in the street or in a temple, before an altar or in a stable, and he listens to those who deserve it'.[22] This is to assert that the church is the community of the faithful, and that to communicate with their God they need no licence from a priest. The attack on the intermediary role of the priesthood, a growing source both of profit and of power, is the chief burden of Henry's case. He elaborated it at two other points where the reformed church was laying an increasing, and expensive, emphasis on the intermediary function. In rejecting prayers for the dead he denied the doctrine of purgatory, and with it William's contention that 'certain sins are cancelled out in the next world by the gifts of friends and the prayers of the faithful' – a point on which William, as a monk, would have strong views, for the great monastic revival of the early twelfth century was founded very largely on the readiness of the living to buy the prayers of the monks for their souls and those of their ancestors. The discipline of the church was even more directly assaulted by the contention that 'the Gospel does not require us to go to a priest for penance'. The insistence on regular confession which was to be enshrined in the canons of the Fourth Lateran Council was already one of the chief objectives of reformers. At this point in the argument William recognized very clearly what was at issue between him and Henry:

> There cannot be reconciliation except through a mediator. We know the priest as a mediator who acts in place of Christ, who was uniquely and especially the mediator between God and man. Therefore we must confess to priests.[23]

It may be significant of the importance of this point that at the end of the section on confession William allows himself one of the relatively few passages of mere invective in his lengthy work, calling Henry a leper who 'must shout unceasingly that you are a leper, a heretic and unclean, and must live alone outside the camp, that is to say outside the church'.

The relationship between popular heresy and the reform of the church has been a central theme of this and many other studies. The judgement of Augustin Fliche that the reform forced men to choose 'between the basest passions of the flesh and the moral teaching of the church'[24] has been superseded, in a more sympathetic generation, by the realization that one of the great stimuli of popular dissent was precisely the reverse, the failure of the church to meet the high expectations of moral renewal which were aroused by the Gregorian reformers. We have seen on several occasions how fine was the boundary which distinguished those who fought for apostolic purity within the church and those whose ideals brought them outside it, so that the heretics have increasingly been regarded by modern historians as the overspill of the reform movement, men who clashed with the church because they loved it too much. It is therefore important to recognize that this was not the case of Henry of Lausanne. His assault was focussed directly on the ideals of the reformers. He attacked them not simply because their efforts produced unpleasant social and economic consequences, although he clearly found those obnoxious, but because they were founded upon a conception of the nature of the church and of the right relations between Christians and their God which was diametrically opposed to his own.

The debate with William shows that Henry possessed a clear and positive understanding of his religious ideal. It was not one which rejected the fundamentals of Christianity, or even of Christian tradition, out of hand. Of the fathers of the church, for instance, he said, 'I accept the New Testament and my teaching is based upon it. If you bring arguments against me from Jerome or Augustine, or other doctors, I will grant them some force, but they are not necessary for salvation.'[25] Those words were shocking from such a source, and in a world where Peter Abelard could cause deep disturbance by drawing attention to the possibility that the fathers might err, but they are not the words of a fanatic. In returning, as he did, to the New Testament for his inspiration Henry did not, in the manner of many a modern fundamentalist, exclude the possibility that his own interpretation of it might be modified by the comments of others, even those who were claimed by his opponents as the champions, and after the apostles as the founders, of Catholic orthodoxy. It is a pity that William does not, by recording Henry's comments on any of the passages from the fathers which were cited against him, allow us to verify his claim that he is willing to treat them with respect, though not with veneration.

What, then, was Henry's idea of a church? It is plain that he despised the corruption and rejected the claims of the church of his own day: reformed or not he would have none of it. He knew his Gospels well enough to cite at least the texts which appeared to support his position, and he is accused of no heresy touching directly the nature or persons of God, Christ, the Virgin or the apostles, except in so far, of course, as heresy itself was alleged to injure them. His position on the sacraments and ceremonies is consistent; he rejects the Catholic versions of them, but not the things themselves. Marriage is not a sacrament, but it is a valid and binding ceremony. Baptism should not be conferred with oil and chrism, for which there is no scriptural warrant, or upon children who are not old enough to understand its meaning – but, *a fortiori*, baptism itself he accepted. 'Mass may be sung, and the body of Christ may be consecrated, if he who does it is found to be worthy.'[26] William claimed that this amounted to postulating a chimera because no man is without sin – but Henry did not say that 'being found to be worthy' meant being without sin, and his position, though certainly heretical, therefore implied a positive affirmation of the eucharist. Quoting from 'Your chapter about penance' William shows him citing the New Testament again: 'James says, "Confess therefore your sins one to another." He says not "Confess to priests" but "Confess one to another".'[27] The suspicion that the repetition implies not simply a denial of the Catholic ceremony, but the commendation of a positive alternative to it is supported by the fact that William's reply begins by discussing the dangerous consequences of confessing 'to peasants and illiterates' as well as by the recollection of Henry's actions at Le Mans.

These are clear indications that Henry's knowledge of the New Testament had given him a vision of a community of the faithful, bound in worship by the reception of baptism and the sharing of sacrament, placing within its framework the social act of marriage, and the discipline of mutual confession. It would be interesting to know whether or not it included a priesthood, but whether through Henry's fault or William's it is impossible to distinguish between his hatred of the clergy of his own day and his view of the status itself. He denied that priests of the present day had the power of binding and loosing, because they had lost it through their sins, and William's angry response suggests that this was a specific reference to the contemporary clergy: 'How can you talk of modern priests, as though priests have had different powers at different times? Did they not sin before as they do now?' He did not record Henry's answer to this question. But when he expounded the doctrine of the Petrine commission, and argued that 'Peter, when he was head of the church, sinned by denying his Lord and master in the passion', and yet did not lose his apostolic dignity in consequence, Henry interrupted, 'Peter repented and made expiation with his tears.'[28] The interruption delighted William, who concluded triumphantly that modern priests also were forgiven when they repented their sins and that Henry had given away his case; he closed the argument without considering that Henry had drawn attention not only to the fact, but to the quality, of Peter's repentence. This suggests that Henry did not deny either the Petrine commission or the apostolic succession, but these in themselves do not amount to the endorsement of priesthood: it might have been held that they applied to all Christians. The argument is drawn from silence, but reinforced by the passage at the beginning of the debate, when Henry asserted his freedom to expound the Gospels with the words 'I was sent by him who said, "Go therefore, teach ye all nations." ' William answered that he would deal separately with Henry's view 'on callings and on being charged with other duties', and later that the apostles specifically charged their chosen successors with the duty of preaching: it was not required of all men, and it would be absurd if everybody did it. Unfortunately he never did deal with Henry's views 'on being charged with other duties', and therefore left no indication of what they were.

While an outright denial of the special place of some of its members in the Christian community would not have been out of place in Henry's thought, however, there is no clear evidence that he made one. It would be unfair to William to suspect him of shrinking from reporting even as dangerous a heresy as this when we owe him so full an account of the rest. It is a general characteristic of the early heresies that they were personal affairs. Henry and his like were prophets, not organizers. That is why their teachings did not survive them. If there was a lack of clarity in his thought at this point it is readily understandable in the light of the central point of his teaching, which is revealed with him, as with others, in his view of baptism.

The denial of infant baptism was, by now, the most universal of all heretical teachings. Henry approached it in a characteristically humane fashion, maintaining that children who died unbaptized would be saved, because 'It is wicked to condemn a man for the sins of others.'[29] According to one of the manuscripts of the debate he applied this even to the children of Jews and Moslems. This involved him in denying two of the foundations of the Catholic faith, the doctrine of original sin, and the principle that a child might be baptized, as William said, 'in the faith of those who baptise them, in the faith of their parents, in the faith of the whole church'. To William original sin was the very raison d'être of the Christian faith: quoting St Anselm's *Cur Deus homo* (a book whose currency was still largely confined to monastic circles), he pointed out that to deny it was to deny the necessity of the incarnation and of the atonement. 'By denying baptism you deny the necessity of benefiting from the death of Christ, and show yourself clearly a Pelagian heretic.' The premises of St Anselm's exposition of the doctrine of the atonement had been that man was steeped in original sin, and that he was not able to redeem it by his own efforts because in his sinful condition he could make no sacrifice great enough. This indeed was not new. His originality lay in the elimination from the process of the devil, who in earlier and cruder theologies of the atonement was entitled by the agreement of God to the souls of all sinners, and therefore, since the fall, of all men. By excluding the devil, however, Anselm threw a still greater weight on the helplessness of man. It was his own inherent imperfection, without the necessity of an external power of evil, that wrought his damnation. He arrived in the world struggling beneath the accumulated wickedness of his fore-bears, a soul already lost, but born that he might have the opportunity to be born again. In such a condition he dare not await maturity before he sought redemption, and it was the crowning mercy of the atonement that, by being received in baptism into the community of the saved, he might participate in their redemption, and be saved in their faith. For the individual soul, therefore, there was and could be no salvation outside the church. The power to seek salvation existed only within the community of the baptized. For the church, on the other hand, baptism was its first and greatest duty. A child who died without it returned to the pit from which he had come; his chance of salvation was lost for ever. When St Bernard complained that in consequence of Henry's work 'the grace of baptism is denied, and Christian children are kept away from the life given by Christ' he described the greatest wickedness that he could imagine, and did not doubt its source. 'This is devilish jealousy, this is the jealousy which brought death into the world.'[30] His words were redolent of the ancient fear: the devil had sent Henry to undo the work of Christ, and bring mankind once more into his dominion.

Henry rejected this view of man, and of God. He maintained that the text 'Suffer little children to come unto me, for of such is the kingdom of God' disproved original sin, because when Christ spoke the words it was not customary to baptize children. Once again, in fact, he saw a Catholic sacrament as a needless elaboration of the original faith. Divine justice did not require infants to be held responsible for the sins of others; on the contrary they were held by Christ to be the model of purity: 'Unless you be converted and *become* as little children, you shall not enter into the kingdom of heaven.' Children did not bring corruption into the world with them: they found it waiting for them when they arrived. The second birth of baptism did not undo the work of the first: it enabled its recipient to return to the situation in which the first had placed him. Until a man was old enough to sin (and William and Henry were agreed that sin could not be committed without understanding), he did not need to be absolved from sin: he might remain, on the contrary, a model, as Christ had shown, for those who had outgrown innocence. From this a second opposition followed, which, though Henry did not state it, is scarcely divisible from his view. For William a sinful soul arrived in the world to be redeemed in the faith of the Christian community. For Henry an innocent soul arrived, to be corrupted. He could hardly, therefore, see the church as a place of salvation. Where for William the evils that he saw in the church of his day were a deplorable, but a secondary human taint on the vessel of salvation, they were to Henry the inevitable manifestation of the corruption which engulfed the innocent soul. That soul came into being endowed, as it was not for William, with the power of good, and its possessor must struggle to maintain it against the forces of worldly evil. 'When the Gospel says "He that believeth and is baptised shall be saved: but he that believeth not shall be condemned" how can you maintain that baptism is possible without faith? He who has not yet attained a state of being able to believe or not to believe cannot believe.'

In Henry's world, man was by nature a better creature, endowed with greater powers, than in William's. But he was also confronted by greater danger, and he could rely on none but himself to extricate him from it. The power to choose good included the power to choose evil, and if men were not born evil they must have embraced it: to deny original sin is to increase not only human freedom, but human wickedness. A man possessed by such a vision must necessarily distance himself from human institutions. They embodied not the mechanism of salvation, but the sum of corruption. Since Henry never doubted the need for salvation his higher view of man inevitably led him to a lower view of mankind. His search for salvation could not but involve the attack on the church, where damnation lay. When he greeted William with the words 'I profess obedience to God, not man,' he proclaimed the only course that could be open to him, and the reply which he evoked described precisely the gulf that separated the heretic from the Catholic. 'It astonishes me', said William, 'that you will not bow your presumptuous neck to the yoke of human obedience.'[31]

To stress the originality of Henry of Lausanne may be unjust to the memory of Peter of Bruys, with whom he was associated, and whose influence upon him is not easy to assess. Like Henry he alarmed the church enough to bring a powerful antagonist against him. The *Tractatus contra Petrobrusianos* of Peter the Venerable, whose learning, vigour, and charm made him distinguished even among abbots of Cluny, is by far the most powerful and sophisticated rebuttal of popular heresy in this period, and our only source of knowledge about the sect which it attacked and its founder. Peter of Bruys was born in the Alpine village of Rosans, and it was in that region of 'bare rocks and perpetual snows' that he preached, probably, for the greater part of his life.[32] He was driven from it by the efforts of the local bishops, and repaired to the diocese of Narbonne where he was much more successful. Towards the end of his life he began to move back towards Provence, and met his death near Arles. As with Henry at Le Mans, to expel Peter of Bruys was not to end his influence. Peter the Venerable's treatise was addressed to the bishops of Die, Embrun and Gap, because, he said, although they had got rid of the heretic his heresy remained in their dioceses, 'not so much defended as whispered about', and he left seeds behind him which might bear fruit if they were ignored.[33] A year or so later Peter added a prefatory letter to the treatise, and the Archbishop of Arles to its addressees. Peter of Bruys was now dead, 'when the zeal of the faithful at St Gilles avenged the flames of the holy cross which he had set alight by burning him with it', but his work was being carried on 'by his heir in wickedness, Henry, and I don't know who else'.[34] The comment that he had been spreading his heresies for almost twenty years completes the sum of the personal information about him which survives.

The manner of his death draws attention to the most distinctive tenet of Peter's teaching. He held 'that holy crosses should be broken and burned, because the instrument on which Christ was so horribly tortured and so cruelly killed is not worthy of veneration, adoration, or any kind of supplication. In revenge for his torment and death it ought to be dishonoured and insulted, hacked by swords and burnt by fire.' This is a new doctrine in the west, and has been thought to suggest some hint of influence from the Bogomils, who also held it. No other such influence, however, is perceptible among Peter's views so that if that is the case it must represent an isolated rumour rather than any direct contact or systematic influence; certainly Bogomils would not have thought it appropriate to dissociate themselves from the celebration of the passion, as the Petrobrusians did, by publicly eating meat on Good Friday. It seems at least as likely that such a belief might be the product of a simple devotion to the person of Christ, uninfluenced by the educated considerations which Peter the Venerable advanced, of the necessity of his sacrifice and of the place which the symbolism and adoration of the cross had assumed in orthodox Christian worship.

Cross-burning is reminiscent of the bitter attack upon the visible images of Catholicism which characterized the career of Tanchelm, and formed part, if Peter the Venerable is to be believed, of a very similar pattern of behaviour. He speaks of 'unheard of crimes in your areas, people rebaptised, churches profaned, altars overthrown, crosses burned, meat eaten in public on Good Friday, priests beaten up, monks imprisoned, women forced to marry by threat and torture'. It may have been such happenings that moved him, with uncharacteristic ferocity, to urge the bishops if necessary to seek secular assistance to extirpate the heresy by force of arms.

The hatred of the church which those words suggest is expressed throughout the teachings of Peter of Bruys. The view which we suspected in Henry of Lausanne is made explicit here: 'there should be no churches or temples in any kind of building, and those which already exist should be pulled down; Christians do not need holy places in which to pray'. Baptism is of use only to those old enough to understand it, and 'the faith of others is of no use to children because they cannot use it', any more than can the dead, whose fate is decided, and who cannot be assisted by 'masses, offerings, prayers, alms or relics' from the living. The denial of the mass is predictable in this company, but the ground on which it was denied is new. According to the Petrobrusians Christ shared the Last Supper only with the disciples, and the words in which he offered himself were intended for them alone, and could have no application for future generations.[35] Where others attacked the mass on the grounds either of the unworthiness of its ministers, or of the incredibility of transubstantiation (which might also lie behind this view, but is not mentioned in the very thorough refutation which Peter the Venerable devotes to it), the Petrobrusian rejection was based on a direct scepticism of the idea that Christ created, or intended to create, a symbolic relationship between his life and his future followers. The implications of that proposition are more radical than any presented even by Henry of Lausanne, for it appears to strike at the root not only of the Catholic church, but of any idea of a church which conceives it as forming a link between the Christian, his fellows in his own and other generations, and their Saviour. To this extent it is of a piece with Peter's other teachings, though it pushes them farther than any of his predecessors had done, but it is difficult to know what weight should be placed upon it. Henry was a man who was neither wholly ignorant of the church's teachings and traditions, nor wholly unsympathetic to what he supposed had once been its nature. His restraints proceeded not from any natural moderation of temperament, but from a sense, to some degree educated, of the nature of religious belief and experience, an ability to inhabit the world of symbol and the search for meaning beyond the merely temporal which is inseparable from the ideas of faith and salvation, whether Catholic or not. There is nothing to suggest that Peter of Bruys had any such background, and what we are told of his movement suggests rather a simple and violent scepticism of everything connected with the claims of a hated priesthood. He and his followers placed themselves directly before an angry God – one, in another of his curious, but surely untutored touches of originality, to whom it was pointless to sing or make music, since 'God laughs at ecclesiastical chants, because he loves only the holy will, and is not to be summoned by high-pitched voices, or caressed by well-turned tunes'.[36] While the propositions attributed by William to Henry of Lausanne display a developed and coherent interpretation of Christian teaching, albeit one which did not win the approval of its orthodox critics, there is nothing to suggest that the consistency of the tenets of Peter of Bruys rested upon anything more substantial than that they were directed with equal passion against a consistent orthodoxy. Peter the Venerable stresses continually that Peter of Bruys preached five important heresies: destruction of the cross, and of churches, denial of baptism and the mass, and of the efficacy of prayers for the dead. The fullness of the *Tractatus*, the learning and sophistication of its author, and especially that one of his motives in writing was 'to soothe the secret doubts of the faithful', are decisive objections to any suggestion that its account of the teaching of Peter of Bruys omits the rebuttal of other major heresies which might appear to be the logical concomitants of those that were specified, or that Peter the Venerable was willing to leave it to his readers to complete his case. In consequence the five principal heresies of Peter of Bruys must be regarded as random shots at a well-built and regularly shaped target, rather than the essential foundations of a rival faith.

The view that Peter of Bruys was a relatively naïve anti-clerical leader, a Provençal Tanchelm, while Henry of Lausanne was an original and creative religious thinker, 'blessed' as they said at Le Mans, 'with the ancient and authentic spirit of the prophets' appears to contradict Peter the Venerable's description, which has usually been accepted, of Henry as the 'heir in wickedness' of Peter of Bruys. To some extent his judgement has been taken at its face value because Peter of Bruys seemed to have elaborated his teaching sooner. That assumption is modified by the recent discovery of the debate with William, which shows that Henry's teaching was formed, apparently, before 1135, and was more consistent with what he had done at Le Mans than used to be supposed, while recent discussion of Peter the Venerable's work has concluded, on the other hand, that his account of the Petrobrusians was composed after and not before the Council of Pisa, between about 1138 and 1141.[37] Nevertheless the careers of the two men overlapped to too great an extent for that adjustment to weigh heavily; if Peter of Bruys had been active 'for nearly twenty years' he had begun, even if he did not die until about 1138, within a short time of Henry's departure from Le Mans. That he started his work a little earlier would not be sufficient to vindicate Henry's originality against Peter the Venerable's description of him not only as the heir of Peter of Bruys, but as his 'pseudo-apostle' and 'hanger-on', or to regard the statement that Henry had 'not only amended his (Peter's) diabolical teaching, but altered it considerably',[38] as anything but confirmation that of the two Peter of Bruys was the innovator.

Peter the Venerable admits, however, that his comments on Henry were based on imperfect knowledge. 'One's soul burns to attack him, and to obliterate his devilish sayings with divine words, but I am not yet quite certain that he believes or preaches these things, and I shall delay my reply until I am fully informed when they were said, and in what context.' His reticence may have been well judged, for 'these things' were the five central propositions of Peter of Bruys, including the advocacy of the destruction of crucifixes. The records of St Bernard's mission of 1145 do not add to our knowledge of Henry's teachings; in fact they say almost nothing about them. But the destruction of crosses was a serious and shocking crime, which is nowhere mentioned in connection with Henry. Bernard's letter to the Count of Toulouse, written early in 1145 to announce the mission, emphasizes that Henry was encouraging absence from mass and the avoidance of baptism and extreme unction, but it says nothing of violence of any kind, and nothing of attacks on churches or the crucifix. It must be supposed, therefore, that the absence of any such doctrine from William's account of Henry's view was not reversed in later life, and that Peter the Venerable was indeed mistaken in attributing it to him. On the other hand the only occasion on which he mentions Henry except as a mere follower of Peter of Bruys is in relation to the rejection of baptism, which we have identified as Henry's most fundamental doctrine; the jibe that Christians were being asked to believe that they would not be saved 'unless after the baptism of Christ we are baptised with that of Henry'[39] implies that on this point the rumours that reached Cluny had correctly identified a difference of emphasis between the two heretics.

Before they met in the area around Toulouse Henry's activity, as far as it can be traced, had been in western and south-western France, that of Peter of Bruys in the south-east, where episcopal action had been taken against him. To suggest that the Abbot of Cluny might naturally suppose the more important heretic to be the one who had been active for a long time in the area which he knew better is, admittedly, to imply that he had missed, or overlooked, the proceedings of the Council of Pisa, or was not caused thereby to revise his judgement, but if he is taken at his word when he says that he knew little of Henry there is no other obstacle to the view that of the two heretics it was Henry who had formed the more coherent and advanced body of teachings.

The lengths of their careers and the quality of the opposition that they aroused stand witness that Peter of Bruys and Henry of Lausanne were not isolated eccentrics who preached to empty air. Both of them evoked great fervour, and led their followers to acts of substantial defiance of the established order. In Henry's case at least it is possible to say something of the nature of this support, the kind of people who responded to his words. Like their predecessors both of them seem to have begun in remote areas, and met greater enthusiasm when they moved into the towns. Henry had his great successes at Le Mans and Toulouse, and Peter made most progress when he left his native Alps for the wealthy littoral of the Mediterranean. 'What he had formerly whispered timidly in wild places and little villages', says Peter the Venerable, 'he now preached boldly to large gatherings in populous cities'.[40] He adds, with the puzzlement with which many an intellectual has noted the failure of progress to carry enlightenment with it, that he had expected that teachings which appealed easily enough to the backward and primitive population of the mountain regions would scarcely survive exposure to the more sophisticated people of the plain, who had been well taught by their preachers and often warned against false doctrine, but he was quickly proved to be mistaken; it is a useful caution against the assumption that the susceptibility of the people of the Languedoc to heresy is attributable to the laziness of their pastors.

Henry, it has been noted already, had preached in the countryside around Le Mans before he entered the city, but the fact that Hildebert allowed him to do so is itself an indication that he had not succeeded in making the nature of his message clear. Among those who assisted him were some of the clergy, who prepared a platform for him and sat weeping at his feet while he denounced the sins and abuses of their order. Two of them, Cyprian and Peter, apparently left the city with him, and remained in his company for some time before they repented and sought the forgiveness of the church, which they obtained in the form of a letter from Hildebert asking that their ill-judged association should not be held against them.[41] It is not untypical of hierarchical organizations that among their younger members are some idealistic enough to wish to dissociate themselves in the eyes of the people from the abuses of their idle and corrupt seniors, and there must have been many of the generation of Cyprian and Peter who entered the reformed church with an eagerness that was quickly soured by the complacency of the chapter. Nevertheless that they returned to the church may suggest not so much that they became less adventurous with age, as that Henry's doctrines were limited in their appeal to the educated.

Henry's oratory 'turned the people against the clergy with such fury that they refused to sell them anything or buy anything from them'. It was therefore among the shopkeepers and small traders who huddled around the walls of the episcopal city that he found support, among the *burgenses* whose dwellings in the *suburbs* were destroyed by the divinely inspired fire that brought them to their senses and enabled Hildebert to reassert his authority. It would, however, be wrong to see here the self-assertion of an emergent bourgeoisie against clerical domination. At Le Mans quite the opposite was the case. The city had been the scene of one of the earliest communal risings in Northern Europe. In 1070, in the purest tradition of the movement, the citizens 'made a conspiracy, which they called a commune (*communio*) and all bound themselves equally by sacred oaths'. They made a stir, and were put down by William the Conqueror. On this occasion, as in Henry's time, they were able to control the city, for they forced the clergy and some of the secular nobility to support them, but they did not get their commune, either then or later. A compelling explanation of that paradox has been advanced.[42] Le Mans was a clerical town. It had in its midst the swarm of petty tradesmen and artisans who supplied the needs of a wealthy clergy, the butchers, bakers, innkeepers and tailors, tanners, skinners, carpenters and smiths. The nature of their economy was well illustrated in 1092, when the county was placed under interdict by the bishop of Mans, who wanted to frustrate a usurpation of the countship. 'The hoteliers, the jesters, the butchers and bakers, the women who sold trinkets of little value, everybody who in normal times made good profits from the affluence of the people of the province', wrote the same chronicler who recorded the doings of Henry, 'murmured angrily against the bishop's enemies, through whom they were deprived of the profits of their business.' It might as easily, if anybody had suggested it to them, have been against the bishop, for pronouncing the interdict.[43]

These were small people who had clustered around the city to scrape a living from the everyday needs of its wealthy clerks. The newness of their community as well as the meanness of their lives is illustrated by the nicknames that they gave each other, not yet urban enough to have regular family surnames, 'Witless', 'Fathead', 'Farter', 'Threeballs'. If they served the church they were also easily subjected to its disciplines over such matters as the regulations on consanguinity, and daily exposed to the arrogance and affluence of its more tactless officers, one of whom they dubbed in their own fashion 'William Who-won't-drink-water'. They were ready enough to rise against the clergy, pull down their houses and beat up those who tried to oppose Henry. He, it seems, commanded their devotion easily; few before him, no doubt, had tried to. He attempted to use his power to bring a measure of stability to their lives when, in addition to preaching to them he organized the remarkable social experiment of finding husbands for the repentant whores. It may seem as ludicrous to the modern eye as it did wicked to the chronicler, but it signalled an attempt to add to the fire of his oratory some practical improvement in the lot of his followers, and goes far to explain the affection in which they held him. There is a certain pathos in the words with which they greeted their bishop when he returned to the city: 'Bless the dirt. Sanctify filth. We have a father, a bishop and a defender greater than you in authority, fame and learning.' The same pathos explains why, for all the precocity and regularity with which they sought to establish their political independence they never got their commune, even when it became easier than it was in 1070. They were small men, struggling on the margin of destitution. They did not produce. There were among them none of independent wealth, of the weavers, or merchants in cloth or spice, who owed their position to manufacture or long-distance trade, and who in Flanders or Lombardy would have stepped forward to make peace between the mob and its masters, and take their natural places as the *bons hommes*, or even the consuls, of a commune established by agreement and charter. Threeballs and Farter were not the material of which the urban revolution was made. Their total dependence on the wealth of the church for their livelihood condemned them to impotence as surely as to the continuous resentment which Henry brought to one of its periodic eruptions.

The story of Le Mans is a welcome reminder that there was no inevitable opposition between the increasing wealth of the twelfth century and the church, which on the contrary generated a great deal of it in one way and another. For instance, Peter the Venerable was doubtless right to attribute the action of the citizens of St Gilles in throwing Peter of Bruys onto his own bonfire to their zeal for the faith. But it was naïve of the heretic to expect an enthusiastic reception for his doctrines in a town which owed its recent and substantial affluence to the international fame of its ninth-century relics. It was the revenue from the pilgrims which turned St Gilles into an important market centre, and the great basilica which began to be erected in 1116, and was still far from completed when Peter died there, was not only a monument to the saint, but a sound and considerable investment.[44] St Gilles was no place to advocate the destruction of church buildings, or to deride the power of saintly bones.

The great city of Toulouse tells quite another story, for it is almost an archetype of the economic revival. Land reclamation proceeded on a large scale in its hinterland during the second half of the eleventh and first half of the twelfth centuries, and the city was munificently endowed with the mills whose multiplication was so clear an index of rising grain production: there were more than sixty of them around the streams running into the Garonne by the turn of the eleventh century. What the countryside did not absorb of the growing population was welcomed into the town, for immigrants to it were granted the first charter of exemption from various exactions before 1067, and again in 1115, and in the new district, the 'salvetat' constructed on land reclaimed from the river between 1120 and 1140. By about the latter date the *burgus*, the newer quarter especially associated with the expansion, was brought within the city wall. From the second quarter of the century onwards there are increasingly numerous references to the men who created and benefited from this flurry of activity, not only in service industries, like provisioning and banking, but in the manufacture of metal, cloth and leather goods on a large scale, and to the moneyers and money-lenders who dealt in a coinage that dominated the whole of the upper Languedoc. As early as 1120 their leaders, the *'bons hommes'*, appear to speak for them, and from 1147 onwards the lists of them are complete, and they pressed increasingly, with a measure of success unknown elsewhere in the Languedoc, for freedom to run their affairs and those of the city without the interference of the Count and his officials. The first trade-guild, that of the leather workers, made its appearance in 1152.[45]

It is not for another generation or so, as we shall see, that the strains and conflicts which were the inevitable accompaniment of such development begin to be clearly visible, but the period of Henry's sojourn in the city was one of great activity. According to Geoffrey of Auxerre, he had only limited support in the city, but of his supporters many were weavers – whose trade later became synonomous with heresy – including some of the most prominent citizens.[46] It would be valuable here to know whether Geoffrey distinguished between the *civitas*, the older quarter, and the *burgus*, where greater support for Henry might be expected, and some of whose leading families were stubbornly heretical in the next generation; on the whole, since he did not know the city well, and the two quarters had recently been enclosed by a common wall, it seems likeliest that he did not. The indications that he gives of the depth of Henry's support are contradictory. The leading citizens, it is to be presumed, did not lightly give their favour to a common agitator, and one of them had been sufficiently impressed, shortly before St Bernard's arrival, to abandon his property and his young son, and repair with his wife to a neighbouring village full of heretics. On the other hand St Bernard made short work of the opposition, if his secretary is to be believed. Henry and his followers fled the city at his approach, and those who remained promised that he would receive no more support from them unless he defended his position in public debate, a formidable undertaking against the century's greatest public speaker.

'Some of the knights promised to drive them out and not to support them in future.' It was another of the ways in which Toulouse resembled the Italian cities more than those of northern Europe that there was among the feudal aristocracy no clear division between town and country. The great families kept their town houses, and gave property in the city to their sons, whose aristocratic lineage reinforced the status of the upper bourgeoisie with which they allied. It is reasonable to assume that at this early stage in its development their influence was considerable, and that St Bernard found in them a section of the urban leadership with which he, familiar with and influential in the seignorial courts of the north, could do business. The measures envisaged were thorough. 'To make sure that this (prohibition) would not be infringed by anybody who might be bribed by the heretics, judgement was pronounced that the heretics, their supporters, and anybody who gave them any help would not be eligible to give evidence, or seek redress in the courts, and nobody would have any dealings with them either socially or commercially.' These measures anticipate those which would be used by the inquisition, and they confirm both that some of Henry's supporters were wealthy enough to be capable of bribery, and that in general they were not thought wealthy enough to withstand the local boycott which is envisaged. It would be useful, from the point of view of the constitutional history of Toulouse, to know more of these knights. At this period justice in the city was still jealously guarded by the count and his officials, and yet it is odd that Geoffrey should omit to mention support from such a quarter in denying the heretics access to the courts.

If comparison is made with the nature and tenacity of support for heresy among the merchants of Toulouse thirty years later it seems that although Henry had made some impact the bulk of his support was, despite Geoffrey's words, among the smaller men; he had made progress since Le Mans, but he had not scaled, and certainly not conquered, the heights. In the countryside his fortunes had been better. Some of the knights 'who hated clerks and enjoyed Henry's jokes' in a telling phrase of Geoffrey's, continued to defend him obstinately, but were persuaded eventually to give up their support for him, once again on the ground that he was not willing to defend himself in debate. Two villages, Verfeil (where St Bernard performed a miracle upon the child of one of the leading heretics) and Albi are named as especially soaked in heresy, and the latter received St Bernard with every appearance of rejoicing. But when he gave up his mission to return to Clairvaux, he regarded it still as 'a land of many heresies', 'in need of a great deal of preaching', and the subsequent history of the region suggests that the Saint was more realistic than some of his historians, who have assumed that his mission was entirely successful. Backed not only by a papal legate, and the bishops, but in principle at least by the authority of the count to whom he had announced his mission in ringing terms, St Bernard was able to persuade the influential to disown Henry, and his oratory had a powerful effect on the rest, but he did not achieve any very lasting result.

Any assessment of the impact of Henry of Lausanne and Peter of Bruys must be a cautious one. They did enough to alarm the church more thoroughly than any of their predecesors had done, and Peter the Venerable evidently did not believe that the threat of Peter of Bruys ended with his life. But there is little to confirm that those fears were well-grounded. His seed did not germinate on the stony ground of his native Alps, and the coastal area around Narbonne, where it is implied that he was most active, never became an important centre of heresy. Only at Toulouse, where some of his supporters lingered long enough to transfer their allegiance to Henry, does he seem to have been remembered for long. There is no real evidence that either of them disturbed the secular lords, who elsewhere were so often in the forefront in repressing outbreaks of heresy. The intervention of the Count of Anjou at Le Mans was apparently designed to safeguard the clerks rather than to put down the revolt, and the knights at Toulouse, if they did include any of the Count's officials, moved against Henry only at the instigation of St Bernard. For the most part, it would seem, their appeal was to the least influential, those who had cause to bewail the exactions and abuses of the clergy without being able to do anything about them. The absence of any indication that either of them left behind him anything more lasting than an affectionate memory is itself an index of the quality of their followers: there were none among them who could inherit the mantle, inspire the faithful, or create any permanent structure. Henry baptized his followers, persuading them that the baptism of the church was of no avail. But after Henry, did any of them take up the office? Nothing remains to suggest it.

Nevertheless the work of Henry, if not of Peter, was portentous for the future. His thought was more complete, and he chose his ground better: the triangle between Toulouse, Albi which he had infected so strongly, and Carcassonne was the region in which the Albigensian heresy would become deeply rooted and widely supported, and it would be strongest after that in the area to the north and west, through Cahors towards Périgueux and Bordeaux, where Bernard had followed in Henry's tracks. The economic changes of the great revival were in full flow when Henry left the backward west for the Languedoc. Their social and political consequences would not become apparent for another generation and more: the trade guilds, the urban patriciate, the '*bons hommes*' were just beginning to emerge when he was in Toulouse. Their members could not, or would not, defend him in adversity, but some of them at least found his message persuasive. His call for the rejection of old and corrupt forms of authority, for a faith which judged a man on his merits and attainments rather than for the meekness with which he played his appointed part in a fore-ordained order, was premature: it would have its day.

Chapter V | The Political Alternative: Arnold of Brescia

On the 13 February 1861, Garibaldi captured Gaeta, the final refuge of the Pope, and the last stronghold of the Bourbons of Naples. A year later the small commune of Loreto, in the Abruzzi, was placarded with posters which read:

> Viva il Papa non re. Viva Arnaldo di Brescia.
> Viva il clero liberale[1]

Thus the decision of the Prefect of the City, to whom Arnold was delivered by Frederick Barbarossa in 1155, not only to hang him, but to burn his body and cast its ashes on the Tiber to prevent its veneration as a martyr's relics,[2] failed to expunge the memory of the first opponent of the temporal power of the papacy whose opposition was revolutionary in deed as well as in principle, and the only heretic of the twelfth century who made fully explicit the implicit threat that dissent was always assumed to bear not only for religious, but for political authority.

The briefest outline of Arnold's life makes it very clear that he was the stuff of which martyrs are made, and his religious, as distinct from his political, enemies did not withhold their admiration. He was born at Brescia, within a few years of 1100, and Walter Map's assertion that he belonged to the minor nobility is consistent with his having crossed the Alps for his education (where he could have followed Abelard's lectures at the height of his early fame, just before the liaison with Heloise and the condemnation at Soissons began to taint it with melodrama), and with his having, apparently, become prior of a house of Austin canons in his native city shortly after his return.[3] He was, said John of Salisbury, 'a priest by office, a canon regular by profession, and one who had mortified his flesh with fasting and coarse raiment: of keen intelligence, persevering in the study of the scriptures, eloquent of speech and a vehement preacher against the vanities of the world'.[4] 'A man', St Bernard added, 'who comes neither eating nor drinking . . . whose life is as sweet as honey.'[5] Like the best saints and heretics he made an impressive death; he refused the offer of his life in return for the recantation of his errors, made a short speech in defence of his principles, knelt in prayer for a short time, and went to his execution.[6] The details highlight a contrast between Arnold and others whose deaths are retailed in these pages. He was not poor or ignorant, like the heretics of Goslar. He was not accused of summoning up demons, like the clerks of Orléans, or of Soissons. He was not accused of spectacular immorality, as Henry or Tanchelm had been, though neither of them had been sentenced to public execution. He was acknowledged to be an able and educated man, austere in his life and steadfast in his principles, and he was executed not for heresy (he was convicted of no doctrinal error, and accused of none by those who knew most about him), but for political rebellion. Upon the decision whether that rebellion was dictated by his religious convictions hangs not only the understanding of Arnold, but a substantial part of any judgement of the nature of the threat that was presented to the world of the high middle ages by the phenomenon of spiritual revolt.

His hostility to 'the vanities of this world' was the aspect of Arnold's teaching that most impressed his critics. When he returned from Paris to Brescia it was clerical wealth that aroused his special anger. 'He used to say that neither clerics that owned property, nor bishops that had regalia, nor monks with possessions could in any wise be saved.'[7] The city of Brescia was fertile ground for criticism of the clergy. Its bishop, Manfred, had been appointed by Innocent II in 1132, apparently as a champion of reform, but he did not succeed in abating the hostility of the citizens, who were in revolt against him from 1135 until he left for Rome to seek papal assistance in 1138. Whether Arnold had any part in this dispute is unknown, though John of Salisbury seems to imply that it was only after Manfred's departure that he 'so swayed the minds of the citizens that they would scarcely open the gates to the bishop on his return'. For this Arnold was deprived of his office by the Pope at the Lateran Council of 1139, and expelled from Italy. He returned to France, where he took up the cause of Abelard, at that moment under attack from St Bernard, in the great dispute which was to culminate in the Council of Sens, at which Arnold was present. There is no sign that his support embarrassed the master as much as it has its historians, but it attracted the hostility of St Bernard for the first time. After Abelard's condemnation Arnold went to Paris, to fill, as it were, the shoes of the disgraced Abelard, 'expounding the scriptures to scholars at the church of Saint Hilary, where Peter had lodged'.[8]

The association, if that is not too strong a word for it, between Arnold and Abelard is an intriguing one, if only because it is the only occasion upon which there is apparently a direct connection between intellectual and popular heresy.[9] It does not, however, survive scrutiny. It is true that Abelard held that the power of binding and loosing was vested only in those prelates who led worthy lives, and thereby came close to the opinion of a number of heretics, including Arnold, that the church had, in this respect sacrificed its authority by its corruption. Yet it is doubtful whether the fact that he held this view attracted much attention, for it is not mentioned by St Bernard, whose opposition to Abelard rested precisely on the fear that his bold speculation might weaken the faith of the simple in the authority of the church. Nor was Abelard a heretic in the strict sense, for although he contested the justice of his two condemnations he did not question the right of the church to condemn him: he was not guilty of heretical pertinacity, and his single reference to Peter of Bruys certainly does not suggest that he had any sympathy with those who were.[10] When Arnold attempted to inherit Peter's pupils he did not do it by preaching Peter's doctrines, but by elaborating his own. 'He said things that were entirely consistent with the law accepted by Christian people, but not at all with the life they led. To the bishops he was merciless on account of their avarice and filthy lucre; most of all because of stains on their personal lives, and their striving to build the church of God in blood.'[11] There is, indeed, no obvious reason why Arnold should have chosen to champion Abelard. His own austerity of life might almost suggest that he had more affinity with St Bernard, who himself drew the contrast, not only acknowledging Arnold's purity, as we have seen, but saying that Abelard 'had nothing of the monk about him except the name and the habit', that he 'proved his life by his behaviour, and his books', that he was 'a monk without a rule, a prelate without responsibility, an abbot without discipline, who argues with boys and consorts with women'.[12] His remarks were, of course, a perfectly clear reminder that Abelard's censures of clerical malpractice were not the outcome of a life of perfect observance of clerical discipline. Nevertheless Abelard had pre-eminently the power of arousing the passionate loyalty of his pupils, of whom Arnold may have been one, and the Council of Sens, with its dazzling constellation both of spiritual and of secular power, was not only the tribunal which condemned Abelard, but a spectacular manifestation of the worldliness of the church's prelates, and the exercise of earthly power in its name, which Arnold detested. The exploitation of such an assembly by the saintly abbot of Clairvaux seems to have appeared to Arnold as mere hypocrisy, for he later denounced him as 'a seeker after vainglory, envious of all who won distinction in learning or religion unless they were his own disciples'.[13]

So uncharitable a view of St Bernard's behaviour was not unique. Some of the stories which Walter Map told against him reflect a very similar judgement, and one of the most respectable of twelfth-century writers, John of Salisbury, recounts the history of the arraignment of Gilbert de la Porée at the Council of Rheims in 1148 with a fastidious delicacy that does not distance him entirely from the opinion which he attributes to the prelates assembled there, that they refused to support Bernard largely because they distrusted his motives.[14] But John and Walter both wrote after Bernard's death, and his reputation was not jealously guarded at the Angevin court. Paris in 1140 was another matter, and the young Louis VII did not hesitate, at the insistence of the saint, to expel Arnold from France. He was still capable of making friends. He went to Zurich, where he received the patronage of Ulrich of Lenzburg, not only the imperial prefect and a close confidante of the emperor, but a member of a family which had been prominently associated with resistance to the political claims of the papacy in Swabia since the time of Gregory VII. It is reasonable to suspect, although the sources have almost nothing to say of this period of Arnold's career, both that that fact assisted his welcome, and that the apparently happy years which he spent in Zurich not only confirmed his antagonism to the temporal claims of the papacy, but did something to form the willingness which he would later display to see in the Emperor the proper defender of religion, and the legitimate source of earthly dominion.

Of Arnold's activity in Zurich we know little except that there is nothing to suggest that it was troubled. Apart from Ulrich he found favour with two men otherwise unknown, Rudolf of Ravensburg and Eberhard of Bodmen, probably local landowners, and with some of the '*divites*', prominent members, that is to suggest, of the townsmen who were now beginning to establish some political identity, though they were still two or three generations from the communal ambition with which Arnold had been familiar in Lombardy. Otto of Freising says that he taught publicly in Zurich, and 'sowed his pernicious doctrine there for some time', but it does not seem that its pernicious qualities were apparent to these notables.[15] St Bernard, however, was not a man to forget his critics, and he favoured Bishop Herman of Constance with a lurid account of the dangers which Arnold represented to the souls of his flock. Herman, another prominent adviser of Conrad III and Barbarossa, was a bishop of the kind that Arnold did not admire, and his entry to the see had been the occasion of a dispute which was expensively settled in his favour by Innocent II in 1139, but St Bernard's letter creates a presumption that he had not moved against Arnold of his own accord, and therefore that Arnold had not attacked him. Nor do we know whether Herman responded to the letter, though it is suggested by the fact that Bernard's next is also directed to an eminent church-man who had alarmed the saint by taking the rebel under his wing. This time it was no less a person than Cardinal Guido (who is otherwise unidentified), papal legate in Bohemia.[16]

Cardinal Guido began his legation to Bohemia in the summer of 1142, and St Bernard's letter to him was written before the death of Innocent II in September 1143. Whether his willingness to shelter a man who was still under the sentence of banishment stemmed from Guido's desire to convert him, as St Bernard conjectured with ironic courtesy, or from admiration for his austerity and sympathy for his ideals, it seems likely that Guido was the instrument of Arnold's return to Italy after Innocent's death, and of his reconciliation with the pontiff. Innocent was succeeded by Celestine II and by Lucius II, who died early in 1145, and it was with his successor, Eugenius III, that Arnold made his peace at Viterbo and embarked upon a lengthy penance in the holy places of Rome. The reconciliation probably took place in 1146, and there is no indication what Arnold was doing before it, except that the very fact of its having occurred suggests strongly that he had not drawn unfavourable attention to himself. Indeed, that the Pope directed Arnold to perform his penance in the city which had since 1143 been in a state of revolutionary war with the papacy, and the scene of successive attacks on the temporal power and wealth of the church, is the clearest possible testimony either that Eugenius was a fool or that he had no reason to suspect Arnold of holding unusually strong views on these questions.

Until this point, in short, Arnold had not been closely identified with any of the causes which he was soon to espouse. There is no evidence that he was associated with a communal movement in Brescia, or that Bishop Manfred's hostility to him was the reaction to any but religious criticism. In taking the part of Abelard at Sens, he shared the view of many distinguished men, in doubting the motives of St Bernard he had done nothing more foolish – though foolish it was – than to say what others thought, and nothing in his sub-sequent association with dignitaries both of the empire and the church seems to have brought him into conflict with them. The purity of his life and his devotion to the ideals of apostolic poverty aroused the admiration even of the one consistent enemy he had made to date, St Bernard. Arnold's outspokeness, his uncompromising proclamation of the severest standards of Christian life, and his readiness to attack deviations from those standards wherever he saw them may at times have made him an uncomfortable man to have around, but no admirer of the abbot of Clairvaux could have taken the view that such qualities were intolerable in a loyal, and even a meritorious son of the church. Eugenius III was just such a disciple, a Cistercian abbot who continued to wear his habit beneath his papal robes, and who, alone among the popes of the twelfth century, was regarded by his contemporaries as a man of humility and exemplary holiness of life. It is possible that the forgiveness which permitted Arnold's reconciliation was not all on one side, for although St Bernard wrote with a special enthusiasm to his former pupil, and the first of his order to be raised to the pontificate, he did not speak only for himself when he said: 'The whole church rejoices and glorifies God, because she has a confidence in you such as she does not seem to have had for a long time in your predecessors.'[17]

The temptation to regard the whole of a man's life and thinking as the path to its natural conclusion is especially great when he is a prophet, or a revolutionary. From 1148 until his death Arnold of Brescia played the second of those parts at least more completely than any other man of his time. He welded religious idealism and political radicalism into a dream of a world order which envisaged a transformation both of church and of empire, a revolutionary programme of singular coherence. Most of the elements of that programme – the detestation of the wealth and temporal power of the church, the exalted role which its reduction would offer to the Emperor, the alliance with the newly wealthy and their communal aspirations – were prefigured in the experiences of his early years. But the reconciliation of 1146 is a powerful testament that the precipitation of those observations and criticisms into a single vision had not yet occurred. It was the consequence of what Arnold saw when he went to Rome as – there is no reason to doubt it – a true penitent under a vow of public silence.

Of the great cities of twelfth-century Italy, and even Europe,

Rome was the most backward. That it was the see of St Peter, the centre of Christendom, and the focus of all the nostalgic veneration for the classical past which dominated the historical imagination of the early middle ages ensured that it should also be a place of corruption, intrigue and petty swindling: nowhere else combined so splendid an image with so tawdry a reality. As the papacy ceased to be the tool of the noble families the families in turn became the satellites of the papacy. The church was the largest landowner by far in the region, and had been, since the chamberlainship of Hildebrand in the 1050s, increasingly concerned with the administration of its properties and powers, the *regalia* which brought it the income, the powers and the preoccupations of worldly government. The city was ruled through the prefect who controlled the police and the criminal courts, and presided over the civil courts; like the *consules Romanorum* who since the beginning of the eleventh century are seen acting as the executives of local justice, responsible for arresting criminals, and carrying out the sentences of the courts, his ancient title concealed the fact that he was no more than a papal functionary.[18]

The church gave the city not only its government but its livelihood. The populace was engaged almost exclusively in providing for the needs of the noble families and their retainers, supporting the ostentation of the cardinals, and fleecing the incessant swarms of pilgrims and tourists who, as ever, provided the greatest part of their income. In the decade which saw the *Ordinary Gloss* and the *Sentences* of Peter Lombard completed at Paris, and the codification of civil and of canon law at Bologna, the most notable book produced in Rome was the *Mirabilia Urbis Rome*, a guidebook to the antiquities of the city. It achieved immense success, and attracts the interest of modern scholars because it is the first example of the genre, and because it displays a lively if unsystematic interest in ancient civilization, and a certain pride in the city's pagan heritage. These qualities only underline the interests which it served – those of the publicans, shopkeepers, moneychangers, sellers of souvenirs, and of the church: its author was a canon of St Peter's. Like the burghers of Le Mans who had flocked to Henry's sermons these people had among them none of independent standing, who owed wealth or influence to substantial trade or manufacture. Rome was the last Italian city of any note to form a commune. The reason is clearly expressed by the fact that the first of its citizens to form a guild, with its own officers, were the farmers.[19]

The years before the accession of Eugenius III to the papal throne had seen relations between the city and the popes at their lowest. The schism of 1130, though it had much wider implications, was precipitated by the desire of the Roman cardinals to retain their control of the papacy through Peter Pierleoni, 'at whose nod all Rome spoke or was silent', and whose supporters enthroned him as Anacletus II.[20] The completeness of his control of the city and of the Roman patrimony shielded them from the consequences of the wars which the resultant schism inflicted on the rest of Italy, but when Innocent II was finally recognized by the Romans in 1138, after the death of Anacletus, he came to the city as a stranger supported by foreigners. Among the Roman families only the Frangipani, the great rivals of the Pierleoni, had supported Innocent from the beginning; the rest sold their acquiescence for cash when the absence of a rival and the convenience of Roger of Sicily left them no more congenial course. Their loyalty was secure only for so long as their interests dictated, and their interest was increasingly, as that of the citizens of more advanced communities long had been, in subjecting to themselves the smaller cities of the region. One of these, Tivoli, succeeded, in June 1142, in inflicting a humiliating military defeat upon the Roman army. Later in the year Innocent in turn got the better of Tivoli, but the papal interest did not require him to exact the total submission which the Romans expected. The Tivolese swore fealty to the Holy See, and conceded the Pope the right to appoint a rector of the city, and to control a number of fortresses which effectively allowed him to secure command over the road to the Abruzzi. From Innocent's point of view it was an excellent bargain. From that of the Romans it denied them the opportunity of avenging their defeat, and left a rival in a position of independent security. They demanded that the walls of Tivoli should be razed and harsher terms exacted. Innocent refused. The Romans stormed the Capitol, from which the government of the city was conducted, and 'wishing to restore the ancient dignity of the city, set up again the order of senators which had lapsed for a long time, and renewed the war with Tivoli'.

The latest historian of these events suggests that the prosecution of the war with Tivoli was the immediate objective of the coup of 1143, and that the reform of civil government followed later, pointing out that when the commune, in the fashion of revolutionary regimes, began to reckon the succession of time from its own inauguration, it did so from 1144, not 1143.[21] When Innocent II died in September 1143 he had not succeeded either by bribery or by the threat of force in recovering his control of the city. The 'renovation' of the senate took place in the following year, and was accompanied by the abolition of the office of Prefect, and the restoration in his place of a leader of the city government appointed by the Senate. His title was *Patricius*, the man Jordan Pierleoni, the brother of Anacletus II, and head of the wealthiest of the aristocratic families, who had had the greatest interest in the subjugation of Tivoli.

Under the leadership of Pierleoni the new regime pursued its policies while Innocent's successors Celestine II and Lucius II tried in vain to bring either the Emperor or Roger of Sicily to their aid. The *regalia* of the Holy See – its temporal rights and powers throughout the patrimony of St Peter – were taken over, and the revenues of the church confiscated. In the city itself the palaces of the cardinals and of those of the nobles who remained loyal to the pope were plundered and razed. Early in 1145 Lucius II, despairing of secular allies, himself led an army into the city, and mounted an attack on the Capitol. It failed, and he died shortly afterwards of a wound, it was said, received in the battle.

Whether by recognition of necessity, or as a mark of a new approach to papal government, Eugenius III abandoned the tactics of his predecessors and came to terms with the republic. In December 1145 he recognized the right of the senators, who were to be appointed annually, to hold their office by his authority. In return for this, the central point of their programme, and one which lasted in essence for two centuries, though not without more bloodshed, the senate restored the revenues of the church, and accepted in place of their Patrician, the reinstitution of the office of Prefect.[22] Our knowledge of these events is scanty, and it is hazardous to attempt a more extensive analysis of them. Nevertheless, it looks very much as though Eugenius followed what was often the method of bringing communal revolts into a posture relatively acceptable to the old order. Jordan Pierleoni, whose office was thus abolished, had had his support from the poorer elements of the city, although he was himself a member of its wealthiest family; what we have described as the central institution of the commune, the senate, may have appeared so less to his supporters than to his relations, and the settlement left untouched the wealth of the church, which had been the object both of communal policy and of popular riot since 1143. In short, it appears that the achievement of Eugenius was to separate the aristocratic from the popular supporters of the republic, and to come to terms with the former at the expense of the latter.

The events of the next two years are not clearly recorded, and two central questions remain matters of conjecture. Rome remained turbulent, and the agreement which Eugenius had reached with the republic at the end of 1145 failed to pacify the city, or to secure his position. On the contrary, by the end of 1148 he was once again contemplating the use of force to suppress the republic. During this period Arnold of Brescia had become a popular political leader in the city, and the Pope regarded his expulsion by the Romans as the *sine qua non* of a fresh settlement. But it is not known why the settlement failed, or when Arnold emerged in his revolutionary garb. Otto of Freising presents him as the initiator, the man who 'aroused almost the entire city, and especially the populace, against his pope'. But Otto was writing in honour of Barbarossa, who had been responsible for Arnold's death, and it is clear from John of Salisbury's account that he exaggerated the extent to which Arnold was responsible; as we have already seen, things had gone far before Arnold reached the city. It is not until July 1148 that he was identified by Eugenius as the source of the trouble, whereas by the end of 1146 Jordan Pierleoni, who had been jettisoned as part of the settlement of 1145, was once more acting as leader of the Romans, and they had renewed their war against Tivoli and Viterbo. This suggests that there had been some readjustment of the political balance within the commune before Arnold emerged as a political figure; that the prefect whom Eugenius had appointed in accordance with the agreement had failed to maintain his position; and that if a division within the republican ranks – obtained no doubt by bribery – had made the settlement possible, the more popular, or anti-clerical faction, had recovered its ascendency, and rejected the settlement. Certainly, Eugenius had to leave the city again by the spring of 1146, to pass the rest of the year at Sutri, Vetralla and Viterbo, and when he left for France in the new year of 1147 he had made no progress towards the recovery of his position.

John of Salisbury implies that it was only after this that Arnold began to involve himself in the affairs of the city, 'preaching all the more freely because the lord pope was occupied in Gaul', and that it was as a religious figure that he made his mark: 'he built up a faction known as the heretical sect of the Lombards [and] had disciples who imitated his austerities and won favour with the populace through outward decency and austerity of life, but found their chief supporters among pious women'.[23] His account of Arnold's own preaching itself contains a progression from denunciation of the avarice of the cardinals, to the preoccupation of the *curia* with worldly affairs, to the hypocrisy of a pope who permitted such wrongs to be done in his name, to the attack on the claim of the church to temporal power, and finally, to the right of Rome itself to political independence. The train of thought is entirely clear; it is presented by a chronicler of exceptional sophistication, who knew the papal court well, and who is our fullest source on Arnold of Brescia; it is unlikely that we shall improve on his account, provided that we remember that he gives us in a single polished paragraph what may represent the evolution of two eventful years. The passage runs as follows:

> He himself was frequently heard on the Capitol and in public gatherings. He had already publicly denounced the cardinals, saying that their college, by its pride, avarice, hypocrisy and manifold shame was not the church of God, but a place of business and den of thieves, which took the place of the scribes and Pharisees amongst Christian peoples. The pope himself was not what he professed to be – an apostolic man and shepherd of souls – but a man of blood who maintained his authority by fire and sword, a tormentor of churches and oppressor of the innocent, who did nothing in the world save gratify his lust and empty

other men's coffers to fill his own. He was, he said, so far from apostolic that he imitated neither the life nor the doctrine of the apostles, wherefore neither obedience nor reverence was due to him: and in any case no man could be admitted who wished to impose a yoke of servitude on Rome, the seat of the Empire, fountain of liberty and mistress of the world.

Arnold was not alone in his low opinion of the Pope and the cardinals. The corruption of the curia was a constant theme of the satirists and a matter of growing concern to serious churchmen. The *Historia Pontificalis* itself relates many episodes that make it easy to see why John of Salisbury, writing before Arnold's career had reached its climax, is temperate in his criticism. While Arnold was preaching at the Capitol St Bernard was composing his *De consideratione*, which was no more sparing in its analysis of the venality of the curia, or less alarmed in its view of the dangers which the political activity of the papacy held for its capacity to give spiritual leadership to the church, and Bernard too identified the relationship between the Pope and the Romans as one of the springs of corruption. 'Who can you quote to me in the city', he asked Eugenius, 'who acknowledged your position as Pope without a bribe or the hope of a bribe?'[24] The consequence of that situation was clear to him. The Pope in the city had become 'successor not to Peter but to Constantine' not only in pomp and circumstance but, much worse, in the weapons he used. He denounced the willingness of Eugenius to bring the republic to heel by force: it must be attacked with words and not with arms, and for the Pope to do otherwise would be 'to usurp the sword which you were twice ordered to replace in its scabbard'.

It is only in the last sentence of John of Salisbury's epitome that Arnold is shown crossing the lines which separated criticism from heresy and heresy from rebellion. To say that the Pope imitated neither the life nor the doctrine of the apostles was one thing; to maintain that on that account neither obedience nor reverence was due to him was quite another. The real originality of Arnold's position, however, lay not in his condemnation of the papal exercise of temporal authority, but in the invocation of Rome 'seat of Empire and fountain of liberty' as an alternative to it. In this he adumbrated what was to become the ideology of the Roman republic, which would be reiterated in the appeals, some probably of his own composition, that the Romans directed to Conrad III and to Barbarossa when they tried to tempt the emperors to assume the duties of their station, and reduce the papacy to the purely spiritual role which became it. The appeal of that ideology, however, was not drawn from a simple polarity between the papacy on the one hand and the Romans on the other. Before Arnold had become involved in the troubles of the city at all Eugenius had succeeded in dividing the forces against him and reaching an accommodation with the nobility. What made Arnold of Brescia so effective, so dangerous and so long remembered was that he now fashioned a thesis which united with the religious aspirations of all those who were shocked by the worldliness of the papal court the political ambitions of those who had been excluded from the deal between the Pope and the nobles.

Arnold was identified as the chief source of unrest in the city in the middle of 1148, as the Pope was returning from France after launching the second crusade. A bull issued at Pavia in July branded him as a schismatic, and denounced him for attacking the authority of the cardinals and archdeacons in Rome.[25] The threat of the most fearful penalties, deprivation not only of their benefices but of their holy orders, attested the presence of clerks among his supporters. A little later he was accused of stirring up the *milites* against the nobles, and in 1152 Eugenius reported to the imperial chancellor that Arnold was plotting, without the knowledge of the nobles and leading men of the city, to appoint a hundred of his own followers as senators in that November, and two more as consuls. It was alleged that he had conjured two thousand of the poor of the city in secret oath to achieve this end.[26]

These allegations had some plausibility, in that Arnold was influential in the city at least to the extent of providing the substance, or even some of the words, of its negotiations with the Emperor. But equally there would have been no point in accusing him of plotting to seize control if he had possessed it already. The object of the accusations, therefore, was to divide the Romans by presenting him not simply as the enemy of the papal curia, but as a threat to all established order by identifying him with the lower ranks of the clergy and aristocracy and with the mass of unprivileged citizenry – with the prospective enemies, that is to say of the nobility whose interest, in the long run, would coincide with that of the papacy.

The assertion that the elevation of the ideal of apostolic poverty had a special appeal to the poor was neither original nor improbable. Otto of Freising, presenting as it were the imperial case against Arnold, draws out another thread. He stresses Arnold's invocation of the vigorous and disciplined government which the ancient Romans had exercised over the city, whose restoration he advocated. Hence, according to Otto, he urged the reconstruction of the Capitol, the restoration of the senatorial dignity, and the reconstitution of the equestrian order. This last proposal points to a new social tension from which Arnold drew sustenance, and suggests why in the end he reinforced the readiness of the nobility to sustain the old order. During the generation immediately before the commune the position of other groups among the laity had changed considerably. The gradual spread of feudal habits and institutions in the papal patrimony was beginning to produce a gradual articulation of the sub-noble military classes. In 1111 barons of the abbey of Casauria had taken an oath of fealty for lands which they held of the abbey, and the word *feudum* appeared in the region for the first time in 1126. At the same time came the earliest references to the obligations of providing and equipping knights for service in the feudal host, and by 1140 the first occurrence of subinfeudation, the most obvious means of meeting this obligation.[27] In this respect the papal lands were backward; the *valvassores* of Milan had won an independent legal position for themselves as long ago as 1037, when the *constitutio de feudis* granted them security of tenure in their benefices, and the right to appeal against their lords to the Emperor or his officers. These are forms of a development which was familiar in the west at this time; the smaller land-holders, who in Italy benefited most from the economic growth of the eleventh century, and the lower ranks of the military orders, were consolidating their position, and requiring recognition of their influence and importance. At the same time the effect of the reforms of papal government in Rome was apparently to diminish the part which these same people had to play in the city. As the reorganization of the curia went forward the part of the local clerks in minor orders who came mostly from these families was diminished. In the last years of the eleventh century, for example, and the early decades of the twelfth, the Papal chamberlain gradually became one of the most important officers of the curia, as he established his control more comprehensively over the collection and expenditure of papal revenues. But in doing so he also diminished the role of two much older dignitaries, the *arcarius* and the *saccellarius*, who found themselves excluded from the executive branch of papal government, and reduced to the part of local judges.[28] The declaration of the Roman commune came, therefore, after a period which had seen the second rank, both secular and clerical, increase its wealth and its military significance, while it had been deprived of status and of influence. The tensions which arose from such a development clearly lie at the heart of the communal movement, and go far to explain the conflicts of interest which are perceptible within it; they also give significance to the proposal which Otto of Freising put in the mouth of Arnold of Brescia, to reconstitute the equestrian order.

The struggle between the popes and the commune lasted until, and indeed beyond, the execution of Arnold in 1155. Its essential elements remained unchanged. Neither side could defeat the other without support; both, therefore, turned to the Emperor. The Pope was less limited than the Romans in the tactics at his disposal, for if the Emperor was his best hope, there was the possibility of Sicilian help as well. Perhaps more important in the long run, the Romans themselves were not united, and even if they had been too much of the interests of the city depended on the papal bureaucracy and the activity which was generated by it, as well as on the position of Rome as the centre of the church and the site of its most revered monuments, for the papal position to be overthrown. The citizens of Rome appealed both to Conrad III and to Frederick Barbarossa to espouse their cause in terms which Arnold himself may well have suggested, and the vision which they painted was a compelling one. In 1149 the Senate denounced the papacy to Conrad III as the usurper of imperial rights, reminding him that even Gregory the Great had not assumed the pontificate without imperial consent. Hence they said, 'it is our earnest and united endeavour to restore the Empire to its position under Constantine and Justinian', to which end they removed every clerical obstacle to Conrad's entry into the city, and had begun to rebuild the Milvian bridge to provide access for his troops.[29]

The prospect they offered to Conrad, who landed at Aquilea in May 1149 on his way back from the crusade, was a tempting one, but he could not have contemplated an alliance with so disreputable a force. On the other hand he was in no hurry to reach a settlement with Eugenius, because his immediate concern was with the possibility of reducing the power of Roger in Sicily, which he hoped to do in alliance with the Byzantine Emperor. Eugenius had concluded a truce with Roger in April, and had received Louis VII in October, after the latter had crossed the Norman kingdom from his landing at Calabria. For a time, therefore, the vacuum which was created by the uncertainties of international diplomacy delayed any effective attack on the Romans, and the assault launched by Cardinal Guy of Tivoli, with the help of the Tusculan and Frangipani forces, was a failure. The negotiations which followed showed again the papal hope of separating the insurgent forces, for the greatest obstacle which they encountered was the reluctance of the Romans to expel Arnold from the city; it was said that he had been promised support under oath, although the nature of the oath is far from clear. It is probably best regarded as the price which the Republic's leaders had to pay for the popular support which Arnold could bring them.

Eugenius settled for what he could get, and returned to the city in the autumn, accepting the restoration of the *regalia* and the patrimony of the church in return for an annual payment of £500 to the Senate and the regions, and a promise not to fortify two strategic points on the Via Flaminia.[30] The agreement strongly resembles that of 1145, in that it was obtained with the help of the territorial aristocracy, and by negotiation with the senate, which was prepared to abandon what Arnold and his followers regarded as their objective, the ending of the temporal power of the church. Eugenius consolidated his alliance and his position at the same time by buying a half share of the town and fortress of Tuscolo, thus ensuring that he was closely linked to the still considerable though declining power of the Tusculani, and by investing in a number of other fortresses at various points of his patrimony. Thus his resistance to the republic drew him yet further into the entanglements of worldly power which had drawn hostility upon the papacy in the first place, and brought upon him also the criticism of St Bernard and of Gerhoh of Reichersberg. The agreement was no more successful than its predecessor, and by the spring of the next year, 1150, Eugenius was forced once again to leave the city; this time it took him almost two years to buy his re-entry, which he contrived shortly before his death.

Before he died, Eugenius was able to take advantage of his success in surviving Conrad III, who died in February 1152. Among the terms of the Treaty of Constance which was negotiated with Frederick I in the following new year were the promises of the Emperor to make no peace either with Roger of Sicily or with the Romans without papal consent, and a guarantee that he would restore the temporal power of the papacy in return for his imperial coronation. The Romans tried once again to outbid the Pope. They told Frederick, in a letter of which Arnold was very possibly the author, that they were glad that he had been elected Emperor by his people, but that only the Roman people possessed that power; they would happily exercise it in Frederick's favour, if he wished, or find themselves another Emperor if he did not.[31] The case against the temporal power of the church was vigorously made, and Frederick rebuked for associating with 'heretics, apostate clergy and false monks who degrade their office by exercising dominion against the Gospel precepts, the apostles' exhortations and the canon law, in contempt of laws human and divine'. The denunciation of the Donation of Constantine as 'the lie, the heretical fable [which is] seen through in Rome so universally that the hirelings and whores confute the most learned in argument upon it' was coupled with an exaltation of imperial power which was expressed by the Roman tag that 'what pleases the prince has the force of law'. Such a view was not easily reconciled, however, with the assertion that the Empire lay in the gift of the people of Rome. Even if Frederick had been disposed to reach an understanding with them he could scarcely have done so on that basis. In fact it was quite impossible. His urgent desire was to receive the recognition of his imperial title, and with it his coronation, from the Pope who had, since 800, been accepted as the proper source of the anointment. Neither Frederick nor his advisers could have acquiesced in a proposal which struck at the very basis of order and authority as they understood them.

The fulfilment of the promises of the Treaty of Constance was delayed by the death of Eugenius, and his replacement by a Roman, and a member of the Subura family, as Anastasius IV. If this represented an attempt by the curia to provide a new basis for agreement with the Romans, as some have suggested, it was not repeated a few months later when Anastasius died. The Englishman Hadrian IV was a much tougher proposition than either of his predecessors, and took the earliest opportunity to confront the Romans with the reality of his power. He refused to recognize the republic, and demanded the expulsion of Arnold from the city, without conditions. When the riots to which this policy inevitably led resulted in the wounding of a cardinal in a brawl Hadrian immediately placed the city under interdict for the first time in its history. It was a serious matter for the city of St Peter to be deprived of the services of the church, and the rapidity with which the ban succeeded is perhaps as clear an indication as any of where Arnold's support lay. The pressure of the mob was reversed within four days, and the Senate found itself with no alternative but to accede to Hadrian's demands. Arnold fled, was captured on the borders of Tuscany by Cardinal Odo of St Nicholas, rescued from a monastic prison by the Viscount of Campagna, and recaptured by imperial troops. The Pope and the Emperor entered Rome together. The Senate offered Frederick the crown, on terms similar to those which had been addressed to Conrad III; he ignored the offer, and was crowned by the Pope, on 18 June 1155. The Romans rose in revolt against the end of their independence which this action represented, and were bloodily suppressed by imperial troops, whom Hadrian duly absolved as just avengers. The new harmony of the two swords was celebrated by the delivery of Arnold of Brescia to the prefect of the city, and his execution.

The history of Arnold of Brescia may seem, on the face of it, to have little to do with the questions which other chapters have discussed. His life was plainly ruled by the conviction that the ideal of apostolic poverty, which was one of the great forces behind the reform of the church in his time, must be practised at every level. The assertion of Otto of Freising that he held dubious, but unspecified, views on the mass and on infant baptism is rejected by all who have studied him in favour of John of Salisbury's judgement that 'he said things that were entirely consistent with the law accepted by Christian people, but not at all with the life they led'. He did not reject the spiritual authority of the church; his endeavour was to preserve it by jettisoning its temporal power. He did not reject the intermediate priesthood; his ambition was to save it from its own corruption. His religious opinions, taken by themselves, were entirely consonant with those of the greatest Catholics of his time, and his criticism of the papacy and its government very little different from that of St Bernard. Yet it is for just those reasons that Arnold is central to the argument. Much of the dissent which was expressed against the authority of the church up to this time proceeded precisely, as his did, from fervent devotion to the ideals which it proclaimed but could not realize. Henry of Lausanne was alone in propounding a coherent alternative view of religion to that which the popes proclaimed, and unusual even in expressing a conscious inclination to draw away from the elaboration of its spiritual role in which the church was engaged. Nothing in Arnold's record suggests that he would have sympathized with those tendencies. He did not lack enemies, and he did not lack, in John of Salisbury at least, a judicious historian. It is inconceivable that if he had attacked the mass, or confession to priests, or the penitential system, or the sacramental view of marriage, as Henry did, we would have failed to hear of it. He was a preacher of eloquence, passion and power, and he preached the same path to salvation as St Bernard.

More than any other figure of his age, therefore, Arnold draws out the stark fact that the history of dissent is not, in the last resort, essentially concerned with opinions about religion. What Arnold had in common with Henry was, in the eyes of his rulers, more important than all the things that separated them. 'He would not bow his stubborn neck to the yoke of human obedience,' and he would not accept what was certainly invoked, the church's claim to license him to preach. He died because he persisted in telling what many good churchmen believed to be the truth. That is why there is a distinct sense of unease in the accounts we have of him. It was rumoured that Frederick Barbarossa later regretted his execution,[32] and Otto of Freising's attempt to depict him as the originator of the troubles of Rome must proceed from some sense of the need to make a sufficient case against him; we do not believe it because we have the words of John of Salisbury, whose chronicle only reaches 1151, but whose comments on Arnold's end would have been so interesting.

Like many radical doctrines, the final views of Arnold of Brescia are strikingly simple. He held that 'it is not the priest's function to bear both sword and chalice, but to preach the word of God, to confirm his teaching by good works, and not to stir up strife throughout the world'.[33] The conjunction of his vision of a renewed apostolic church with the desire of the Romans for communal liberty suggested a clear remedy for both ills. The replacement of papal power by imperial authority, rooted in popular consent in the city of Rome, would cleanse the church and confirm the popular institutions of the city at a blow. The two ideas could be united because their appeal was to the same people, those who found their religious or their political aspirations frustrated. They were doomed to defeat because they united not only their friends, but their enemies. In the long run, the Roman aristocracy could abandon neither the wealth nor the power which accrued to it through its close interconnections with the church, and was always ready to deal with any of its members who should attain the papal throne. The papacy itself could abandon neither the right not to be judged by the followers of the faith which it led, nor the temporal power which, whatever its less reputable attractions, was indispensable to the maintenance of a machine to govern the world: however uncomfortable St Bernard might be about the means by which leadership must be exercised, he knew that there were in the end no other. And the Emperor, much as he might have liked occasionally to be without the pope, could not place his position at the disposal of the restless and venal citizens of a single city.

The case of Arnold of Brescia illustrates very completely the analysis of twelfth-century power upon which the case for coercion was based. It showed that dissent and rebellion could not be separated. Arnold's achievement – largely, we have argued, an accidental achievement – was to unite in his person the two greatest revolutionary forces of the age, religious dissent and the spirit of the commune. Neither in the end made a revolution, and it was the paradoxical success of Eugenius III and Hadrian IV that in their response to him they showed why. Religious dissent was killed by force, and the radical political aspirations of the early commune by aristocratic and, where it existed, plutocratic domination of the urban governments which consequently found that they could get on well enough, after a little adjustment, with the church and with royal power. In 1188 Clement III, the first Roman pope since Anastasius IV, reached an agreement with the Senate which ended the conflict that had begun in 1143. The Senate was recognized, but its members, and other representatives of the city, were to take a vow of fealty to the pope. The *regalia* and the properties of the church were restored, in return for a variety of financial payments, some to recur, and others once only, both to individual senators and city officers, and for general purposes such as compensation for those who had acquired church revenues, and the upkeep of the city walls.[34] It was, in essence, the same as the agreement which Eugenius III had made in 1145, and again in 1149, and which the senators had failed to persuade the people to accept. There was still nothing in it for those who cherished the memory of Arnold of Brescia.

Part Two | The Little Foxes

Chapter VI | The Problem of Evil

Is not purification really . . . to separate as far as possible the soul from the body, and to accustom it to collect itself together out of the body in every part, and to dwell alone by itself as far as it can, both at this present and in the future, being freed from the body as if from a prison?[1]

Socrates' question expected the answer yes, and has generally got it. The civilizations which have grown around the Mediterranean have been notably, though certainly not exclusively, marked by the conviction that a man listens to the call of his bodily appetites at the cost of blunting his incorporeal faculties, whether he calls them his soul, his spirit, or his mind. Nothing could be more mistaken than to attribute to the Judaic or the Christian traditions in which its expression has been most familiar the authorship of a tension which, at its simplest level, is familiar to everybody who has drowned a sorrow, and gone to work with a hangover. If it is not logically inescapable it is humanly certain that the elevation of the spirit must be accompanied by the humiliation of the flesh. The poetry and the philosophy of Christianity have tapped the seam with power and subtlety, and we have seen one of the richest moments of its exploitation as a dynamic force in the renewal and expansion of Christian life in the eleventh and twelfth centuries, and in the increasingly coherent and formidable expressions of dissent which accompanied it. About the middle of the twelfth century the tradition of Catholic asceticism which the heresies had channelled towards their own goal was joined and overtaken in the west by a different resolution of the same conflict, which would give western heresy its final and definitive shape, bringing it at last into stark juxtaposition with the Catholic civilization into which it had been born, but with which it could not live.

The problem which is posed by the warfare of body and soul may be resolved by translating the war to a cosmic plane. The process was seen clearly by one who spent much of his life studying its consequences, the inquisitor Anselm of Alessandria. 'A Persian named Mani once asked himself, "If there is a God where does evil come from? And if there is no God, where does good come from?" From this he deduced the existence of two principles.'[2] That is, that the universe was the work of two creators, one responsible for what was spiritual and good, the other for the material and evil. The dualist solution – the conclusion that each man is a battlefield, within whom the forces of two Gods are at war – is the final expression, or as some would have it the final abandonment, of the hostility between desire and ideal which is periodically fanned to the point of mortal agony by the force of religious enthusiasm. It is to be expected that the cultures which ringed the Mediterranean, which were all in their ways heavy with the sense that man's appetites draw him constantly away from his highest callings, should regularly have produced dualist movements. Since they all drew on a common and complex heritage they share a great deal, and it is always difficult to decide when they are kin to one another and when we are presented with a new manifestation of the old and universal tendency. The greatest of them was that which was founded by the prophet Mani, (216–76), whose faith provoked a universal hatred which has robbed him of the acknowledged place he deserves among the founders of great religions.

Mani was born in Mesopotamia, the Syriac-speaking province of the Persian Empire in which Christian traditions were more deeply rooted than the Zoroastrian religion of the Sassanids. He was a missionary of genius, and his followers had brought his message to Spain by the fifth century, while it was still a Roman province, and by the eighth to China, where their communities still flourished four hundred years later. Their tenacity and determination are best recalled in the *Confessions* of St Augustine, whose majestic rhetoric was deployed throughout his life against what he regarded as the most dangerous of the temptations to which he had succumbed in his youth. The relief which he found from the sense of his own wrongdoing, and of the outrageous wrongs which the one God of the Christians seemed to license, bring us closer than any medieval writing to understanding the power of Mani's message.

> I thought that it is not we who sin but some other nature that sins within us. It flattered my pride to think that I incurred no guilt and, when I did wrong, not to confess it so that you might 'bring healing to a soul that had sinned against you'. I preferred to excuse myself and blame this unknown thing which was in me was but not part of me... And it seemed to me better to believe that you had created no evil than to suppose that evil, such as I imagined it to be, had its origin in you. For, ignorant as I was, I thought of evil not simply as some vague substance but as an actual bodily substance.[3]

In Carthage and in Rome Augustine lived among the Manichees, and eagerly awaited the arrival of a famous leader of the sect who might answer the questions which were too deep for the simpler talents of their local devotees. Faustus failed, when he came, to satisfy him, but Augustine was an unusually exacting critic, and the patience, charm and companionship which he found among them brought the Manichaeans converts throughout the Empire, and especially in the fertile crescent from which their founder had come.

The life of the Manichee was firmly directed towards the suppression of 'the unknown thing which was in me, but not part of me'. Mani adapted from the Zoroastrian cosmology of the world in which he grew up the conception which permitted a radical solution to the problem of evil, that the universe was ruled by two powers, each of them absolute and eternal, which warred with each other.

The realm of evil was the kingdom of matter and of the body, pitted in desperate struggle against the realm of the spirit. Plant and animal life alike were composed of matter intermixed with fragments of light, whose salvation consisted in disentangling themselves from the matter or the dark, to return to the kingdom of light from which they had come. This would be achieved by observance of the three 'signets' (*signacula*) which provided a comprehensive code of dissociation from every aspect of material existence. The signet of the mouth governed cleanliness of thought and speech, and the avoidance of every form of enjoyment through the mouth. Meat, with its special association with procreation, was to be avoided above all, and the true Manichee must live on the fruit and vegetable substances which contained a high proportion of light: melons, oil and fruit juices were especially commendable. The signet of the hand controlled behaviour, and was dictated by the need to avoid every action, even the uprooting of a plant, which could harm life in any form, and thereby cause particles of light to be reimprisoned in matter. The signet of the loins forbade every form of sexual activity and especially reproduction, which perpetuated the kingdom of the dark.

The severity of these prohibitions dictated the structure of the sect, for they could not be enjoined upon all its followers. Most of them, it appears, did not practise the precepts of Mani. They were 'Hearers', who confined themselves to being taught his doctrines, and providing support for the 'Elect' who were separated by their observance of the signets from every task and pleasure of material existence. The Hearers might marry or (like Augustine) keep a mistress, though one sect had children only by adoption, and they were not prohibited from eating meat. They fasted and abstained from intercourse on Sundays, and probably at other times of the year, though it is not clear whether they joined the Elect in the month of fasting (perhaps a forerunner of Ramadan) which preceded the great annual feast of Bema, the commemoration of Mani's death from exhaustion, after nearly a month in heavy shackles in the prison of the Persian king Bahram I. We know little of the ritual life of the Manichees, but it is doubtful whether it was of elaborate character. The feast of Bema itself may be thought to have

had some sacramental character from the fact that after it had been
served by Hearers they withdrew, and the Elect were left alone: a
miniature has survived which is thought to depict this ceremony.
Whether there was any ceremony equivalent to baptism, as initiation
to the ranks either of the Hearers or the Elect, is very doubtful and
the only regular rituals which seem to have been carried out were of
a confessional nature, unless such a character be attributed to the
feeding of the Elect.

The Elect were comparable, in orthodox terms, with the monastic
rather than the clerical order. Complete observance of the signets
made them constantly dependent on the service of the Hearers.
They could neither earn, nor gather or prepare food: each of them
must always be accompanied by a Hearer who would attend to his
bodily needs. When the Hearer brought bread to the Elect it was
consumed only after disavowal of the guilty deeds which had
produced it:

> I did not mow thee, did not grind thee, nor knead,
> Nor lay thee in the oven,
> But another did do this and bring thee to me.
> I eat thee without sin.[4]

In this way the body of the Elect was maintained in a state of purity
which made it capable of extracting the fragments of light from the
matter which was fed into it, whence they might pass through the
column of light which joined the earth to the moon, and thence to
the sun, to regain the kingdom of light.

The surprise that is often expressed that so seemingly negative
a faith could command such widespread and stubborn adherence
– for no sect was persecuted so universally or so cruelly as the
Manichees – is misplaced. The sense of the wickedness of man, and
of the evil which was wrought by human passions in a world where
the powerful regularly indulged their appetites in a host of manifest
wrongs, was certainly not peculiar to them. From the monks of the
Egyptian desert to the heads of the great Roman families who found
in their neo-platonist interpretation of classical literature as a cult of
purity and austerity, the adoption of rigorous personal discipline
was universally accepted as essential to the pursuit of the good:

like the monks whose work he set out to undo Julian the Apostate dedicated himself to his mission with a vow of chastity. As their monks for the Christians and the Buddhists, the Elect of the Manichees provided for their ordinary followers a repository of virtue; to contribute to their support was to participate in their freedom from evil. Yet Mani offered more than these things. Those who comment on a faith which they do not possess commonly make the mistake of emphasizing its rules at the expense of its appeal to the imagination. Few Protestants have contributed much to the history of the Catholic liturgy, and there are no Manichees now to recreate the passions which gave substance to the bare skeleton of prohibitions and prescriptions which are easier to comprehend. The hymns and prayers of the Manichees which survive – and they have survived against formidable odds – contain much of haunting beauty.[5] The myth which Mani preached is reconstructed hesitantly and incompletely, but it deserves its place among the explanations of the universe and the predicament of mankind which have provided the basis of most of the great religions. The juxtaposition of the gentle harmony of the world of Light with the noisy chaos of the kingdom of the Dark; the heroism of Primeval Man who set out as a champion knowing himself doomed to defeat, but laying the seeds of distant victory by insinuating his own particles of light into the darkness which devoured him; his redemption by the Spirit of Light, when he struggled free from the monster and demons which would have held him for ever in the pit into which he had fallen; the column of light which constantly transferred the victorious particles that he had left behind, so that the moon waxed as it received them from the earth, and waned as it passed them on to the sun – these are themes which suggest how successfully Mani had added to the morality which would quiet the stirrings of the flesh a myth to satisfy the yearnings of the spirit. This is why, to the puzzlement of the casual reader, Augustine's description of his disenchantment with Manichaeism is so largely concerned with its incompatibility with classical physics, and why long before he met St Ambrose, doubt had been sown in his mind by the *Categories* of Aristotle. Manichaeism was not a negative or pessimistic faith. It enabled the Hearer not only to recognize and disown the evil he already knew, but to find himself a humble participant in the cosmic battle which raged between the forces of Light and Dark. He contained within himself the fragments of good which had been so stirringly deposited by the epic ordeal of Primeval Man, and he was offered a path of liberation which would lead him to the stars. To him, Mani was the prophet of freedom.

The ideas and legends of Manichaeism were or might have been drawn from so great a variety of sources that the question whether it should be regarded as a Christian heresy or a distinct religion is scarcely intelligible. Mani was known to his followers as the Envoy of Light, and referred to himself as the Prophet of Jesus Christ. The division of creation between the realms of God and Matter, Light and Dark, Truth and Lie, and many of the elements of the myths with which he accounted for the creation and pointed to the redemption of man, were taken from Zoroastrianism, but Jesus was the redeemer.[6] Both the Buddhists and the gnostic sect of the Marcionites have been suggested as possible inspirers of the division between the Hearers and the Elect. Among other gnostics who preceded Mani, Bardaisan of Edessa described the attack on Light by Darkness, some of the Mandaeans among whom Mani may have been brought up advocated dietary and sexual abstinence with special fervour, Marcion's scepticism of the Old Testament laid a critical foundation which enabled Mani to reinterpret such parts of the New as seemed to him authentic. The present trend is to see the Christian rather than the Zoroastrian tradition as that from which dualism – the belief in two eternal principles – sprang, but it is also noticed that Mani's own division between God and Matter is not explicitly stated by him to have been a division between God and God: we dare no longer assert with full confidence that Mani was a Manichee.

The purpose of this list is not to indicate the range of disagreement among Manichaean scholars, or to show how even the most elementary statement about the sect and its founder is fraught with formidable difficulty, and how far from completion is the task of tracing the filiations and kinships between all these strands of religious tradition to produce a received version of 'the origins' of Manichaeism. We may, with pardonable relief, leave the navigation of that maze to others. Its significance for the future of what some still refer to as 'the dualist tradition'[7] is to point out that the innumerable faiths of the ancient Middle East were woven through each other so intricately, shared so much in their heritage and preoccupations, travelled so many of the same paths in their internal development, that the construction of tables of descent and influence between them is not only next to impossible, but of very limited value. The fame and hatred which Mani achieved, and the force of his challenge to Christianity, and especially to the young Augustine, who became its most prolific and influential expositor, were so great that for a thousand years after his death Christian commentators everywhere greeted as 'Manichaeism' every manifestation of irregularity which had any point of similarity with what they knew of his teaching, and some which had none. The truth was more complex. In Plato and in neo-platonism,[8] in Judaism, in Christianity, and later in Islam there were many threads which might lead a man conscious of his own sin to renounce the flesh, and to elevate the threat of evil to the point where it assumed an autonomous, godlike, power. Dualism was not a tradition. It was a recurrent answer to an ever-present question.

The conditions which had prevented the appearance of heretical movements in the early medieval west did not prevail in the Byzantine world. Indeed a comparison of the two is almost sufficient to account for the placidity of western Europe before the eleventh century. The dominance of Christianity and the habit of lay literacy continued in the east without a break. Religious life was conducted, at every social level, with an exuberance which would have denied the ecclesiastical hierarchy the monopoly of debate, teaching and the regulation of the religious life even if it had had the immense advantage, like its western counterpart, of shaping the basis and guiding the destinies of new and primitive political authority, instead of accepting its place as the companion in principle and servant in fact of an ancient and sophisticated autocratic monarchy. The complex and shifting social structure which went with advanced economic and cultural standards, and with the incessant struggle to assert and defend hegemony over subject peoples both civilized and barbarous, and the constant movement of men and ideas across territories as varied in their history as in their geography, created frequent opportunity for difference of opinion on the principles and practice of Christianity which the subjects of the Emperors, and on occasion the Emperors themselves, exploited with boundless enthusiasm.

The history of Byzantine heresy, in short, is a subject of Byzantine complexity. In considering those parts of it which ultimately impinged on the west it is necessary to cling firmly to the recollection that while the possibilities of contact and influence between one stream of heterodoxy and another are endless, and endlessly debatable, they all derived ultimately from the same confluence of sources that was displayed in Manichaeism – of which by far the most important was the New Testament – and that in discussing and classifying them the Greek churchmen were very much more interested in their doctrinal content than in their historical antecedents. By the tenth century there was almost no heresy which human ingenuity had failed to devise, and none, therefore, which might not be characterized as a reassertion of an ancient heresy, either in its pure form or mixed with others. Much scholarly blood has been spilt in the debate over the extent to which the continuity of labels is indicative of continuity of traditions. It is emphasized, therefore, that the discussion that is offered here has an eye to the future rather than the past, and is intended not to characterize Byzantine heresy *tout court*, but to record the appearance of those parts of it which may subsequently have influenced the west.

The writings of Symeon the New Theologian (c. 949–1022) offer an entry to monastic thought in his time at a point which is undeniably close to the gnostic pattern of speculation of which Mani had been the most startling exponent.[9] Symeon stood in a tradition of mystical thought stemming from the Pseudo-Dionysus which had been influential in Byzantium long before it was introduced to the west through the translation of Eriugena. Leaning heavily on the epistles of St Paul, he emphasized the pursuit of purity through renunciation to the point where he made a clear division between the visible and invisible worlds, and held that there was 'no union, knowledge or communication between the two'. The true Christian must use the eyes of the spirit to detach himself from the preoccupations of the visible world, attaining it chiefly by the practice of continuous prayer. True authority could only be vested in the pure in heart, and not, therefore, in worldly hierarchies; baptism in water was only a prefiguring of baptism in the holy spirit, which itself must be a conscious act, and consequently (it is implied) not open to children. Symeon's teachings, in brief, show clearly how the mystical contemplation which was deeply embedded in Byzantine monasticism might lead its devotee along paths which had been followed by heretics in the past, as they would be in the future. As early as the eighth century St John Damascene had seen in it a manifestation of the Messalian heresy which had been one of the most abominated, if most obscure, of ancient deviations. The Messalians appeared in Syria in the middle of the fourth century, and their existence was noted in that region from time to time until the seventh. They were known to the Greeks as the Euchites, or sometimes the Choreutes – the Praying People, or the Dancers, – because their faith was notable for its emphasis on the continuous performance of religious exercises, rather than on speculation. They repeated the Lord's Prayer in endless chains, and believed that by doing so they would eventually achieve union with the Holy Spirit. After three years of such devotion, combined with the most uncompromising bodily abstinence, initiation brought the novice into a state in which (according to their enemies) he might do as he liked, because being now separated entirely from his mere flesh he could not sin with it. Satan, they held, was the elder, and Christ the younger son of God, who as the Holy Spirit entered a human body for a time, though he did not unite himself with it. Mary, therefore, had no claim to special veneration, and the cross on which Christ was crucified was abhorred as an instrument of torture, rather than venerated as one of redemption.

The pattern is one which has become familiar. Without entering into any debate on filiation, it will be observed again how easily the sense of evil led those who were hounded by it from austerity into a sect characterized by a division between novices who did not undergo its full rigours and initiates whose claim to freedom from the bonds of the flesh gave rise to lurid beliefs about their behaviour,[10] and how the combination of the horror of the world with the espousal of the Christian Gospels generated unorthodox views on the relation between God, Christ and the Devil and on the nature of Christ and the sense in which he 'became man'.

It has been thought that Messalians may have been introduced into the Balkan provinces of the Byzantine Empire in 757 when Constantine V garrisoned Thracian fortresses with Armenian heretics who included some from Mytilene, where the Messalians had been described before. It is more certain, and at least as plausible, that John Damascene, like a number of his successors in the following three centuries, was learned enough to recognize in the descriptions he had read of them errors which were similar to some which he had observed among his enthusiastic contemporaries. It is proper to follow him in describing as 'Messalian' the strong tendency to carry the mystical separation of soul from body far in the direction of cosmological dualism which characterized much of the Byzantine contemplative tradition of the tenth and eleventh centuries, and which was a significant part of the environment in which the Bogomil and Paulician heresies evolved, provided that in doing so we leave open the question whether there was a direct influence of the ancient upon the medieval 'Messalianism', or simply a new assertion of the same patterns of asceticism.

If Constantine V brought Messalians to Thrace in 767 it was by accident, for his concern was with another and more dangerous heretical people, the Armenian Paulicians. During the early part of the ninth century they became an even greater nuisance, and conducted regular and well-organized military raids into the territory of the Byzantine Empire, to which their subjection was spasmodic and imperfect. The occupation and destruction of their capital city of Tephrice in 871-2 was one of the notable achievements of the Emperor Basil I, and greatly diminished although it did not end their capacity to inconvenience his successors. About 970 John I Tzimisces, following the same familiar policy of moving the troublesome among his subjects to areas where their aggressiveness might be put to use against other enemies, settled more Paulicians around Philippopolis, and in 988-9 Basil II moved large numbers of Armenians, doubtless including many Paulicians, again to Macedonia. The Paulicians clung tenaciously to their faith, and their heretical and military traditions combined to preserve their communal identity when they were settled as colonists in a foreign land. The trouble of converting so notoriously ferocious a people seldom seemed worth undertaking, though Alexius I had some success in that direction at the beginning of the twelfth century. Their community survived the Byzantine Empire and the Turkish invasions, and if they were converted to Roman Catholicism in the seventeenth century, they still called themselves 'Paulines' when they were described by Lady Mary Wortley Montagu in 1717.[11]

The Paulicians were long regarded as the transmitters in chief of Manichaeism to the Byzantine world. Their good and evil Gods were sharply distinguished from each other and locked in conflict with the vigour which was appropriate to the religion of a military people. They resolved the problem of the nature of Christ in the most frankly dualist manner, by maintaining that his body was human only in appearance – the docetist heresy. Hence Mary was not his mother, but a mere conduit who had assisted the disguise of the holy spirit, worthy of no special reverence. Every doctrine and tradition which could not be found in the New Testament was rejected, including notably the special standing of the saints, the authenticity of miracles, and the practice of infant baptism. The New Testament itself was interpreted in an allegorical fashion, which might conceal diversion from orthodox belief by a willingness to express a heretical one in the same words; when a Paulician denounced those who would not venerate the cross, for example, he did so with the private knowledge that in the language of his sect, the cross was not the artefact, but an allegory of Christ with his arms outstretched. By the same technique Christ's commendation of his body and blood at the Last Supper was held to refer to his words and teaching, and the eucharist therefore was denied. The Paulician journey through the world of evil was attended, in short, by the rejection of every orthodox development of doctrine, and every orthodox comfort of ritual.

The history of the Paulicians in Armenia is known chiefly through the *Historia Manichaeorum* of Petrus Siculus, a work whose authenticity is hotly disputed.[12] It purports to be the work of Basil I's ambassador to Tephrice in 870, based on the observations which he made during a nine months' stay in the city; it has been argued, on the contrary, to be a composite work, put together at the court of Constantinople in the middle of the tenth century, for the purpose of demonstrating the Manichaean descent of the Paulician communities at Philippopolis. Happily the protagonists of the debate, at variance on every other point, are agreed on the one that matters here, that the Paulicians were not descendants of the Manichees, and not therefore a crucial link in any historical chain of dualist religion. If Peter of Sicily is authentic the dualism and docetism of the Paulicians were acquired before and not after they left Asia Minor. Even in that case, however, Peter's description of them as Manichees is to be regarded not as an informed historical judgement, but as another example of the habit of medieval observers, eastern and western alike, of attributing to Mani direct responsibility for every manifesta-tion of the two doctrines which were regarded as central to his heresy. In fact neither the memory nor the mythology nor the writings of Mani had any place in the religion of the Paulicians, and their selection of books of the Scriptures which could be regarded as authentic was not identical with his; they used the whole of the New Testament, 'in exactly the same text as ours, word for word' says Peter of Sicily, except the Apocalypse and two Epistles of Peter, and to it they added nothing but the letters of their great missionary Sergius (d. 835). As their name suggests, their beliefs derived from an intense, if unorthodox, respect for the writings of St Paul, to be accounted for not by the absorption of other heretical inspirations, but as a direct return to the primary sources of evangelical Chris-tianity.

It was probably in the middle decade of the tenth century that the Tsar of Bulgaria sought advice about a new heresy which had appeared in his kingdom. What he had to say about it is unknown, but the analysis which he received from the Patriarch Theophylact of Constantinople, that he was confronted by 'Manichaeism mixed with Paulicianism'[13] has been central to most discussion of the origins of the Bogomil heresy. The first, and only substantial, direct evidence of the nature of Bulgarian Bogomilism in its early stages is a little later, apparently shortly after the death of Tsar Peter in 967. Cosmas the Priest does not indicate over what period, in what areas or in what detail he had observed the heresy of which he writes with first-hand knowledge, and he has the disadvantage of the unique source, that he cannot be checked. Nevertheless his *Sermon* against the heretics engenders confidence.[14] It is avowedly based on direct knowledge of, and even discussion with, the heretics; its author's insistence that the vicious lives of some monks and extravagant teachings of others bear much of the blame for the currency of the heresy lends him a degree of objectivity; and the fullness of his account, which runs to some forty printed pages on the heresy itself, and almost as much again on the weaknesses in orthodoxy which encouraged its spread, frees his reader from the constant need to fill lacunae by inference which condemns so much discussion of these lost religions to irredeemable uncertainty. Above all (unlike Theophylact) Cosmas had the rare and precious quality of leaning upon his own knowledge, and not upon what he had learnt from old books. For a chronicler, as for a historian, the lack of a conceptual framework has its disadvantages, but they are least important at the beginning of the quest.

Bogomil (meaning 'beloved by God') began to preach his heresy in Peter's reign (927–67) and it was spread by his followers who went, Gospel in hand, from village to village, winning converts by the modesty of their demeanour as well as the attractiveness of their teachings: they were 'lamb-like in appearance, gentle, modest and silent, always pale from hypocritical fasting'[15] and thus attracted the simple and uneducated whose inquiry for the road to salvation they answered with caution and humility. Their teaching was based on the New Testament, and what they could not find in it was rejected. Saints' days, miracles and fasts, and confession to priests were human not divine ordinances. The liturgy of the church was the work not of the apostles, but of St John Chrysostom, and the veneration of icons, relics and holy ornaments was superstition like that of the pagan Greeks, prohibited by St Paul's refusal of authority to gold and silver objects made by men. They regarded infant baptism with particular horror, and would turn away and spit if they saw a very young child who had been baptized. Even more notorious was their hatred of the cross, which they regarded as no more than the instrument of Christ's agony: they would say 'If someone were to kill the son of a king with a piece of wood is it possible that this piece of wood could be dear to the king?"[16] Like the Paulicians they interpreted Christ's words at the Last Supper as a commendation of his teachings – the body and blood were the Gospels and the writings of the Apostles – and therefore held the bread and wine of communion to be a meal like any other.

Bogomil's interpretation of the commands of Christ rested, according to Cosmas, on a cosmological dualism. The whole of the material universe, earth, sea, sky and stars, sun and moon, were the creation of the Devil, the younger son of God and lord of the World, who constantly attacked men like a mad dog, and had perpetrated the miracles of Christ to deceive them. Christ was the elder son of God, and Cosmas, who is the only authority to make him so, explains it as the interpretation which Bogomil placed on the parable of the prodigal son. No explanation of his nature is offered; that the cult of the Virgin was condemned in terms so insulting that they could not be repeated[17] would be consistent with docetism, but also with horror of every orthodox elaboration on the simple message of the Gospels. The Bogomils abjured the consumption of meat and wine, and procreation, and some at least embraced poverty to the point of begging for their food from house to house.

There is clearly a consistency between the conviction that the Devil (Mammon) was the lord of the material world, and the abjuration of material pleasures and goods. Nevertheless it is striking that Cosmas, who argues with the Bogomils at every point, does not connect them explicitly. On each point his debate is conducted solely in terms of the correct interpretations of the scriptural passages upon which the Bogomils based their teachings, which suggests at least that Cosmas does not recognize their adherence to any other authority. The doubt thus raised as to how fully and consistently the dualism of the Bogomils had been worked out in his time is strengthened by the reasons which he gives for the spread of their beliefs. If the hatred of the church, and the denial of authority to its priests was to be attributed, in his view, to their vicious and greedy habits, the positive doctrines of the heretics are likened with equal firmness to the dissemination of distorted precepts from monastic circles. He denounces the monks who maintain that salvation is impossible in this world, and therefore undermine belief in the validity of marriage, who abandon their wives and take the tonsure irregularly to go on pilgrimage of their own accord, or who leave the monastery and abandon its rule to make their living by begging in the towns. 'If what makes you become a monk is the conviction that the world is a pollution, if you condemn the married state, holding that it is impossible to be saved while living in it, you are endorsing the position of the heretics.'[18]

These points are emphasized because they imply a disagreement between Cosmas and the Patriarch Theophylact about the roots of Bogomilism, at least if Theophylact's description is taken to imply a historical as well as a doctrinal judgement. Much that Cosmas describes may reflect the influence of others on the Bogomils. The insistence on chastity as indispensable to separation from the world (a doctrine which the Paulicians did not hold) and the recognition of no prayer except the Lord's Prayer, which they repeated in long sequences, may be thought to point to Messalian influence, which, through its monastic milieu, is consistent with the views of Cosmas. The insistence upon discarding all that was not in the New Testament, and some of the allegorical interpretations of it (as of the Last Supper, but not of the crucifixion) are common to the Bogomils and the Paulicians, but also to many others; and though the world was the realm of the Devil there is no unambiguous sign in Cosmas' account either of the myth and the horror of matter *per se* in Manichaeism, or of the independent existence of the evil principle, and the conviction of the illusory nature of the incarnation, which would be associated with the Paulicians. In short, while, like every other group that we have considered, the Bogomils may have drawn piece-meal upon the vast and miscellaneous repository of heretical traditions which was so prominent a part of Byzantine Christianity, they cannot be regarded as a simple product of one or two of them without doing violence to the best evidence that we have.

The attribution of the appearance of Bogomilism to the presence in tenth-century Bulgaria of devotees of more ancient heresies is vitiated not only by the absence of decisive evidence, but by the presence of almost every alternative stimulant that might be postulated. Tsar Peter's Bulgaria was a land rich in misery, showing signs of a multitude of social and religious tensions so varied that it would be more difficult, if it had been necessary, to explain the absence of heresy than its presence. The conversion of Boris the Great to Christianity in 865 was associated by the *boyars* with the acceptance of Byzantine domination, understandably enough since the Byzantines themselves regarded the expansion of Christendom as co-extensive with that of their own civilization. It was followed by a series of revolts which culminated in 893 with Boris' emergence from the monastery to which he had retired to depose his eldest son, Vladimir, and put in his place his second son, Symeon 'the half-Greek' who could be relied upon to maintain his father's Christianity. Symeon remained faithful to his religion, but he chose to assert his independence by the prosecution of a series of bloody and ultimately disastrous wars with the Empire which left Bulgaria at his death in 927 'with its economy in ruins, its army decimated in distant adventures, its aristocracy seething with humiliation, and its peasantry with discontent'.[19] The peace which Peter concluded with the Greeks at the beginning of his reign married him to the grand-daughter of the Emperor Romanus, and left his Archbishop of Preslav with the title, assumed in Boris' time, of Patriarch, but these concessions amounted to no more than a tactful expression of the essential truth that henceforth Bulgaria was to be, both in church and state, the loyal satellite of the Empire. In such circumstances it was inevitable that the insecurity of a crippled peasantry should lead to the extension of great estates upon which their position had changed for the worse, and of these estates many were the possessions of the monasteries and bishoprics from which Greek clergy spread simultaneously the message of the Gospel, and of political domination. It is a matter for debate whether the extent to which this process was carried in the tenth century was sufficient to justify its description as the feudalization of Bulgarian society (a term which some would prefer to reserve for the eleventh century), but it is clear that the position of the peasantry had deteriorated substantially, and that the end of the wars was accompanied by the appearance of new groups of poor, deprived of their place on the land and driven to domestic or labour service, or simply to vagabondage.[20] In the towns too (much more advanced than in the west at this time), a host of small tradesmen and artisans had found through exaction and impost that their livelihood was threatened almost as much by the peace as it had been by the war. At every level, in fact, between Bulgaria and Byzantium, between Tsar and boyar, between each of them and the rest of the population, tension and grievance mounted.

The teachings of Bogomil, as they are described by Cosmas, leave no difficulty in identifying the audience to which he appealed in this miserable forum. Obedience to the divine law was explicitly held to dispel obligation to human order; the heretics 'revile the wealthy, hate the tsar, ridicule the elders, condemn the boyars, regard as vile in the sight of God those who serve the tsar, and forbid every servant to work for his master'.[21] In short, the implicit challenge which the contempt of the world necessarily holds for worldly authority was spelt out clearly enough by Bogomil for at least one reporter to be left in no doubt of it. In the nature of things it is impossible to estimate the practical effect of such teachings, which are commonly less than those against whom they are directed fear or allege, but they offer a vivid sketch of the emotions which assisted their formulation. The hatred of the church which accompanied them was the result of its Greek direction, of its social privilege, and of its spiritual success. The violent aversion to baptized children for example, may have been the expression of a conviction that baptism, which had sometimes been directly forced during the conversion of less than a century before, acquired in addition to its religious significance a flavour of subordination, either to the Tsar or to the Greeks. Symeon was a great builder of churches and monasteries, especially in the province of Macedonia, which is the likeliest birthplace of Bogomilism, but he left his subjects in no position to pay cheerfully for his ambition to lead a cultured people. The questions which Boris I put to Pope Nicholas I[22] when, in 867, he thought that the Roman church might suit him better than the Greek suggest that the predilection of the latter for elaborate ritual and its tendency to equate Christian precepts with Byzantine cultural values had already aroused hostility among his subjects, which they would express again when they listened to Bogomil preachers. He asked, for example, whether Christianity really forbade bathing on Wednesdays and Fridays, and the wearing of trousers, and whether it was true that the holy chrism which was used in the sacraments was produced in, and obtainable only from, the Byzantine Empire. On the other hand the strictures which Nicholas pronounced upon Greek tolerance of marriage in priests cannot have increased Bulgarian respect for the moral standards of the Greek clergy when Boris decided in 879 that Rome was not for him after all.

The identification of the orthodox church with so extensive a variety of oppressive forces, and the miseries and dislocations of Bulgarian society in the time of Bogomil combined to produce a situation in which great spiritual power accrued to those who escaped identification with the sources of the troubles from which they offered escape. The vigorous development of monasticism manifested not only the ambition of Symeon and the extension of Byzantine influence under his successor, but also a widespread desire for holiness, for peace and for seclusion from the horrors of the world. The monasteries satisfied those aspirations with mixed success, but they were supplemented, and often preceded by hermits and holy men who took upon their shoulders, to the admiration of crowds of pilgrims, the sins and problems of their fellow men. Cosmas was careful to except the hermits who lived in the mountains from his strictures on those who claimed to live the holy life without subjection to a monastic rule. The most famous of them, John of Rila, who became the patron saint of Bulgaria, must have been almost an exact contemporary of Bogomil. He died in 946, after a life of splendid deprivation, lived in a hollow oak tree, and later in a cave. The same overlapping of function and appeal which occurred in early twelfth-century Europe between the hermits, preachers and monastic founders on the one hand, and the heresiarchs on the other, delivered the consolation and leadership of the Bulgarians at a time of special hardship both to the saintly hermits and to the emissaries of Bogomil.

This account of the Bulgarian Bogomils of the tenth century is notably incomplete in the light of what is known about the development of Bogomilism in the Byzantine Empire during the eleventh and twelfth centuries. The absence of a wholly dualist theology, and of the docetist Christology which ought to have accompanied it, of clear evidence that the sect was divided distinctly between Hearers and Elect, and of the ceremony of *teleiosis* which later signalled that distinction, raise problems of continuity as acute for the future of the 'dualist tradition' as for its past. Rather than assuming that Cosmas' account was incomplete, but implies the existence of some or all of these things, there is much to be said for supposing that the religion which Bogomil preached was not a fully fledged dualist faith. The whole field of Balkan and Byzantine heresy still holds many puzzles for those equipped to solve them, but it appears to the unskilled eye that the historians most sceptical of assertions of continuity between different heresies have often been those whose views have lasted longest. In the east as in the west each closer study offers fresh warning against the too ready assumption either that bodies of heterodox teaching were passed intact from one time or place to another, or that heretical thinkers have often presented their visions and teachings in a state of logical completeness which, after all, has usually evaded innovators in other fields of thought. If attention is paid to the circumstances of its genesis rather than to its intellectual structure what Cosmas describes has a certain coherence. The simple Christian, beset by a score of physical and moral dangers, was offered a theology incomplete but sufficient to account for his predicament, and a code of behaviour which removed him alike from danger and temptation, and encouraged him to despise his afflictions as he bypassed them on his way to salvation under the guidance of preachers whose poverty and humility warranted their freedom from earthly contamination. There is no reason to suppose that such virtues were wholly vitiated in the eyes of the poor by a certain lack of intellectual completeness.

In 1018 the Bulgarian Empire fell to Basil II, the Bulgar slayer, and Macedonia, together with Thrace and the north-eastern provinces which correspond to modern Bulgaria, became part of the Byzantine Empire. The troubles of Peter's reign were renewed, as the Byzantine administration set about recovering the costs of the war by imposing a variety of new taxes with vigour and efficiency, the spread of the great estates increased the power and stimulated the rapacity of the landowners, and the church, the chief spiritual agent of the new domination, grew in power and wealth. Bogomilism was a religious, not a political movement, and the pacifist convictions to which it always adhered (unlike the Paulicians) forbid any crude suggestion that it became a force of 'national resistance'. At the same time such circumstances were bound to strengthen its hold among the Bulgarians, if only because it was now the greatest of the heresies which alone could be described, in any sense, as popular institutions. On the other hand there is some reason to suspect that Bogomil missionaries had begun work within the Empire, as far afield as Asia Minor, before 1018, and the abolition of frontiers with the conquest certainly assisted it to spread widely within the Empire during the eleventh century.

The dissemination of Bogomilism through the Byzantine lands exposed it to a new variety of influences, and a new level of sophistication both among its converts and its commentators, and it is not always easy to tell one from the other. The links between the Bogomils and some of the monasteries, and the readiness of the heretics to avoid detection by outward conformity which Cosmas had noted are more strongly marked later. Euthymius, a monk of the great monastery of the Peribleptos in Constantinople, saw the trial and investigated the doctrines of John Tzurillas, at Acmonia in Phrygia, some time before 1025.[23] He described how the followers of Tzurillas, whom he regarded as the first teacher of a 'newly appeared heresy' in the region, and who was a Bogomil, took part in church services, accepted the sacraments and appeared to venerate icons and crosses, even had their children baptized, to avoid detection. Tzurillas himself became a monk, and encouraged his disciples to follow his example in placing his wife in a nunnery. His decision took advantage of a feature of Byzantine monasteries which greatly aided the concealment or development of heresy in them, that (unlike those of the west) the individual monk was left free to follow his own path of sacrifice and speculation without being compelled to participate in regular corporate activity. Euthymius later discovered that four monks of his own monastery were Bogomils, who could provide him with a convenient source of information on their beliefs. This close interpenetration of heresy in the citadels of orthodoxy, to which there is no parallel in the west, had important consequences. It meant that the generally easy-going Byzantine authorities were seized by occasional panics against infiltrators, one of them strong enough to allow a Patriarch of Constantinople to be deposed as a 'Bogomil' in 1147. It also increased the opportunities for various strands of orthodox and heterodox ideas to interact with each other; in particular, each successive account of Byzantine Bogomilism shows a greater degree of Messalian influence, until after the middle of the twelfth century the distinction between the two heresies ceased to be drawn. Finally, it introduced the Bogomils not only to new materials for the construction of their ideas, but to new techniques, as they gained converts who were educated and sophisticated, some of them, by about 1110, from among the aristocratic families of the capital.[24] The heresy which would begin to reach western Europe by the middle of the twelfth century was in a state of continuing development, and the beliefs of its adherents differed from each other not only at different times, but as they came to include a heterogeneous variety of people from different parts of the Empire. The necessarily schematic description of Byzantine Bogomilism which follows in no way implies that it was an unvarying, much less a monolithic faith.

The teachings of Bogomil were most complete in their moral and ethical precepts, which remain common to all the subsequent accounts of it. Apart from the report of Euthymius Zigabenus, who compiled his *Panoplia Dogmatica* at the command of Alexius I, that the prohibition of animal foods had been extended to include eggs and cheese, there was nothing significant to add. The account of Zigabenus also provides the first definite information that the sect had assumed the structure which was typical of its kind. He describes their procedures of initiation, which involved two ceremonies, apparently identical in kind, but separated by a period of 'more rigorous training, a more continent life, purer prayer'.[25] The first was called *Baptisma*, and was itself preceded by a period of prayer and confession; we may infer that it admitted the recipient to the rank of believers or hearers. After the further period of preparation 'they seek for proof as to whether he has observed all these things and performed them zealously. If both men and women testify in his favour they lead him to his consecration.' The supplicant knelt and faced east, a copy of St John's Gospel was laid on his head, and his co-religionists laid their hands upon him while they recited a hymn. On the second occasion of its performance this was the *Teleiosis*, which conferred upon the recipient the status of *theotokos*, and full initiation. Initiates of either degree became members of the church, and were assured of salvation provided that they committed no grave sin and adhered to the strict discipline of daily and nightly prayer which was laid down for them.

It is one of the most regrettable of the many deficiencies in our knowledge of Bogomilism that we know so little of its organization. Western sources make it quite clear that there were 'bishops' before the end of the twelfth century, but not when or how they emerged. On the other hand the missionary success of the movement in the eleventh century may be thought to imply the existence of a hierarchy within it,[26] and Euthymius of the Peribleptos claimed that they had divided the Empire between them by lot, in imitation of the Apostles, for conversion. Without taking him too literally it is reasonable to suppose that there was a measure of organization, and that the dedication of the Bogomils to their work may have been marked by ritual steps such as the *Baptisma* and *Teleiosis*. The conjecture is strengthened by the difficulty which all ascetic sects encountered in imposing on all their members disciplines whose observation was socially unacceptable, or alternatively of accepting the allegiance only of the few who could undergo the full rigours which it would ultimately call for.

The progress which is clearly set out as Bogomilism advanced was in the fields of theology and cosmology. Cosmas described a system in which the material world was the work of the Devil, who was in turn the younger son of God, but which offered little explanation of how this state of affairs had come about, or of the process of redemption from it. By a century later there was a great deal more. In addition to Euthymius of the Peribleptos we have from this period the *Secret Supper* or *Interrogatio Johannis*, a dialogue between Christ and John the Evangelist which survives in two western versions, but had been brought to Lombardy from Bulgaria at the end of the twelfth century. It is in general agreement with the accounts both of Euthymius and of Zigabenus, but since it is rather closer to the former may be supposed to have been eleventh century in composition, as well as Bulgarian in origin.

Satanael was the elder son of God, acted as his ruler (the unjust steward of St Luke) over creation, and sat on the throne at God's right hand. Overcome by a desire to equal his father he went into rebellion, stealing souls according to Euthymius of the Peribleptos, or tempting angels to transfer their allegiance to him in the versions of Zigabenus and the *Secret Supper*: in the latter one of the inducements was a promise to reduce their taxes. He was expelled from heaven, created the earth and its firmament as his own kingdom, and succeeded in confining the soul of an angel in the body of Adam: the accounts of the method vary. Euthymius of the Peribleptos had it that the soul kept escaping, until the Devil stopped up the anus through which it had always escaped with his hand, and vomited over it the flesh of every unclean animal which he had eaten, to make a seal; in the *Secret Supper* the angel was simply persuaded to enter the body of its own accord, and in Zigabenus the Devil appealed to God to send down a spirit to Adam on condition that the man thus created should belong jointly to them both. Finally Zigabenus and the *Secret Supper* provide for the continuity of the race by saying that the Devil created Eve in the same way as Adam, and seduced her to beget Cain before teaching Adam how to follow his example. The explanation of the earliest version, that of Euthymius of the Peribleptos, is therefore rather coarser than the others, making the Devil depend for his success on violence rather than his capacity to mislead by appealing to the vanity or credulity of the angels who became his victims.

The place of Christ in the drama is also progressively explained. Euthymius of the Peribleptos adds to the account of Cosmas the information that the heretics rejected the Christian doctrines of the Second Coming and the Resurrection, both entailed by the essentially evil nature of matter. It is left to the *Secret Supper* to explain how God, taking pity on the captive angels, sent one of his own angels in the disguise of a woman, through whose ear his second son, Christ, might enter the world in the guise of a man. This is the first clear statement of the docetist heresy, the necessary freeing of the Saviour from the incarnation which was repellent to the dualist mind. In Constantinople Christ was rescued from the flesh by the neo-platonist strain in contemplative mysticism and by the academic neo-platonism which was influential in the schools of the capital at the same time, and became the Logos, the Word, who on his descent into hell revealed himself to Satanael, bound him in chains and deprived him of the last syllable of his name, which had symbolized his creative power, before returning to heaven to sit on his Father's right hand.

With these developments the evolution of Bogomil's teaching had been worked out in all its essentials, and its further progress is noted not in Byzantine but in western sources, which we shall consider below. One aspect of that progress, however, must be considered. By the end of the twelfth century one of the Bogomil churches, the *ecclesia Dugonthiae*, associated with Constantinople, had espoused the doctrine of absolute dualism. Satanael, the evil power, was no longer the creature of God, but an uncreated eternal principle. The independence of the evil power had occasionally appeared in ancient dualist cults (Mani's Matter was eternal, though it is not clear that he personified it), but has been notably absent from this account of Bogomilism. So long as the belief in 'the dualist tradition' prevailed it was supposed that absolute dualism was the true tradition of Mani, from which less whole-hearted heretics deviated. Indeed one distinguished authority went so far as to suggest that Bogomil himself was an absolute dualist, and that the mitigated version which we have seen was the result of a reform or schism after his death.[27] The Paulicians have been popular candidates for the position of importers of absolute dualism into Bogomilism at one stage or another of its development, and it is true that their cosmology distinguished sharply between the good and evil gods. Even if it is assumed, however, that Peter of Sicily, upon whose account of Paulician theology this view chiefly rests, is what he says he is, closer examination of Paulician teaching throws doubt on his understanding. Not only had the Paulicians entirely failed to absorb any of Mani's myth or writings, but their benevolent God was so far removed from the world of matter that his existence had little impact on it: the Paulicians did not advocate any of the austerities which were otherwise the universal concomitant of dualist cosmology because they believed themselves to be wholly the creation of the evil God. The good had no power in the world, and they knew nothing of him, except that he had sent an angel (Christ) to inform them of his existence.[28] Whatever the ancestry of this belief it was wholly different not only from the dualism of Mani, but from that of the absolute dualists among the Bogomils and Cathars of the thirteenth century, who shared the myths and traditions of their co-religionists except where they had to be modified to allow Satan to be eternal. The most satisfactory way of accounting for their appearance therefore seems to be by internal logic, in the same manner as the docetist Christology was gradually evolved because it was appropriate to the rest of the Bogomil vision. Mitigated dualism did not, after all, provide a complete solution to the problem of evil. If there was no evil before the rebellion of Satan what tempted him to rebel? The answer is provided by a myth of the mitigated dualists of Lombardy, which says that he was seduced by the four-faced beast which dealt in the primeval chaos, while an earlier stage on the road may be indicated by the fact that, in the *Secret Supper*, there was a hell, shielded by a flame of fire, which Satanael was unable to penetrate when he made the tour of his dominions which immediately preceded his rebellion.[29] These were germs sufficient to enable some of the educated Bogomils of Constantinople to bring their beliefs finally to a state of coherence, at some time between the composition of the *Panoplia Dogmatica* of Zigabenus, (1110–18) and the first appearance in the west of an emissary of the absolute dualist *ecclesia Dugonthiae* in the early 1170s.

To recount the development of Manichaeism and Bogomilism has plainly been to observe in fuller form the elaboration of the same ideals and aspirations which had produced rebellion against the western church since the beginning of the eleventh century. The heightened sense of evil which produced a horror of worldly satisfaction, and loosened the willingness of its possessor to accept the ministrations of a manifestly corrupt clergy as the offices of the true God, driving him to rely instead on the inner sense of his own knowledge of the good, was the commonest of the personal forces which might lead a man to heresy. The question which therefore arises is what the nature of the connection between them was. Adhemar of Chabannes, who described the heretics who appeared in

Aquitaine in 1018 as Manichees, inaugurated a tradition that is still represented by the greatest modern scholar in the field,[30] of regarding heresy in the medieval west as an alien force, the kindling of sparks left dormant since antiquity, or the result of the activities of Bogomil missionaries who, as we have seen, began to carry their religion from Bulgaria at almost exactly the moment when dissent appeared in the west. None of the heretics from Leutard of Vertus to Arnold of Brescia is described fully or clearly as though he were a Bogomil, or had unmistakeably fallen under Bogomil influence, but almost none of them did not exhibit, in some detail or other, a trait which might plausibly be described as neo-manichaean. The avoidance of meat, the condemnation of marriage, the dislike of infant baptism, the rejection of the mass, the designation of the Roman church as the agent of iniquity, the reliance on the New Testament and not the Old, the initiation by the laying-on of hands, all appear in Europe, and may be thought to arise from a conviction of the irredeemable evil of the created universe. It is possible to construct a table which shows the appearance of each of these points and others in eleventh- and early twelfth-century heresies taken *en bloc*,[31] though none of them individually contributes much to it. The accumulation of these parallels has been thought by some to show that (as this case has been deftly summarized) the western evidence 'is consistent with the view that we are shown by the sources a variety of aspects of a Bogomil iceberg',[32] which accounts for the appearance of popular heresy in the medieval west.

On the other side is the opinion which has been, in effect, the premise of the early chapters of this book. Taken point by point all the attitudes and opinions expressed by western heretics may be derived from the scriptures, and the preference for those particular interpretations to the ones which were promulgated by the church can be accounted for partly by the dominance within the church itself of the apostolic and evangelical spirit which contrasted the virtues of simplicity and austerity with the luxury and laxity which prevailed among its priests, and partly by the emergence of dislocations and discontents which the church could not answer.[33] The attribution of responsibility for the origins of western heresy to the Bogomils rests ultimately on a failure to account for it otherwise, for there is not a single instance (and this is agreed on all sides) in which we are persuaded to concede the presence of an identifiable Bogomil in western Europe before 1143. Further, the assessment of early heresies in the west as a group, rather than one by one, is justifiable only if they are held to have the character of a movement, to share with each other enough of doctrine, organization, and visible connection to embrace them all in a single explanation. My contention[34] has been, on the contrary, not only that evidence of any such coherence is entirely lacking, but that what evidence there is shows that the incidents of heresy in the west were as varied as the men who preached them and the circumstances in which they appeared, that what they had in common is little more than what was universally there to be reacted against.

It is for the reader to decide whether the origins of western heresy have been sufficiently accounted for without recourse to the hypothesis of Bogomil penetration. There is, however, no difficulty, if its dismissal be accepted, in explaining the amount that Byzantine and western heresies had in common in the eleventh century. The argument of this chapter has been that the problem of evil was deeply sunk in the roots of the civilizations which grew around the ancient Mediterranean, and that a rich variety of solutions to it was embedded in every part of the Christian inheritance. In every case the first impulse was to turn to the Gospels, where there was to be found a simple code of personal purity, neighbourly charity, and the subordination of human to divine precepts. Suggestions for their elaboration abounded in the writings of the received fathers of the church and of the innumerable visionaries and prophets who had failed to join their number. No historian dare maintain that some of these ideas did not reach eleventh-century Europe by an unknown route through time or space, however hazardous he may know either journey to have been. It is perfectly possible that the Gundolfo who is dubiously alleged to have infected peasants near Arras with heresy in 1025 might have picked up his ideas from some Bogomil rumour in Italy,[35] or that Peter of Bruys derived his hatred of the cross from an unrecorded Bulgarian contact,[36] or that the chain of prayer which was maintained by the pious at Monforte was Messalian in inspiration, and there is room for legitimate difference of opinion as to how close a similarity is needed to sustain such suspicions in the absence of any concrete evidence.[37] It is equally true that the community of ideas which existed within orthodoxy on either side of the Mediterranean was sufficient to make observers on both turn to St Augustine for the elucidation of the unknown, to find in the early fathers accounts of the lurid orgies of which Psellus accused the Bogomils, and Paul of St Père de Chartres the canons of Orléans at almost exactly the same time, and in terms which bear the same close resemblance to the same passage in Justin Martyr.[38] It was the same devotion to the same scriptures which led reformers on both sides to point to self-denial and the embrace of poverty as remedies for the similar ills of both their churches, and which suggested to Ratherius of Verona that God must be perceived by the *interiores oculi*,[39] as to Symeon the New Theologian that only the eyes of the spirit could show the Christian the path to salvation. And for all the differences between them, neither church had the means to ensure that such enthusiasms and insights could always be contained within the bounds of orthodoxy.

The debate about the origins of western heresy does not depend in the end on the vain attempt to trace the paths of error through the labyrinth of eastern and western Christian tradition. The possibility of heterodoxy was always present, but that is not sufficient to explain the transformation of heterodoxy into dissent. The search for eastern bacilli behind the expressed ills of the church in the eleventh and early twelfth centuries may not be entirely fruitless, but it does not reveal any wholesale exportation of the doctrine, organization or myth of any earlier heresy. In that respect the middle of the twelfth century saw the beginning of a great change.

Chapter VII | The Arrival of the Cathars

The appearance of Bogomil missionaries in Europe was announced with admirable clarity by Eberwin, prior of the Premonstratensian house at Steinfeld near Cologne, when he wrote to St Bernard in 1143 to ask him to direct the force of his eloquence against a new heresy. Its devotees, he claimed, were 'rising on every side from the depths of the abyss, in almost every church, as though their leader is released, and the day of the Lord is at hand'. 'There is a verse in the wedding song of the love of Christ and the church which you must deal with,' he continued (St Bernard was at the time in the middle of his task of composing a sermon upon each verse of the *Songs of Songs*), ' "Catch us the little foxes that destroy the vines", which is appropriate to this problem.'[1]

The heretics of whom Eberwin wrote had come to the attention of the ecclesiastical authorities because they could not agree among themselves, and in the course of their disputes they had permitted their enthusiasm to exceed their discretion. They were examined for three days by a council composed of both clerical and secular notables presided over by the archbishop before they were put to the stake. The execution was carried out by the people despite the resisance of the clerks, and if, as seems probable, the Annals of Brunweiler for the year 1143 refer to the same incident, three who escaped from Cologne were burned at Bonn by Count Otto of Rheineck.[2] That there were two heretical sects and not one drew the attention of the council to differences of doctrine between them, and ensured that what Eberwin says of them is the result of what he saw and heard himself, the beliefs of particular people at a particular time, described without the preconceptions which distort so many of the earlier narratives.

Eberwin distinguished carefully between the 'new heretics' about whom he was particularly worried, and the 'other heretics in our area', who clearly belonged to the tradition of disillusioned apostolic idealism which had become familiar in the preceding decades. The characteristic conviction of the latter was that 'the apostolic dignity has been corrupted by involvement in secular affairs, and the throne of St Peter by failing to fight for God as Peter did has deprived itself of the power of consecration which was given to Peter. Since the church no longer has that power the archbishops who live in a worldly manner within the church cannot receive it and cannot consecrate others.' Hence they held the sacraments of the church valueless, including the mass, and preached a faith of puritanical individualism. Marriage, except between virgins, was 'mere fornication' (which is enough to undermine the occasional description of these people as 'Henricians'), all observances of the church which did not date back to the time of the apostles were condemned, the intercession of saints and other penances for sin were rejected, because forgiveness would follow true repentance alone, and, inevitably, baptism could be conferred only upon adults who understood its meaning. In short, if the authority of the church was denied more radically and the necessity of personal purity asserted more fiercely than usual, there was nothing in this which differed significantly from the persuasions of their western predecessors and contemporaries.

Those with whom they are contrasted are a very different case. Their defence was conducted by two of their number 'one who was called their bishop, with his companion', who when they saw that their deployment of authorities from the New Testament was failing to make any impression offered to produce others of their faith more expert in its teachings to defend it better. It is, incidentally, remarkable that Eberwin seems to imply that this offer was not accepted: the rawest recruit to the Dominican inquisition would not have missed such an opportunity. But it was one of the points that he was most anxious to stress about the new heretics that they claimed to be members of an ancient church, which had been hidden since the time of the martyrs, 'and persisted in Greece and other lands, and these are the heretics who call themselves apostles and have their own pope'. In this they contrasted ominously with the more familiar sectaries who 'deny our pope, but at least do not claim to have another one instead'.

The heretics expounded their teachings clearly. Their claim to be apostolic was founded on their total rejection, modelled on that of Christ and his disciples, of every form of wealth and property; even the common possession of the orthodox monks and canons seemed to them to violate this principle. They described themselves as *pauperes Christi*, fleeing before persecution from one city to another, like the apostles before them, devoting their lives to 'fasting, abstaining, working and praying by day and night'. They omitted from their diet every product of coition, including milk, and they rejected the Catholic sacraments, though they went veiled to mass. Their own observances were in the daily consecration of their food by the recitation of the Lord's prayer at table, and the baptism of the Holy Spirit, performed by the laying-on of hands in the manner described in the Acts, without water. These two ceremonies were performed by those of their number who were known as the *electi*, the highest of their three grades: there were also the *credentes*, who were present at prayers during a probationary period before they became *electi*, and the *auditores*, or hearers. The translation from each grade to the next was achieved through the ceremony of the laying-on of hands.

This precise and circumstantial description leaves no room for doubt. Eberwin had witnessed the examination of converts to the Bogomil faith (his silence affords a reasonable presumption that the men themselves were not foreigners) who were quite ready, once apprehended, to expound their convictions in the naïve belief that their hearers would perceive the truth: they said that they themselves would be willing to rejoin the Catholic church if they saw their masters confuted, though otherwise they would die – as in the event they did – rather than betray their faith. Only their vague assertion of the antiquity of their church is at variance with this conclusion, and that illusorily, for Christians must necessarily believe that they practise the religion of the apostles. That they were uneducated men is suggested not only by their own modesty, but by Eberwin's comment that though they rejected marriage he could not discover why, 'either because they dared not tell it, or (more likely) because they did not know it': there is no reason to suspect him of irony. We shall see again that the first converts to the new faith in the west were simple people, not equipped to pursue the theological subtleties of their belief – upon which Eberwin's account touches not at all – travelling in the fashion described here, surreptitiously from one place to another, and including both among their *credentes* and *electi* women as well as men. Eberwin saved this point for the end of his letter, confident that it would arouse St Bernard to action.

The points of Eberwin's narrative which make it decisively clear that he had seen something of which there is no earlier western description are the sacrament which in its nature and function is identical with the *teleiosis* of the Bogomils, which became the *consolamentum* of the Cathars, and the organization of the sect, with its hearers, believers and elect, and its bishops. The second of these is exactly repeated in a letter which the clergy of Liège sent to Pope Lucius II just over a year later, at the beginning of 1145.[3] They also had tried to save evangelists of 'a new heresy', which they said was spreading from the village of Montwimers in Champagne, from an angry mob. They succeeded in rescuing most of them, and one whose name was Haimeric repented his heresy and was sent to the Pope for absolution. Like Eberwin's letter this one was based on direct encounter and on information volunteered (in some sense) by at least one of the heretics, but since its purpose was to warn the Pope of Haimeric's arrival it was much briefer. It mentions one custom, characteristic of the Bogomils, which Eberwin had not, that the heretics forbade every form of oath-taking, and it remarks as he had that they protected themselves by occasional conformity, 'pretending to take our sacraments to conceal their wickedness'. Otherwise there is nothing new: the clerks were shocked by the comprehensive rejection of the Catholic sacraments, and filled with the gloomiest forebodings of the popular success which the heretics were achieving.

These two letters mark a watershed in the development of heresy in the medieval west. Even if it is accepted, as it has not been in the foregoing pages, that any of the earlier heretics who were discovered in Europe had been significantly influenced by the east, it remains true that we have here first-hand and unambiguous evidence of direct missionary contact, which we shall continue to trace over the next four decades as it carries new doctrines and forms of religious organization through western Europe, to become Catharism. The nature of the infiltration remains obscure. The only direct statement that survives about it is mythical rather than historical. In the second half of the thirteenth century the Lombard inquisitor Anselm of Alessandria tried to preface his description of Catharism with a précis of its history.[4] From the early 1170s, when the new religion reached Italy it is precise, though brief, and accords well with the earlier sources; before that it is better in the spirit than in the letter. The religion had been founded, according to him, by Mani, who preached in Bulgaria; 'later' Greek merchants trading in Bulgaria were converted, and brought the infection to Constantinople, where it was passed to the Franks who 'went to Constantinople to conquer the land'; later again some Slav merchants came from Bosnia to trade, and took the heresy home with them, and after this the Franks went home from Constantinople, and spread the heresy in their own country.

Anselm had his information, presumably, from Italian victims of the thirteenth-century inquisition, and it is easy to see how he and they blended authentic memory with preconception. That Bulgaria was the birth-place, but Constantinople the centre of propagation of the heresy is as accurate as the idea that Mani worked in Bulgaria is groundless and it appears that Bogomilism did indeed spread to

Bosnia in the early 1140s, at about the same time as we have seen it in Cologne and Liège.[5] But was it memory or preconception that characterized its carriers? The crusades have indeed been credited, and on more serious grounds, with the importation of dualism into Europe as of syphilis and leprosy.[6] Soldiers both in the first and on the second crusade encountered Paulician communities on their path, and it is not ridiculous to suggest that they might have been influenced by them, and brought their ideas home again, though, as we shall argue later, it is with Bogomil rather than with Paulician influence that Europe is chiefly concerned. But there are serious grounds also for reservation. If our sources are to be trusted the major turning points of the impact of eastern on western heresy happened just before crusades rather than immediately after them, in the 1140s and 1170s; the first converts who come to our notice were wandering artisans, not members of the crusading classes; and the parts of Europe where the heresy first appears are not, on the whole, those which are thought to have contributed most to the crusading movement. In any case a certain lack of perspective is inherent in the proposition, for our interest is not in contact with the east in general, but with Constantinople in particular, and by the middle of the twelfth century the crusaders represented a very small and a very untypical part of the contact between that city and western Europe. When Anselm wrote, a hundred years later, popular memory doubtless recalled the military connection most vividly, but it was a surer instinct which prompted him to identify trade as the medium of propagation in two out of his three cases. A glance at a map will strengthen the suspicion that the real force in the dissemination of Bogomilism to Europe was the same one which carried it (according to Anselm) from Bulgaria to Constantinople and thence to Bosnia; it entered along the great Danube–Rhine route, which carried a rapidly increasing volume of trade, and from the Rhineland spread again along the paths established by commerce, to Flanders, England and Champagne, whence it made its way slowly to southern France. Just as Manichaeism shrank with the Roman world in the fifth century,[7] its successor in the twelfth expanded with the economy and culture of its time.

This general observation, however, by no means amounts to an assertion that heresy was peculiar to, or propagated particularly by 'the merchant classes', men of whom the slightness of our knowledge mocks the importance of their activity. They might establish routes, but there is no reason to suppose that they monopolized their use. The suddenness with which dualism spilled from Constantinople, reaching northern Europe and Bosnia, so far as we can tell, almost at the same moment, suggests that it was precipitated by events rather than processes. In 1140 a monk named Constantine Chrysomalos, whose work was influential in monastic circles, was condemned as heretical on the charge that he taught Messalian and Bogomil doctrines on a number of points, including baptism, confession and the study of the Gospels, and the accession of Manual I to the imperial throne in 1143 was followed by renewed prosecution of suspected Bogomils; it was through his friendship with one of those accused, the monk Niphon, that the Patriarch Cosmas II was deposed as a heretic early in 1147.[8] These episodes suggest that the atmosphere of the capital in those years was congenial to persecution, both in and outside Constantinople. Perhaps it was not only in the seventeenth century that new worlds made accessible by commercial expansion seemed to offer haven to those whose puritanism made their homes uncomfortable.

If this view is unavoidably speculative it has the merit of consistency with such facts as break surface, and with the constant association which is noted between the dissemination of heresy and the mobile poor, and particularly with the artisan crafts which were compatible with a wandering life, among which that of the weaver rapidly became synonymous with the idea of heresy itself.[9] The image of the heretic which strikes the note associated with these decades is that of the people who 'came to Cologne from Flanders, and stayed secretly in a barn near the city' in 1163, or of the 'Manichees' denounced by the Council of Rheims in 1157 – it is a general condemnation, not associated with any known group – who 'hide among the poor and under the veil of religion labour to undermine the faith of the simple, spread by the wretched weavers who move from place to place and often change their names, accompanied by women sunk in sin'.[10] Nevertheless, while it is true that most of those who were detected are described as newcomers, it is well to remember that, especially in small communities, it is the new-comers who are most closely scrutinized and most readily blamed for newly discovered problems. We can only guess that poor heretics were more numerous than rich ones, but we can be sure that they were more likely to be accused, and if accused more certain to be punished.[11]

During the two decades after Eberwin sounded the alarm the new heresy clearly established itself around the Meuse, Rhine and Moselle rivers. A glimpse of how it was done is revealed by the settlement, in the court of Bishop Nicholas of Cambrai between 1164 and 1167, of a dispute between the abbot of Jette and a clerk named Jonas, who claimed that he was entitled to the curacy of Neder-Hembeek in the diocese of Cologne.[12] It had indeed been granted to him by the abbot of Cornelimunster, from whom the patronage passed to the abbot of Jette in 1155, but it was now adjudged that he had forfeited his right to it on the testimony of no fewer than four bishops, or their successors, that Jonas 'had been convicted in their courts of the heresy of the Cathars, and excommunicated'. These convictions were the result of at least two, and more probably four, separate trials, in the diocese of Cologne between 1151 and 1156, of Trier after 1152, and of Liège between 1145 and 1164, and again between 1164 and 1167. The implication is that Jonas had been presented to the benefice before 1155, subsequently been converted to Catharism, and moved from one place to another, as his activities were checked, over a period of ten or fifteen years. It also appears that on the first three occasions at least the bishops were content to rely on the traditional sanction of expulsion from the diocese as a sufficient response to his heresy.

This pattern is confirmed by Eckbert of Schönau's *Thirteen Sermons against the Cathars*, composed in 1163, and based upon the author's encounters with them over a period of some fifteen years during which he disputed with them, and examined them, both at Bonn and at Cologne;[13] he was to come across them again some years later at Mainz. Between 1143 and 1163, therefore, the triangle between Liège, Cologne and Trier not only introduces us, in two sources, to the word Cathar, but provides for the first time a full and detailed account of those to whom it was applied. Eckbert had heard of one Cathar who when offered the body of the Lord on his death-bed responded with a debating point which they made – it was to become a common one – about the mass. If it were really true that all the bread that Christians took in communion was the body of Christ, they told this man, his body must have been consumed by now even if it were as big as a mountain: in deference to the regional landscape they used a local illustration.[14]

The *Sermons* of Eckbert of Schönau were in some respects a direct fore-runner of the inquisitorial treatises which are the chief source for the popular heresies of the thirteenth century, in that they endeavour to present a complete exposition of the beliefs of the heretics based upon interrogation of them. As a young man in the early 1150s Eckbert was a canon at Bonn, and there with his friend Bertolf he used to enter into argument with the Cathars he met, and to befriend those who thought better of their ways, and rejoined the church. Open debate implies the absence of coercion, but Eckbert's later knowledge was gathered in a more formal capacity. He questioned one important Cathar in the presence of Archbishop Arnold of Cologne (d. 1159) and another at Bonn 'because we suspected him of being a Cathar', and he gives it as one of the reasons for writing his sermons that they would assist others in the examination of heretics.[15] It seems, therefore, that the decade of the 1150s saw an increasing desire on the part of the authorities to pursue the new heresy, which may have encouraged the neighbours of five Flemish immigrants to Cologne in 1163 to report them for not going to church, with the result that they were brought before an ecclesiastical court, and when they refused to abjure handed over to the secular power and burnt.[16] In the circumstances the secrecy with which Eckbert reproaches the Cathars so bitterly is understandable, and makes it important not to exaggerate the authority which is accorded to what he says. A good deal of it is hearsay, and since (unlike the inquisitors) he wrote as much to provide refutation of the Cathars as to assist in their identification, he gave their beliefs a greater degree of completeness than he knew them at first hand to possess. Eckbert, more frankly than any of his predecessors, believed that 'this sect with which we are concerned undoubtedly owed its origin to Mani', and although he knew that some of their beliefs were not associated with the ancient Manichees, and that they differed occasionally among themselves, he attached a selection of St Augustine's anti-Manichaean writings to his book 'so that my readers can understand the heresy properly from the beginning and see why it is the foulest of all heresies'.[17] In fact some of the differences which he perceived among the heretics whom he came across arose because some of them were Cathars and others were not: like Eberwin, Eckbert was confronted by both old and new strands of heterodoxy, but unlike Eberwin he failed to realize it because his intellectual training and preconceptions led him to place a monolithic interpretation on the evidence that he found.

When Eckbert wrote the Cathar church was settled and organized in his region. He refers repeatedly to their 'doctors' and 'masters', sometimes meaning the originators of the doctrines which he condemns, but at others his contemporaries: among those whom he interrogated was one 'a man of no small name, who had come back to his own people from the school of the Cathars', and on being asked what was taught there replied briefly that 'they adjudge false and ridiculous everything that you believe and everything that the church does'.[18] The conclusive evidence of the development which the new heresy had achieved is Eckbert's description of its 'baptism':

> The wretch who is to be baptised, or catharized, stands in the middle (of the meeting) and the archcathar stands by him, holding a book which is used for this office. He places the book on his head, and recites blessings – or rather curses – while those who stand around pray, and make [him] a son of Gehenna . . . they call this baptism by fire. . .[19]

Eckbert had this account from a man 'expert among you' who had himself undergone the ceremony, but later renounced it. It is, of course, the baptism of fire and the holy spirit which was described by Eberwin, and later, as the *consolamentum*, by Rainier Sacchoni and his fellow inquisitors, the single sacrament which marked each stage of progress among the Cathars. Eckbert goes on to name two of the 'archcathars' as Arnold of Cologne and Thierry of Bonn, saying that both of them had undergone the ceremony of consolation with their 'accomplices' and 'companions':[20] the second word (*socii*) completes the story, for it is always used, as it had been by Eberwin, of the travelling companion of a Cathar bishop. The burnings of 1143 had failed to accomplish their purpose, and in these two diocesan seats at least the Cathars had set up, as would become their habit, their own hierarchy in opposition to that of the Catholics.

It comes as no surprise that Eckbert is able to provide a comprehensive account of the beliefs of the Cathars, though at two points at least he confuses them with others. While some insisted that Christian baptism was altogether invalid, and that which has just been described alone efficacious, others confined their attack to infant baptism, on the familiar ground that there could be no faith without comprehension. And while some denounced marriage absolutely, 'and promise eternal damnation to those who remain in the married life until their death', others, 'the followers of Hartwin', held that 'only that marriage is righteous which is between virgins, and they ought to have one child and then separate and not meet in the marriage bed again'.[21] These two differences are just those which Eberwin had noted between the Cathars and their rival heretics, whose successors must have been the followers of Hartwin. No Cathar of any stamp held Catholic baptism appropriate for adults, or could have commended the generation of even a single child, while the promise of damnation to those 'who remain in the married life until their death' reflects the custom which was normal among the Cathars, as it had been among earlier dualist sects, of rendering the prohibitions acceptable to the majority of the faithful by requiring them to be observed only late in life. Thus it was that 'those who have become perfected members of their sect avoid all meat'.[22] The appearance of the hierarchy shows that the Cathars now had regular and settled followers, and that the necessary division between the 'elect' who had received the *consolamentum* on the one hand, and the 'believers' on the other had become an ordinary feature of their organization.

In this setting it is to be expected that the sacraments and disciplines of the Catholic church will be rejected, and Eckbert devotes his attention in particular to the denial of purgatory, and with it of prayers, alms and masses for the dead, and to the assertions that 'the whole order of priests in the Roman church will be damned', that the mass is pointless, and the doctrine of transubstantiation a fraud, though once again the practice of occasional conformity is noted: 'they will go to mass and even receive the eucharist with the people among whom they live, to prevent their infidelity from becoming known'. He is able to add a little, though rather vaguely, about their observances. Like Eberwin he knew that the Cathars referred to the recitation of the Lord's prayer at their daily meals as the consecration of the body of Christ, and he also claims that they tried particularly to avoid association with the Catholic celebration of Easter, and replaced it among themselves by an autumn commemoration of the death of Mani, the feast of Bema. The latter assertion, however, exemplifies the weakness of Eckbert's method, for he cites as his authority not the testimony of any of the Cathars whom he had questioned or heard of, but St Augustine's *Contra Manichaeos*, to which he turned for an explanation of what was probably true enough, that the Easter celebrations were especially disliked by the heretics.[23] Neither among Bogomils or Cathars is there any reason to suppose that *Bema* was remembered, for the sufficient reason that, whatever their orthodox critics might say, none of the heretics regarded Mani as the preacher of their message or the founder of their sect.

In the development of the Bogomil church the elaboration of theology and myth appears to have followed the working out of the code of behaviour and worship, and the rejection of orthodoxy. At least as they appear in the sources, theory followed practice rather than practice theory, though it remains arguable whether this reflects the evolution of the doctrines themselves, the emphasis with which they were presented to the people, or the order in which they were perceived by orthodox observers. The same was true in the west. Eberwin of Steinfeld did not say that the teachings of the heretics whom we have identified as Cathars followed from a dualist conviction that matter was the creation of an evil God, and his annoyance that they would not or could not tell him why they condemned marriage suggests that neither he nor they were aware of it. Eckbert had a clearer understanding of this, but even in his case it was uncertain, and his knowledge on this point was changing during the period of which he wrote. On the eating of meat he was confident: the Cathars abstained from it not for the same reason as monks and other Catholic ascetics, but because it was the fruit of coition and unclean. In private they had an even worse reason, 'that all flesh is made by the devil, and therefore must not be eaten even in direst necessity'.[24] But this knowledge did not inform the remainder of his exposition of their teaching, and his discussion of marriage reveals his uncertainty of its implications. It has already been observed that in the part of it which referred to 'the followers of Hartwin' he mistakenly confused with the Cathars votaries of a sect of native western enthusiasm. The remainder[25] dealt with two propositions, neither of which involved the direct condemnation of procreation *per se*. In the first place, and with some confidence, he expounded the orthodox view of Christian marriage as a divinely ordained institution, albeit a state inferior to celibacy, and he derided as hypocritical because physically impossible the ideal of the heretics that man and woman should live together without copulation. This argument was well-honed because it had long been in use against enthusiastic advocates of universal celibacy; it was not only against Cathars that it needed to be deployed.[26] A second argument is presented more diffidently, and is of considerable interest.

> I know one of your secrets, part of the secret wisdom which is the foundation of your heresy, that you hold about marriage. I heard it from certain men who left your sect. . . You say that the fruit which God forbade the first man to eat in paradise was nothing other than the woman whom he had created. . . Hence you hold that the whole human race which is descended from them was born of fornication, and nobody therefore can be saved except by the prayers and blessings of those who among you are called *perfecti*.[27]

This information, it seems, was comparatively new to Eckbert, and not part of the public teaching of the Cathars which his first argument was designed to rebut. The conclusion already arrived at about the state of the Cathar church in the Rhineland is here confirmed by the first use of the word 'perfect' to describe the true Cathars, those who had taken the *consolamentum* and were thereby enabled to minister to their fellow believers, and Eckbert continues, quite rightly, to explain that the 'chief masters' of the heretics were called

'Cathars' because *Catharos* (from the Greek) meant pure. The story which he had heard takes us still further, for the identification of Eve with the forbidden fruit is made in a number of myths of the monarchist Cathars of two generations later, and the version which he gives is very close to that attributed by our earliest source on the Cathars of Lombardy to Caloiannes and Garattus, leaders of sects which had their consecration respectively from the Cathar churches of Bosnia and Bulgaria.[28]

Another 'reliable man who recognized their perfidy and the wickedness of some of their secrets and left their sect' brought Eckbert the news that the Cathars believed that Christ 'was not truly born of the Virgin, and did not truly have human flesh, but a kind of simulated flesh; that he did not rise from the dead, but simulated death and resurrection'. Once again it seems that the information was recent, for the rather short sermon which is directed against it refers to it as an assertion made 'by those who know you well', and remarks that 'if it is true' Eckbert has been wasting his time in composing his extended defence of the eucharist as the body and blood of Christ. Characteristically, he adds that he is quite ready to believe it, because it is in St Augustine.[29] Since it is the first clear assertion of the docetist heresy in the west his surprise may be forgiven, and will act as a useful caution against the tendency to take it for granted that any earlier accusation of heresy on the nature of Christ (such as that professed by the clerks of Orléans) refers to docetism.

Eckbert was still more tentative about the last heresy which he discussed, saying that he did not know whether it was generally held in the sect, or only by some of its members who disagreed with the others, and his surprise was compounded by the observation that it was not attributed by the fathers to the Manichees. This was the doctrine that human souls were in reality those of apostate angels which had fallen to earth at the creation, and could be saved from their corporeal bodies only if they belonged to the sect. This belief had only come to light during the interrogation of those who were burned at Cologne in August 1163, shortly before Eckbert began to compose his sermons.[30] It is perhaps because they had come recently from Flanders that he wondered whether it was universally accepted among the Cathars. It has been pointed out that the source of the story as he heard it is almost certainly the *Secret Supper* which was composed in the eleventh or early twelfth century,[31] and a copy of which reached Italy at the beginning of the thirteenth through the agency of Nazarius, bishop of the Cathar sect of Concerezzo, and successor of that same Garattus whose belief about the forbidden fruit we have already seen shared by Cathars described by Eckbert.

Eckbert's *Sermons*, then, if they have been rightly read, reveal the Cathars of the Rhineland at the very beginning of their development. The words 'Cathar' and 'Perfect' themselves appear for the first time, and with them is an organized church with its teachers and bishops, and regular arrangements for the performance of the *consolamentum*. Although Eckbert could not distinguish Catharism clearly from the non-dualist enthusiasm which had long expressed the dissatisfaction of western Catholics with the standards and services of their priests, its theology and myth were in the process of formation, stimulated by direct and apparently repeated contact with the modified dualist, and Bogomil, church of Bulgaria, most probably through the medium of its votaries in Constantinople. Since the distinctions which Eckbert observed among the heretics of whom he wrote have often been held to imply the presence not only of the moderate, or Bulgarian, Cathars, but also of the Dragovitsan church which held that the Good and Evil principles were both eternal and absolute, it is important to emphasize that a closer reading of his work does not support that view. Everything that he says is consistent with, and accounted for by, the influence of the modified dualists alone.

While Eckbert of Schönau was observing the establishment of Catharism in the Rhineland another new sect was beginning to make its presence felt in northern Europe. In 1163 Archbishop Henry of Rheims accused of Manichaeism some burghers of Arras who belonged to a group described as *Populicani*. Shortly afterwards some thirty *Publicani* whose leader was Gerard came to England from Germany and tried, with little success, to make converts to their sect. In that much-governed country it was not long before their activities were noticed by 'certain curious men', and they were examined at a council at Oxford, denounced as heretics, and handed over to the king for punishment. They were driven from the city at his command, and since it was strictly forbidden to give them food or shelter they did not long withstand the rigours of winter. In 1167 'certain heretics called *Deonarii* or *Populicani*' were arrested at Vézelay, and seven of them were burned when they failed satisfactorily to answer the charges against them. Finally, between 1176 and 1180 a young English clerk named Gervase of Tilbury set eyes on a beautiful maiden working in a vineyard outside Rheims. When she refused his ardent invitation to amorous pleasure 'Master Gervase realized at once that she belonged to the blasphemous sect of *Publicani*, who were being searched out and destroyed all over France, especially by Count Philip of Flanders, who punished them unmercifully with righteous cruelty', and the maiden's modesty led her to the stake, since she refused every inducement to abjure her heresy.[32]

Publicani and *Populicani* are probably derived from the same vernacular term as *Piphiles*, the name by which 'Manichees' were denounced by the Council of Rheims in 1157, and which Eckbert of Schönau gives as the Flemish equivalent of 'Cathars'.[33] It has been usual to follow him in the assumption that the movement of Bogomil missionaries which we have traced up the Rhine was following its natural course, and spreading through Europe from the Low Countries as the canons of Liège had warned it would in 1145. The assumption was a natural one, and there was much to support it. The missionaries of the *Publicani* were both men and women, rejecting the sacraments and denying the authority of the Catholic church. The persistent virtue of the maiden of Rheims, who told Gervase that 'If I lost my virginity and was once corrupted there is no doubt that nothing could save me from eternal damnation,' is consistent with the assertion of Ralph of Coggeshall and of the authorities at Vézelay that they denied the legitimacy of matrimony, and would not eat meat or any other food which was the product of coition. That the sect had secured something of a foothold was suggested both by the ability of the townsmen of Arras to offer Archbishop Henry the very considerable sum of six hundred marks of silver to leave them alone, and of the girl at Rheims to call to her assistance an old woman, also a member of the sect, who defended their heresy with such skill that 'she must have had great knowledge of the whole Bible, and had plenty of practice in this kind of debate'. Similar skill and forthrightness were exhibited by Gerard at the council of Oxford.

It seems plain that the *Publicani* were members of a dualist sect, and the geography of their appearances suggests that if they came from outside Europe it was by way of the Rhine and the Danube. Neverthelessthere are some curious differences between them, if they are taken as a group (as they clearly should be), and the Cathars described above. There is no echo of the assertion that they concealed their heresy by occasional conformity; on the contrary, they seem to have made little effort to conceal it at all. There is no suggestion that they had any hierarchy, or any sacrament of their own such as the *consolamentum*. Most strikingly, when Gerard was questioned at Oxford, he did not hesitate to convict himself of heresy by denying baptism, communion and matrimony, but 'answered correctly on the nature of Christ':[34] he did not, that is to say, subscribe to the docetist heresy which Eckbert had noted with such interest. It would be wrong to insist too strongly on the negative aspects of such fragmentary evidence, though William of Newburgh was a careful and accurate chronicler, or to forget that such a haphazard exodus as we have postulated for the Bogomils from the Eastern Empire would be likely to have been accompanied by a loss of coherence among them. It is worth noting, all the same, that the differences which thus appear between the Cathars and the *Publicani*, especially since although they were accused of not eating meat none of them admitted it, are not unlike those between the Bogomils and the Paulicians, who were more agressive in the avowal of their faith, did not practise the avoidance of meat, and had no division between Elect and Believers which the institution of the *consolamentum* necessarily created. Although their beliefs were dualist in origin, they did not affect their lives so directly as those of the Bogomils, or lead them to the profession of the docetic heresy, because of their belief in the powerlessness of the good God to influence events in this world. This adds interest to Ralph of Coggeshall's remark, at the end of his account of the heretics at Rheims, that 'some of those who have investigated the secrets of their sect say that they believe that God does not concern himself with human affairs, and exercises no power or influence over the created world'.

It must be conceded that such plausibility as the suggestion that the *Publicani* represented Paulician rather than Bogomil influence in the west may have is of very slight importance. In the new environment the differences between the two which always kept them apart in the Balkans must have seemed of little moment compared with what they had in common. The *Publicani* did not retain any distinct existence, even in name, for more than twenty years or so, whether because they merged with the far wider Cathar movement, or because the persecution to which they were subjected was successful. They have been invoked in the past to account for the difference between absolute and mitigated dualism which appears among the Cathars, but it is neither plausible nor necessary to attribute that role to them, either in Bulgaria or in the west, to which absolute dualism was brought directly from Constantinople, and to Italy not Flanders, in the 1170s.[35] The *Publicani* of the 1160s seem to have been less sophisticated in their heresy than Eckbert's Cathars, not more so, and if their separate identity were clearly established its significance would lie not in any distinctive contribution which they made to the development of Catharism after they arrived, but in the detail which they add to the picture of the first appearance of Eastern heresy in the west. It is easy to share the vision of Eckbert and his catholic contemporaries, who saw their church being menaced by a powerful and united external enemy; the truth is more probably that the accidents of trade, travel and spasmodic persecution deposited haphazardly the newcomers whose church was formed in much the same way as the delta of the river by which they came.

Although the Cathars had before them in the Rhineland a long history of persistent independence, which would eventually lead to the bloodiest of inquisitorial massacres at the hands of Robert the Bugger and Conrad of Marburg, they achieved a much less dominant position over the currents of dissent in that part of Europe than they would later do in the south. Their arrival had been marked by clashes with heretics already established, and Eberwin of Steinfeld seems to have regarded the older group as the aggressors. Its teaching stemmed from the conviction that the involvement of the church in secular affairs had interrupted the apostolic succession, that 'the throne of St Peter, by failing to fight for God as Peter did, has deprived itself of the power of consecration which was given to Peter'.[36] Hence the orders of contemporary priests were not valid, because 'the archbishops who live in a worldly manner within the church' could not ordain them legitimately. Where the priesthood goes, the sacraments follow, and they rejected them all except that of baptism which, as is to be expected by now, should be conferred only on adults. The intermediary function of the church was inevitably denied. The intercession of saints, the performance of fasts and penances, the doctrine of purgatory, prayers and offerings for the dead, were all rejected. The mutual support which the venality of the contemporary clergy and admiration for the purity of the primitive church so often gave each other was here in abundance. All observances that were not laid down by Christ and the Apostles – for which, that is to say there was no direct Biblical authority – were condemned as superstitions, and if Eberwin does not say that they were held to be impositions nourished by the greed of the impostor clergy that is the clear implication of the doctrines that he reports.

In this there is a strong reminiscence of Henry of Lausanne. The combination of the rejection of the catholic priesthood with the advocacy of adult baptism suggests very strongly that these heretics had worked out some ceremonial of their own. Like Henry and his followers they lived in a world too dangerous to allow them to entrust their salvation to any hands but their own, facing the judgement of a God who would forgive their sins without outward panoply of penance if he knew their repentance to be sincere, and who would decide in the terrible moment of death whether their souls should pass to rest or damnation. There is, however, one clear difference between their beliefs and Henry's, in the strong assertion of sexual austerity. The conviction that marriage was fornication unless it were contracted between virgins, and that even they should live in celibacy after the birth of their first child, was derived from the instruction that man must not put asunder what God has joined, which was held, therefore, to mean that the first coupling created an indissoluble union between the partners. There is a coherence between the stern implication of that view, that human actions once committed are inescapable in their lasting consequences, and the salvationist spirit which imbued the remainder of their teaching, but it suggests that they did not share Henry's confidence of the essential innocence of man.

The beginning of the argument of these nameless heretics, that the spiritual power of the clergy was nullified by its temporal pre-occupations, is the same as that which Arnold of Brescia expounded at the same time. In this there is no coincidence, for unless it were in Rome itself there was no part of Europe where such views would be as vigorously stimulated as in the cities of the Rhine. The prince bishops had long devoted themselves with consistency and determination to the government of the Empire and the defence of their privileges against the townsmen: it was seventy years since the citizens of Cologne had sought their liberties by rising in support of Henry IV to be bloodily suppressed by their archbishop. His twelfth-century successors were great men in their way, but none of them preserved any reputation either for personal holiness of life or for diligent attention to his pastoral responsibilities; Rainhald von Dassel, to whom Eckbert dedicated his *Sermons*, was not only Archbishop of Cologne but imperial chancellor and, for the ten years before his death in 1167, the closest adviser of the Emperor and a dominant figure in the politics of the Empire. The churches for which such men were responsible might be magnificently endowed with the rewards of their temporal success, but the statues and reliquaries which they accumulated with such enthusiasm can scarcely have appeared as monuments to their concern for the souls of their flock.

At least one parish priest shared the disgust of his parishioners. Some time in the early years of the pontificate of Alexander III – that is, at about the time that Eckbert wrote – Albero, who held the benefice of Mercke near Cologne, was convicted of a series of heresies which followed from the proposition that the mass had no validity if the hands which performed it were unclean. A monk of the abbey of Altenberg, of which Mercke was a dependency (which suggests that Albero himself may have been a member of that community, though he is not so described) wrote a pamphlet in refutation of his errors.[37] According to him they were developed not only from the Gospels, but from the writings of the Popes, and pre-eminently the reforming Popes. Albero cited the decrees of Nicholas II, of Alexander II, and most of all, inevitably, of Gregory VII. They had led him to the conclusion that impure hands could not confer the sacraments, that the prayers of the corrupt would not be of assistance to the dead, and that in the evil times in which he lived the altar was more often surrounded at the elevation of the host by legions of demons than by the angels of whose presence the faithful were generally assured. If a criminal priest should confer the sacrament it might be validly received by those who did not know of his crimes, but not by those who did.

Albero trod dangerously at the boundary of discipline and doctrine. He seems here to have argued by analogy. Urban II had ruled, at the council of Piacenza in 1095, that sacraments received from a priest who was not validly ordained would nevertheless be valid if the recipient did not know that the hands from which he received them were not those of a true priest.[38] Albero maintained that the rule which applied to a priest whose orders were false held also for one whose morals were culpable. But the difference between the validity of the priest's orders and his personal purity was crucial; upon it depended the whole question of what the church was. Every claim of the Catholic church followed from the doctrine that its sacraments were transmitted by the apostolic succession, and their validity lay in that succession, and not in the person who might represent it at a particular moment. When Urban conceded, therefore, that a false priest could bless an ignorant Christian he did not depart from, although he relaxed, the rule that the power of the church lay in its succession. When Albero applied the same argument to hold that the personal wickedness of the priest should be regarded in the same way he confirmed, in effect, that he had broken with the principle of the apostolic succession, according to which the priest was simply the conduit through which divine power passed. What is essential about a conduit is not that its walls should be clean, but that it should be properly connected to its source. Hence the importance of the distinction which Albero's adversary hammered home. Sacraments received from a heretic, or anyone who had not the orders of the church, were *imagines*, fakes, mere charades; sacraments received from a catholic priest, however scarlet his sins, were true sacraments, and they were no less true because the discipline of the church required that the faithful should avoid taking them from tainted hands except *in extremis*. It is the constant argument. The heretic was he who gave individual merit priority over catholic legitimacy.

Little is known of Albero apart from this teaching. His critic says that he was a man whose own habits commanded the respect of the populace, and gave force to his dangerous doctrines. After he had been convicted of heresy he had been prepared to put the veracity of his convictions to the test of fire. The outcome is unknown. The existence of the pamphlet, which is not intemperate in tone, and is generously garnished with passages from the scriptures, the fathers and the popes that tell against Albero, together with careful explanations of how he misinterpreted the passages from their works which he had used to buttress his own case, suggests that the monastery which had the patronage of his parish felt a duty to undo his work. Like the *Contra Petrobrusianos* and the *Sermons* of Eckbert of Schönau, it has the appearance of being intended for the use of those who might wish to preach against the teachings of the heretic. It is another testimony to the power which a priest might gain from the admiration of his parishioners. Albero's influence rested on the purity of his personal life no less than on his rhetorical skill. A recurring theme of the pamphlet tells much of the story. Again and again, it is explained, he has confused the consequences of heresy with those of immorality. For example, he had been deeply impressed by the remark of the prophet Isaiah that evil priests are the destruction of the people. His adversary is most anxious to have it understood that Isaiah's remark referred not, as Albero supposed, to the behaviour of the priests, but to their opinions. The vigilance of the people must be transferred from discipline to doctrine, and their faith in the church must not be weakened by the frailty of its ministers.

· · ·

The differences between the heresies to which the Cologne region gave birth of its own accord and those which were brought to it by the missionaries from the Balkans lie in questions of theology and organization. The grievances to which they appealed were the same. That the differences were adhered to with such passion that the two groups quarrelled publicly in 1143, and remained distinct after twenty years more, is a reminder that men do not adopt beliefs for which they are prepared to die simply for negative reasons, and that common hostility to the church did not give them, as Eckbert of Schönau and his orthodox contemporaries were wont to suppose, common cause with each other. Nevertheless the ability of so many shades of dissension to attract support shows that by the middle of the century the desire to seek salvation by a personal path, and to reject the authority and mediation of a priesthood whose way of life provoked constant disgust, was widely felt and passionately obeyed. This situation did not leave the parish clergy untouched, and Albero of Mercke was not alone among them in taking the side of his parishioners against his superiors. The complaint that the heretics, of every variety, included priests among their converts was now universal: Cyprian and Peter, who had accompanied Henry of Lausanne from Le Mans, had many successors. Little is known about them, for St Bernard's complaint that 'clerks and priests, both young and old, are leaving their churches and congregations and are often found in the company of heretics of both sexes'[39] is as precise as most. It is not a surprising phenomenon. The twelfth-century church beckoned both to talent and idealism, and therefore created disillusion. In the preceding generation disappointed idealists sought the desert and the cultivation of personal holiness; by the thirteenth century the institution of the friars completed the replacement of the contemplative by the pastoral life as the principal focus of clerical idealism; in the interval heresy and the fringes of heresy were particularly attractive to those who felt that the official church was not responding quickly enough to the changing needs of its members.

The most complete expression of the tension between developing lay piety and ecclesiastical authority which is thus displayed in the Rhine cities comes, unsurprisingly, from the neighbouring region of the Low Countries. Heretical preachers had found an early welcome among the restless poor of Europe's first industrial region and the disjointed history of the *publicani* demonstrated the continuing capacity of dissent to find a welcome there. The career of one priest whose combative spirit has made him uniquely well documented among the humbler members of his profession offers a vivid portrayal of the trials of those who attempted to resolve their problems and pursue the path of reform and pastoral dedication within the bounds of orthodoxy.

Lambert le Bègue – the stammerer – was the very model of a devoted parish priest. When he was ordained in the diocese of Liège, shortly after 1160, he was given the charge of a tumbledown church which belonged to the canons of St Paul's. He set about repairing it with his own hands, filling the holes in the walls, providing windows, painting it and finding the candles and other furnishings which the dignity of the services demanded. As such men do he attracted to his mass women of strenuous devotion, who hung upon his every word with careful attention, and conducted themselves at communion with ardour that put him to shame. 'How can I describe', he said, 'with what contrition of heart, what outpourings of tears, what reverence and trembling without any of the common jostling and clamour, they received the body and blood of their Saviour?' When they returned home they spent the rest of their Sunday in prayer, contemplation and chanting, and Lambert, to encourage them, made a rhythmical translation of the Acts of the Apostles – a significant choice – into the language they spoke. In short, as his parishioners testified, he followed his vocation with diligence and determination.[40] The innocent, of whom Lambert was one, might suppose that any bishop would be glad to number such a priest among his clergy. In fact Lambert reached the nadir of a tempestuous career when his bishop imprisoned him on trumped-up charges. In 1175, five priests who supported him were deprived of their benefices and driven from the diocese, and his lay followers were harried, driven from their homes and even imprisoned in their turn.

In the three letters which Lambert addressed to the anti-Pope Calixtus III for redress of these wrongs he had no difficulty in disposing of the charges of heresy that had been brought against him.

They were evident distortions and malicious misconstructions of his words, as that he had said that the mass might be celebrated with milk when he had answered contemptuously in some argument that to do so would be no more futile than to use water, or that he told a man whose cloak bore the crusader's cross that it was vain to seek God in Jerusalem because he had been eaten at yesterday's mass.[41] That Calixtus III, who reigned at Rome with a full apparatus of papal justice at his disposal, should have upheld the cause of a humble and awkward parish priest against so powerful a bishop as Rudolph of Zahringen is a sufficient assurance that there was no substance in these calumnies, which Lambert refuted with eloquence and ease. His crime was enthusiasm, and having been led by enthusiasm to assault the habits and customs of his colleagues and superiors; he belongs to the long line of those who made the mistake of telling the truth.

Lambert le Bègue was a puritan, in a surprisingly unanachronistic sense of that word. It appears most strikingly in his discussion of sabbath keeping, another issue upon which he had been accused of heresy. He had been horrified to see his parishioners, instead of keeping the Sabbath as his holy women did with decent solemnity, enjoy themselves in 'mimes, plays and dancing girls, taking their holiday with drunkenness and gambling, flocking around armies of wicked women, and eyeing them, or dancing with them through the grounds of the churches and over the graves of their parents and relations, singing obscene songs and indulging in lewd gestures', and he had told them that if they could not use their leisure in a more seemly way they would do better to work at tasks which were at least not evil in themselves; it is a view that has often enough been expressed since his time. His attack on the pilgrimage movement brought him closer to the nerves of his fellow priests, whom he accused of having their priorities wrong when they sought their salvation in Jerusalem, and left their flock in misery at home. Did the fathers of the church ordain 'that prisoners should be redeemed, guests entertained, the hungry and thirsty refreshed, the naked clothed, the widow consoled and the flock protected, or that trips to the Holy Land should multiplied'?[42] It was an uncomfortable question, and shows why what commended Lambert to his lay followers did not seem so attractive to his clerical colleagues. He went further when he preached against 'the perverse and detestable practice which prevailed in the city and the towns around it of exacting payments, openly and irreverently, for baptizing children, bringing the sacraments to the sick and the last rites to the dying, and burying the dead',[43] and by cutting down the number of masses celebrated for the dead, whose multiplication he saw as little more than a spiritually empty source of income to the priests.

Like many radicals Lambert believed himself a conservative, defending established values against the erosion of corrupt times. One of the high points of his quarrel with his superiors was his intervention at a diocesan synod convoked by Bishop Alexander in 1166, at which he quoted the decrees of the Council of Rheims in 1148 which had forbidden the baptism of children more than three at a time (an obvious shortcut for the indolent), the practice of looking for prophecy and divination in the mass, and the wearing of fashionably tailored and brightly coloured clothes by the clergy. He also cited the ruling of Alexander's predecessor, 'Henry of blessed memory', who had ordained him, that the sons of priests should not be admitted to orders, and in doing so tells much of his story. He had entered the church at a moment when a reforming bishop was intent upon its improvement, he had flung himself into the work, and he was appalled by the backsliding of Henry's worldlier successor; he attacked, by forcefully expressed precept and popularly acclaimed example, the abuses of those who cared more for their own profit than the care of the faithful, and, inevitably, he made bitter enemies. He was vindicated by Calixtus III, who ordered his release from prison, the restoration of his benefice and those of the few priests who had supported him and the end of the persecution, and he died in Liège in 1177.

The history of Lambert le Bègue does more than fill out the saga of clerical indolence and extortion against which the heretics so regularly protested, and show how the tensions which they exploited existed not only between the church and the laity, but within the church itself. It brings clearly to light the tangled relationship between religious reform and social change which is so constant, and yet so imprecise a motif of the twelfth century. Lambert's insistence on the wretchedness of the people, on the need for the relief of poverty and distress before indulgence of the journey to Jerusalem, picks out the fact that the church was now faced, for the first time in its history in western Europe, with the pastoral implications of urban poverty. Even his lurid sketch of popular leisure, of the whoring and dancing in the churchyards of a Sunday, however highlighted by his own puritanism, remains an expression of urban and rootless squalor rather than bucolic lightheartedness. His comment that the journeys of pilgrims were too often financed by 'robbery and theft, swindle, fraud and other kinds of wrongdoing', and that even some of those who acquired their wealth honestly 'have seen their fathers in need and yet shut their hearts to them and set out for Jerusalem and other holy places at great expense' evokes a world of rapid commercial expansion where even honestly made fortunes could place a heavy strain on traditional social ties. His own followers were not all among the poor, and it would be a crude error to suppose that only they were affected by the process of change. But if the difference between rich and poor was not new its importance was more nakedly and more universally displayed, unsoftened by the ancient hierarchies and extensive family ties of rural life. It was not the difference of class, but mobility between class and class which fractured customary solidarities and added instability to indigence.

The complexity of any consideration of the social context of early heresy, and the inescapable fragility of its base, are well illustrated by the notorious association which it had with weaving. The romantic picture of the spinners in their workshops, intelligent artisans with time to dream of utopias as they chatted with their customers, will hardly stand serious contemplation. The association itself is clear enough, from the assertion that it was the weavers who cherished the memory of Ramihrdus to the plain fact that by the middle of the century the word 'textor' signified both weaver and heretic so indifferently that it is not always easy to guess in context which is meant. More pointed is the constant tendency of heresy to move along the routes of the cloth trade, first suspected when it came to Arras from Châlons as early as 1025, and so clearly demonstrated by the Cathars and *Publicani* of the 1140s, '50s and '60s. But weaving was not a homogeneous trade; on the contrary, it was perhaps the first European industry to display the whole range of industrial society from prosperous capitalists to sweated labour in the workshops, and from international merchants to wandering journeymen. The tendency to rebel against the church embraced them all: the council of Rheims in 1157 blamed 'the wretched weavers who move from place to place' for spreading heresy, but it is difficult to guess from what other business the men of Arras might have earned the six hundred marks of silver with which they tried to bribe the archbishop of Rheims six years later; it has rightly been pointed out that those who fled from Constantinople adopted a trade fit for fugitives, but Eckbert of Schönau remarks that at least one of their converts was a man 'of no small name'; if Lambert le Bègue expressed most concern for the poor he also remarked that some of his followers were rich enough to buy off their persecutors.[44]

There is no difficulty in proposing a theory of heresy to fit either class – the poor in their desperation, or the fortunate in pursuit of a faith which would express their new-found independence and self-esteem; both are plausible, they are not inconsistent with each other, and we have noted and will note again many instances where either or both may seem to be true. Since the early medieval church was constructed for a system of society much simpler than that which in fact confronted it by the twelfth century, especially in the Low Countries, it is natural that the seams should have burst in more than one place. But it was the fact of adjusting to change, rather than the circumstances in which it placed each of them individually, that the heretics and rebels had in common. The men of Arras who were arraigned before Archbishop Gerard in 1025 expressed their desire 'to earn our food by the labour of our own hands, to do no injury to anyone, to extend charity to everyone of our own faith' within a few years of the first signs of the emergence of a privileged *bourgeoisie* in that city. By the end of the century Bernold of Constance had noted the spread of the habit, among lay people in towns, of living together, both men and women, under a form of religious rule, and under the spiritual direction of local priests, and some association of the kind seems the likeliest explanation of the fragmentary references to the burning at Liège in 1135. Early in the thirteenth century the distinctive religious institution of the Low Countries had appeared, communities of lay women bound by no vows, but living in common, pursuing their ordinary walks of life, and finding in their association spiritual and, no doubt, social consolation. That movement began in Liège, and spread rapidly to Cologne. The chronicler Gilles d'Orval was mistaken in believing that the Béguines derived their name from Lambert, who seems to have had no association with any organization of this kind, and died a generation before their existence is clearly established. Yet Gilles was not far wrong, for it is plain that the women who prayed and read together with Lambert's encouragement, and for whom he made vernacular translations of scripture, were only a step away from Béguines.[45]

Another suggestion for the derivation of the Béguines' name almost certainly as wrong, but almost as nearly right, is that it was a corruption of Albigensian, which is to say Cathar. It was of the essence of lay piety and those who encouraged it – St Francis and his various followers are another case in point – that they wavered on the verges of orthodoxy, implying as they did by their very existence an enterprising dissatisfaction with the provision of the church that seemed especially dangerous to the orthodox mind when it was expressed by those who had not undergone clerical training. In this may lie the solution to a minor problem about the Cathars, that the regions in which they first established themselves were not those in which they had the most universal success. Both in its religious and its social contours the area of northern Europe in which they first appeared was well equipped to receive them; there were many, for one reason or another, who would lend them a willing ear. But because those conditions had existed for a long time there was competition. The citizens of the Low Countries had already begun to form the habits of association and the pursuit of common purpose which might readily be transferred from the political scene to the religious (and *vice versa*), and by a curious irony, if the bishops of the Rhine cities effectively retarded the political development of their subjects they did not prevent them from seeking and creating their own structures of faith and worship. The doctrines which the Cathars preached were new, and it would be wrong to suggest that they did not, so far as it can be seen, find many converts, but they would fare better where the ground was clearer.

Chapter VIII | The New Heresy in the South

Catharism became far more important in the Languedoc than in the Rhineland, but there was no Eberwin of Steinfeld to announce its appearance there with comparable clarity. We have instead a curious and undated letter in which a monk from Périgueux, whose name was Heribert, sought to warn his fellow Christians of false prophets whom, it is only too clear, he did not know by direct acquaintance.[1] They embraced poverty and spurned the sacraments and authority of the church, they attracted the allegiance of nobles who relinquished their property and of clerks, monks, priests and nuns, and their dealings with the devil were made manifest by the sinister fact that 'nobody is so stupid that if he joins them he will not become literate within eight days, so that he can be reconverted neither by argument nor by example', as well as by an unnatural capacity to escape from imprisonment. 'Even if they are bound in iron chains and shackles, and put in a wine butt turned upside down on top of them, and watched by the strongest guards, they will not be found the next day unless they choose to be and the empty butt will be turned up again full of the wine which had been emptied from it.'

For all its absurdity Heribert's letter suggests that he had come across something more than a precocious Houdini. His scraps of information include genuine novelties which are suggestive of Bogomilism. The followers of Pontius, whom he names as their leader, 'genuflect a hundred times a day', and instead of 'Glory be to the Father' they say 'For thine is the kingdom' and 'thou shalt rule the created universe for ever and ever Amen'. The formula, which encouraged Heribert to believe that he was writing of devil-worshippers, is reminiscent of that which, according to Cosmas the Priest, was used by the Bogomils to appease the Lord of the (created) World, while they addressed their worship to the God of the immaterial universe.[2] 'If one of them does attend mass in order to conceal his heresy he does not say the canon and does not receive communion, but spits out the host behind the altar or into a mass-book.' Like the special dislike of the cross which Heribert also records, this practice of occasional or apparent conformity was, in the East, specifically and consistently associated with the Bogomils.

Such scraps of information can hardly be alleged to amount to a systematic or irrefutable record of the appearance of Catharism in the *midi*, but they do reflect in these particulars a more direct similarity to Bogomil belief and practice than had been noted in the region before. It is a great pity, therefore, that Heribert failed to put a date to his letter. It certainly will not do to assume, as many have, that it must precede St Bernard's visit to Périgueux in 1145, for there is no ground for supposing, any more than he did himself, that wherever he went Bernard eradicated heresy for a generation.[3] It is a better guide that a copy of Heribert's letter appears in the *Annals of Margam* under the year 1163,[4] not only because whenever he came across it the annalist would most likely have put it where he thought it belonged, but because in that year a Council at Tours expressed alarm about 'a new heresy which has recently appeared in the region of Toulouse, spreading like a cancer step by step to neighbouring areas, and has quickly invaded Gascony and other provinces'.[5] Although official assertions of novelty are always to be treated with caution these words do suggest that something different was afoot in a region which was notorious for its susceptibility to heterodox preaching.

The assertion that Bogomil-influenced dualism did not appear in the Languedoc much before the 1160s is novel enough to make one wish for better evidence. Yet no recognition of the inadequacy of these two scraps can disguise the uncomfortable fact that there is nothing before them. The firmness with which the dominance of Catharism in the Languedoc by the beginning of the thirteenth century has identified the region ever since as the theatre *par excellence* of western dualism makes it difficult to realize how little there is to support the universal assumption that that dominance was the result of a steady diffusion of popular heresy in the region for two centuries previously. In fact the references to such activity there are very few by comparison with those for northern Europe, though they seem swollen by the glamour of Peter of Bruys and Henry of Lausanne. Yet with those two exceptions, neither of whom conceived his heresy or began his mission in the Languedoc, and neither of whom needed the help of any eastern influence to formulate his ideas, there had been only three occasions in the century and a half before this time when heretical activity was recorded. Adhemar of Chabannes had noted the appearance of preachers of celibacy and poverty, 'denying baptism, the cross and all sound doctrine' in Aquitaine in 1018, and said that some were caught and burned at Toulouse, and that Duke William of Aquitaine presided over a council at Charroux which resolved to eradicate them. In 1119 the Council of Toulouse called upon the secular powers to constrain heretics who rejected the sacraments and the authority of the church; whether or not, as some have held, it referred to Henry of Lausanne or to Peter of Bruys, nothing in the canon points to dualist rather than native anti-clerical tenets among those condemned. Finally, much has been made of the comment of Geoffrey of Auxerre, who accompanied St Bernard in 1145, that among Henry's followers in Toulouse were some '*de textoribus, quos Arianos ipsi nominant*'.[6] A phrase which it is natural to translate as 'weavers whom they call Arians' has been rendered 'heretics whom they call dualist heretics', and that these 'Arians' had established bases in the villages outside the city as well as in Toulouse itself has been held to mean that the

Cathar implantation of the Languedoc was well advanced by 1145. Yet it is easily shown that such a translation, based on the meaning which was attached to the words *textores* and *ariani* by the end of the twelfth century, has neither philological justification in their use before 1145, nor historical support from the context of Geoffrey's letter and the other records of St Bernard's mission, and that Henry's supporters were far more probably weavers indeed, who had transferred their allegiance to him after the death of Peter of Bruys.[7]

The paucity of the record may, of course, be accounted for by the familiar assertion that the ecclesiastical authorities of the Languedoc were lax in their duties, and that the insidious and extended diffusion of heresy appears so little in the record because they failed to check it. This view greatly exaggerates the difference between the state of the church in the Languedoc and in the rest of Europe. The record reveals, on the contrary, that although both Henry and Peter had lengthy careers in heresy, there is no occasion when we know that dissidence was preached in the Languedoc without a rapid response, including the invocation of the secular power, from the church: there is no measuring its effectiveness, but this is not a point on which the argument from silence can be held legitimate. On the other hand, the record also shows that when heresy appeared in the region, and especially in and around Toulouse, it met an immediate and enthusiastic response, and that by the time of Henry of Lausanne at least that response was not confined to the poorest orders of society. From this it follows that there is no reason to be surprised if the new heresy of the Bogomil missionaries from the north spread rapidly (as the Council of Tours alleged) and entrenched itself deeply when it reached the Midi in the 1160s. By that time the devotees of Henry and Peter had been without a prophet for fifteen years or more, and the region seems to have been very much less richly equipped than the urban communities of the low countries in forms of association and traditions of popular evangelism which might give expression to religious aspirations that the church could not satisfy, or to the discontents that its privilege and corruption engendered.

The assembly which was convened at Lombers, between Albi and Castres, in 1165, also casts some doubt on the alleged apathy of the prelates of the region, for it was attended by the archbishop of Narbonne and the bishops of Albi, Toulouse, Nîmes, Lodève and Agde, six abbots and a variety of other ecclesiastical dignitaries, as well as by representatives of the lay power ranging from the countess of Toulouse and two of her husband's most powerful vassals, the vicomtes of Béziers and Lavaur, to 'most of the people of Albi and Lombers and various other townships'.[8] This was not a formal council of the church, but a sort of extraordinary general meeting which seems to have been arranged by the bishop of Albi to examine and secure the public condemnation of certain men, 'enemies of the faith', who called themselves *bons hommes*, and had been impugning the doctrines and priesthood of the church. To secure their attendance the bishop had promised them that no oath would be imposed upon them and instead of conducting the proceedings himself he left the bishop of Lodève to question the heretics before a panel of 'assessors' chosen by both sides. The form of the meeting does much to account for the ease with which the heretics – as they turned out to be – had established themselves, for it was modelled on secular process, and assumed a basis of equality between the disputants. It can hardly be supposed that the bishop (however scarlet his sins) would have selected such a forum by choice, or that he would have secured the presence of the heretics by a safe-conduct if he had been able to compel it. In short it appears – and here there is a very stark contrast with northern Europe – that the church was acting almost wholly without the support of the secular power, as the outcome of the assembly would confirm.

The demeanour of the *bons hommes* before their interrogator demonstrated a similarly striking confidence of their security; they displayed neither the fearful indignation that they should be suspected, nor the defiant stubbornness of the prospective martyr that were usually adopted by men in their position, but an aloof condescension in evading the questions when they could, and counter-attacking when they could not, which suggests a certain contempt both for the bishops and their power. They said that they recognized the authority only of the Gospels, the Acts, the letters of the apostles and the Apocalypse, and were prepared to discuss their interpretation, but they would not answer questions about their faith. They avowed as much of their teaching as was not plainly heretical, and refused to go further. Asked whether husband and wife who slept together could be saved 'they would only reply that men and women are joined because of lust and fornication, as Paul said'; whether confession should be to priests or to any layman 'they replied that James only said that they should confess to be saved; they did not aspire to be better than the apostle, or to superimpose anything of their own as the bishops do'. It is the tone of these responses, rather than their content, that is interesting. They followed, formally at least, the Bogomil practice of avoiding either falsehood or a direct confession of heresy, and yet did so in a manner which made it perfectly plain that they were not in the least concerned to persuade the assembly of their innocence, or to conceal the real nature of their convictions. To these responses they voluntarily added an assertion that the Gospels forbade the swearing of any oath whatsoever, and a swingeing attack on the morals and behaviour of the bishops and priests, 'ravening wolves, hypocrites and seducers, men who want to be bowed to in the streets, to have the most prominent seats or sit at the top table in banquets . . . not good teachers but mercenaries, who should not be obeyed'.

Although the bishop of Lodève did not succeed in exacting any incontrovertible admission of heretical doctrine from his ingenious adversaries it is impossible to suppose, from the temper of their replies, that he was wrong in denouncing them as heretics who rejected the authority of the church, and the validity of its sacraments of baptism, mass, confession and matrimony – in short, though he did not say so, as Cathars. Their reaction was of a kind with their conduct throughout the examination. They called him a heretic in his turn, repeated their eloquent and savage denunciation of prelacy and priesthood, and added insult to injury by turning to the assembled people, pronouncing a full confession of Catholic orthodoxy, and absolutely refusing to confirm it by oath. Even through the threadbare pages of the record of the assembly they make it perfectly clear that their intention was to avoid an indisputable formal conviction of heresy, but not for a moment to conceal the real nature of their faith and practice. All that the bishop of Albi could do about it was, rather lamely, to confirm the verdict which his colleague had pronounced, and warn the knights of Lombers against giving the heretics any support in the future.

If, by the nature of the assembly, the Council of Lombers does not reveal much that is positive about the substance of the heretics' beliefs it speaks volumes about the situation in which they found themselves in 1165. They enjoyed the support of the knights – the same who had 'hated clerks and enjoyed Henry's jokes' in 1145 or their descendants – and by implication also of at least some members of the higher nobility whose presence at the meeting did not inhibit this plain demonstration of contempt for the church. Like the heretics themselves the laymen were prepared to go through the form, by attending the meeting and, in some cases, by depositing fines with the bishop of Albi as surety that they would abide by its outcome: the church was not set openly in defiance by those who were supposed to be its disciples and protectors. In this a pattern was set which was to remain characteristic of the nobility of the Languedoc, from the Count of Toulouse downwards, for the next two generations: there was no open declaration of support for the Cathars, but equally there was a perfectly obvious disinclination (from whatever motives it may have sprung in any particular individual) to act against them. The contrast with the secular rulers of northern Europe, who had so often embarrassed churchmen by the enthusiasm with which they urged coercion more vigorous than canonical practice yet permitted, could scarcely be clearer, and it created a situation in which the bishops were helpless. They had turned out in force, they had examined their adversaries in detail and at length, and shown everybody what they were up against, they had pronounced a verdict and a warning which would remain ineffectual. They had mounted a demonstration: they could do no more.

The Council of Lombers is, in a sense, the last episode of Cathar prehistory. Up to this point the story of the Cathars and of their various predecessors has been pieced together from a heterogeneous variety of sources most of whose creation and survival was, to whatever degree, a matter of chance, and for most of whose authors, chroniclers, biographers, letter writers, heresy was incidental to their main theme. Some of them, like the monk William and Eckbert of Schönau, had attempted a systematic description, and even indicated as far as they could what they believed to be the historical antecedents of the incidents and doctrines to which they drew attention, but beyond the general, and generally imprecise, assumption that the new heretics were the descendants of Mani and Arius there was no collective attempt to counter the threat which they represented by tracing the development of their sects and teachings in contemporary times. The early thirteenth century saw the creation of a body of men who were charged by Christendom with the task of eradicating heresy. They soon found that knowledge was the first weapon in their armoury. If the enemy was to be tracked, identified and convicted it was necessary to know the patterns of his movements, organization and daily life, as well as to be able to distinguish clearly between the different strands of heterodoxy so that each might be traced to its end, and eliminated. The manuals of the inquisitors therefore provided not only an official but a pragmatic account of what had been discovered through the activity of their authors. Moral denunciation might be taken for granted, but it was less efficacious against the present danger than precise information. As always official history had its dangers; many suffered because the inquisitors became too confident that they knew what they were looking for and would not be satisfied by less, and no doubt their account of the heretical movements suffers from over-systematization and over-emphasis on the aspects of doctrine and practice which would be of direct assistance in their task. Nevertheless their achievement, based upon the multiplied personal interview which is once more in vogue among those who would bring classified knowledge to the aid of social ills, is an impressive one, and necessarily alters the pace and focus of the present narrative.

The inquisitors had no doubt that the regions in which the Cathars were most dangerous were the Languedoc and the cities of Lombardy and Tuscany, and although they assumed that the heresy had a very ancient history the accounts which they compiled point unmistakably to the decade or so after 1165 as the period of formative importance. The change is clearly marked by Anselm of Alessandria whose account, written about 1270, becomes precise and circumstantial at that point, after some vague introductory commentary which supports the present conclusion, that emissaries of the Bogomil heresy entered Europe by the Danube and the Rhine before finding their way south to the Languedoc, where they had a considerably greater success. 'Because it was the Bulgars who led the Franks astray', he says (his Franks, contrasted with the *Provinciales*, included the inhabitants of the Rhineland and the Low Countries) 'heretics are known as Bulgars all over France. The Provençals, who are neighbours of the Franks, were converted by them, and the heresy spread among them so much that they made four bishops, of Carcassonne, Albi, Toulouse and Agen.'[9] Thus, without providing any clear chronological assistance, Anselm summarizes development up to approximately the point which had been attained by the time of the Council of Lombers, or shortly afterwards. Thenceforward, as he follows the path of the heretics into Italy, he is more exact.

A long time after this a French notary came to Lombardy to the district of Concorezzo in the county of Milan. There he met Mark, a native of Colonio nearby, and converted him. Mark in turn converted his friends, John the Jew, and Joseph. Mark was a grave-digger, John a weaver, and Joseph a smith. One of them went to Milan, to the eastern or Corencian gate, and converted a friend of his called Aldricus de Bando. The converts had a meeting with the notary, who sent them to Roccavione, near Cuneo, where some French Cathars had settled. The bishop of the heretics was not there, but at Naples. They found him there, and stayed for a year. Then Mark was made a deacon by the imposition of hands, and the bishop sent him back to his native Concorezzo to preach. Through his preaching the heresy spread widely in Lombardy, and later in Tuscany and the March of Treviso.[10]

This was the foundation of the Cathar church of Concorezzo, which remained the largest of the Cathar communities of Italy, and continued to have close links with Bulgaria, the home of the modified dualism which it professed. We have no means of dating Mark's conversion precisely, or guessing what Anselm meant by 'a long time'. It was probably later than 1165, when we have with the Council of Lombers the first clear indication of the success of the heresy in the Languedoc, but earlier than the mid-1170s, when the Italian Cathars were thrown into confusion by the arrival in their midst of a missionary from Constantinople who told them that their Bulgarian *consolamentum* had no validity. By that time they had spread enough to have congregations at least in Milan, Florence, Mantua and Desenzano, near Lake Garda, as well as in the March of Treviso. Of the French Cathars in Naples we hear no more, except that Mark met a deacon in Calabria near the end of his life: the Norman kingdom of Sicily was one of the regions which demonstrated most completely that heresy did not flourish where secular government was strong.

Shortly before Mark's death his apparently flourishing infant church was visited by a trauma which was of formative importance in the development of western dualism. A man named Papa Nicetas, from Constantinople, bishop of the church of Dragovitsa, visited Lombardy and told Mark and his followers that their orders, which derived through the Languedoc from Bulgaria, were not valid. After some hesitation they accepted his authority, and the *consolamentum* of his church, which (whatever its origin) differed from the church of Bulgaria in many points of doctrine, and most importantly in the belief that the evil God was not the fallen son or steward of the good, but himself eternal and uncreated. This was the first appearance of absolute dualism in the west. Its immediate consequences for the Italian Cathars smacked more of farce than of high drama. The conversion itself was a matter of no great difficulty, for all Mark's followers seem to have accepted it. The trouble started after Nicetas had returned to Constantinople, when another traveller, called Petracius, brought some alarming news to the Lombards. Nicetas, it seemed, had received his *consolamentum* from another Dragovitsan bishop called Simon, and Simon had been found in bed with a woman, and subsequently discovered, as such men are, to have committed other grave sins.[11] From this it followed that the *consolamentum* which he had conferred on Nicetas, and Nicetas in turn on Mark and his followers, was invalid. The whole sacramental basis of Italian catharism was wiped away, and damnation stared its votaries in the face. Nothing could have better demonstrated the sound sense of the Catholic insistence that the power of the sacrament must not depend on the purity of the priest than the events which followed.

The sources do not agree whether the bombshell fell just before, or just after the death of Mark, under whose leadership the Italian Cathars had remained united. His successor was John the Jew, one of his original converts, and it was around John that the debate over the *consolamentum* raged. Peter of Florence and his party insisted that John's orders were not valid, and went into schism; Nicholas of the March persuaded the Cathars of his region to do the same. After some years an attempt was made to restore unity, and on the advice of a bishop of the Languedoc to whom they went for advice, lots were chosen between John and Peter, and the winner would go to Bulgaria to renew his *consolamentum*. Neither party would accept the other's leader, but after more anxious quarrelling they chose two more candidates, Garattus from among John's followers, and John the Judge from Peter's, and the lot fell on Garattus. The adherents of both parties agreed to accept him as bishop, travelling companions were chosen and money collected to send him to Bulgaria to renew his *consolamentum*, and the end of the schism was thankfully anticipated by the faithful. Once again they were deceived by human weakness. Shortly before his departure Garattus was surprised, by two witnesses, with a woman. A new cause of division was added to the old, and the question was raised whether the promise of obedience which the Cathars had taken to Garattus was still binding upon them. After much anxious debate they took themselves once more to the bishop in the Languedoc who had advised them before. On his recommendation they turned again to John the Jew, who had so willingly resigned his claims in the cause of unity, and remained untouched by the disgrace of his putative successor, and this time success was achieved. John went to Bulgaria for ordination, and on his return was accepted by the Lombards and led them until his death, when he was succeeded by Mark's other original companion, Joseph the smith.

The treatise *De heresi catharorum in Lombardia* which recounts these events, compiled shortly after the turn of the century, is the first intimate account of the life of a heretical community written with what looks like inside knowledge. It reveals nothing of its author except that he was a Catholic, but the circumstantial freshness of his narrative, and the capacity he shows to write of the disputes with a clear understanding of the position of those who took part in them assert that if he was not a Cathar who had been converted to Catholicism he was a remarkably talented historian. In either case he shows us vividly for the first time the difficulties which beset a movement of enthusiasm when it confronted the necessity of giving itself permanent leadership and regular institutions. One explanation of the inability of the earlier heretics to found permanent sects is well displayed in the events which followed the death of Mark. Although no impression is conveyed of his talents or personality, it is plain that he was an effective evangelist and a compelling leader. With the help of his first companions he made converts in several places, and while he was alive they remained together; his prestige was enough even to allow him to accept the allegation of Nicetas that his *consolamentum* – in principle the whole basis of the sect which he had founded – was invalid, and to accept new orders, and with them a new theology, without creating any division among his followers. But as soon as he was dead division arose around the simple question, where did the true succession lie? The importance of the scandal levelled at Simon and at Garattus lies not in whether it was true but in how easily the unyielding moral purity of the Cathar creed laid its devotees open to the dangers of intrigue and personal ambition. The leaders of the local communities saw in rumour-mongering the opportunity to enhance their influence. Peter of Florence exploited the doubt over Simon's *consolamentum*, and three or four others took the same advantage of the unfortunate Garattus: Nicholas of the March not only went to work on the reputation of Mark himself, but discredited John the Jew as he did so: he 'set about stirring up disagreement among the Cathars. He asked them, "What do you believe about Mark? Do you believe that he made a good end, or not?" They replied, "Yes we believe that he made a good end." "John the Jew says that Mark made a bad end, and because of this he wants to go abroad to receive the *consolamentum* again." '

The effect of these disputes went beyond personalities. For any Cathar the rehabilitation of the *consolamentum* was a matter of urgency, for only by receiving it from an impeccable source could the burden of the flesh be cast off, and salvation hoped for. While the dispute continued there was a constant danger of not 'making a good end' – dying in a state of purity, having received a *consolamentum* unvitiated by one's own sins or those of others. Many, therefore, could not be content to await with patience the resolution of the debate between the claimants to Mark's succession.

> Before the date at which they had promised to give Garattus companions and expenses for his journey to Bulgaria some heretics from Desenzano formed a congregation, chose John Bellus as their bishop, and sent him to Dragovitsa to be ordained... The community at Mantua and their followers chose Caloiannus to be their bishop, sent him to Sclavonia, and when he had been ordained he served as their bishop. In the same way a man called Nicholas [the adroit politician] was selected by the congregation at Vicenza, and sent to Sclavonia for ordination to be their bishop when he returned.[12]

The dissensions which followed Mark's death, in short, not only accentuated the divisions between the congregations of his followers in various places, but caused them to turn for their *consolamentum*, and with it their doctrines, to three different sources. Mark's own inspiration had come, by a long and circuitous route, from the *ecclesia Bulgariae*, and when he died he was in Calabria, on his way to renew it in Bulgaria. His successors did the same, and their links with Bulgaria remained close: it was from Bulgaria that one of them, Nazarius, would bring the *Secret Supper* in the early years of the next century. The church of Bulgaria, wherever its precise location may have been, was the repository of the earliest traditions of the followers of Bogomil, before their teachings had been modified in Constantinople. Their dualism was incomplete, their evil power the rebellious son of God, their Christ still partly corporeal, and in these fundamental doctrines as in more elaborate myths, the Cathars of Concorezzo, always the most numerous of the Lombard heretics, remained faithful to their traditions.

The church of Sclavonia, or Bosnia, to which the Cathars of the north-east, Mantua, Vicenza and the March appealed, quite naturally since they were neighbours by land or by crossing the Adriatic in the north, had been founded from Constantinople in the 1140s, and its teachings therefore reflected a later stage in the evolution of dualist thought. God himself remained ultimately one, and Lucifer, the evil power, was his creation. But while Nazarius was in a minority among the Concorezzans, and that a generation after their establishment, in denying that Christ had assumed human flesh, the Sclavonians were fully docetist and held that Christ, the Virgin and John the Baptist were angels whose bodies were simulated. The Sclavonians (who soon came to be known as Bagnolans after the birthplace of one of their leaders, Orto of Bagnolo) remained distinct from the Concorezzans in doctrine and as churches, but by the end of the century each recognized the *consolamentum* and orders of the other as valid.[13]

The church of Dragovitsa, which Nicetas had represented and to which the Cathars of Desenzano, near Lake Garda, became directly affiliated during the confusion after his and Mark's deaths, differed more sharply from the other two. Whether Dragovitsa was in Thrace or Macedonia is uncertain,[14] but Constantinople was the effective centre of the church which bore its name. The demeanour of Nicetas in Lombardy suggested plainly that he regarded himself as the missionary of an organized and aggressive evangelical body. When he told Mark and his companions that their orders were invalid, that they must begin all over again under his instruction, he proclaimed that his was a church of uncompromising purity. It is this attitude, consistent with the view that the Dragovitsans were a breakaway movement from traditional Bogomilism, and not simply the theological difference between modified and absolute dualism, which accounts for the continued hostility between the Dragovitsan, or as it came to be called in Italy, the Albanensian church on the one hand, and those of Concorezzo and Bagnolo on the other. The rift endured for as long as Italian Catharism, and in the middle of the thirteenth century, according to Rainier Sacchoni, those on either side of it were convinced that the others were bound for damnation. Even when the personal divisions which generated the struggle for Mark's succession had been resolved, therefore, they left a permanent legacy of doctrinal separation, and made the history of Italian Catharism that not of one heresy, but of three.

These events can be placed with some confidence in the early and middle years of the 1170s. Anselm of Alessandria, writing in 1270, says that it was in 1174 that Mark and his companions 'brought the heresy from Naples to Lombardy' to begin their mission,[15] and though he may have put it a year or so too late he cannot have been far wrong. Italy was the meeting place of the three streams of dualism which had developed in the Byzantine world over the past century or so. We have followed the Bulgarian tradition, which Mark represented, up the Danube and the Rhine, and south to the Languedoc in the 1150s and '60s, before it was brought to Milan by the notary who converted Mark. That after his death some of the Cathars of Mantua, Vicenza and the March went for their *consolamentum* neither to Bulgaria nor to Constantinople, but to the *ecclesia Sclavoniae*, suggests that there may already have been some contact with it before Mark's time. Finally Nicetas had introduced the newest and most advanced dualist theories and the aggressive organization which accompanied them from Constantinople, where their development had probably been comparatively recent.

Such indications as orthodox sources provide tend to support Anselm of Alessandria's chronology. Florence was put under interdict in 1173 'because of the activity of the heretics there', and it may not be accidental that in calling them 'Patarenes' the chronicler used the name which was particularly associated with the Bosnian dualists. It was from Florence that the first Cathars went to Orvieto 'in the time of Bishop Rustico', who died in 1176, and it was about 1176 also that 'the heresy of the Cathars began to spread in Milan, and to cause growing dissension and schism'.[16] These random reports cannot be clearly identified with any of the events recorded by the *De heresi catharorum in Lombardia* and Anselm of Alessandria, but it may be suspected that the open conflict in Florence and Milan reflected the upheavals after Mark's death rather than the early progress of his mission, not only because it is in them that the best sources point to the seeds of vigorous disagreement but because in general the Cathars, like their Bogomil ancestors, seem to have avoided flaunting their beliefs too provocatively before the orthodox. Although they reached Orvieto as early as 1176, for example, it was not until a dispute between the city and the papacy caused confusion among the Catholics more than twenty years later that their presence became a matter of notoriety.

While the modified dualism of the Concorezzans and Bagnolans retained the loyalty of most of the Cathar churches of Italy the Dragovitsan absolutism which Nicetas had brought to the west quickly became dominant in the Languedoc, and it seems that the process by which it did so had something in common with the Italian experience. In 1177 Count Raymond V of Toulouse wrote to the Abbot of Citeaux to seek assistance in dealing with heresy in his chief city. He said that the heretics denied baptism and the eucharist, rejected penance and the resurrection of the flesh, disdained the sacraments of the church, and 'worst of all, have introduced two principles'.[17] This is the first explicit statement in a western source of the presence of absolute dualism. The Count had already decided to invoke secular coercion against it, and concluded by telling the Abbot that he had appealed to Louis VII of France for support in his intention.

To ask at what moment the two principles had been introduced to Toulouse is to confront one of the most difficult of the many perplexing documents of early heresy, the so-called *Acta concilii Caramanensis*. This curious text, purportedly copied in 1232 for Pierre Polha, Cathar bishop of Carcassonne, describes how Papa Niquinta – generally agreed to be Nicetas – addressed a grand meeting of all the leading Cathars of the Languedoc, instructed them on the organization of the dualist churches of the east, and administered the *consolamentum* to them, and how on his advice they set up a commission to define the respective jurisdictions of their bishops of Toulouse and Carcassonne. The general burden of this story accords closely with what is known both of the mission of Nicetas to the west and the subsequent development of Catharism in the Languedoc, but the contradictions and obscurities which abound in the text itself constitute a powerful case against its authenticity.[18] The problems are largely resolved, however, by the recent suggestion (which is summarized by its author in the Appendix on page 285) that the *Acta*, if genuine, is not the record of a single meeting, but a conflation of two or even three distinct accounts, of an assembly convoked to hear Nicetas and receive the *consolamentum* of the Dragovit-

san church from him, the address which he delivered, and the final
conclusion of the boundary commissioners. This insight permits the
conclusion that, while the date of 1167 which the *Acta* gives for the
events it records is either a mistranscription or the error of a
subsequent editor, it may be regarded as an authentic description of
the organization of the Cathars in the Languedoc at the time of
Nicetas' mission to the West, shortly after 1174.[19]

The Council was attended by three Cathar bishops, each accompanied by his *consilium*, Robert d'Espernon from Northern France
(*ecclesia Francigenarum*), Sicard Cellerier from Albi, and Mark of
Lombardy, who had presumably accompanied Nicetas from Italy.
There were also present the *consilia* of the churches of Carcassonne
and Agen (or, less probably, Val d'Aran), and the men of Toulouse,
who wished to have their own bishop, and chose Bernard Raimundi,
while on the advice of Sicard Cellerier the men of Carcassonne
chose Guiraud Mercier, and those of Agen Raimund de Casalis.
Then both the newly elected and those already named as bishops,
including Mark, received the *consolamentum* from Nicetas.[20]

If the *Acta* is taken here at face value it reveals a series of Cathar
congregations at various stages of development now, under the
leadership of Nicetas and Sicard Cellerier, to be placed on a regular
and uniform basis. There had been bishops among the 'Franks' –
though not necessarily within the Capetian realm – since the time of
Eckbert of Schönau, and either they or the Cathars of the Languedoc
had provided the first contact with Mark and his companions in
Lombardy. That Sicard Cellerier was already a bishop confirms the
tradition that the church of Albi was the senior Cathar congregation
of the Languedoc, and Sicard himself must have been the successor
of Oliver, who had been the principal spokesman at Lombers. Since
1165 churches had been founded at Carcassonne and Agen, which
therefore had *perfecti* and *consilia* – that is, a recognized collective
leadership – but as yet no bishop; Toulouse also had a church, but
there is no mention of a *consilium*. This situation is consistent with
the rapid expansion of Catharism in the Languedoc in the 1160s
which has been postulated, and the problems which it posed are
readily envisaged. It was natural that each new community should have
its own leadership, both in reflection of the Catholic organization

which was so familiar, and because no other solution would have been practicable. But what should be the relations of these leaders to each other, and how should their areas of responsibility be defined? Here the experience of Nicetas was put to use. He explained to the assembly how in the east there were five churches, each of which was autonomous within its own boundaries, 'none of them doing anything to gainsay another', so that there was peace between them. He advised that this pattern should be imitated by the churches of Toulouse and Carcassonne, and men chosen by each to work out its boundary with its neighbour. The commission thus elected recommended that the boundaries of the Catholic dioceses should be followed (which would have the obvious advantage that everybody knew where they were), and it was agreed that this should be done, and that neither would attempt to exercise authority in the other's territory.

The administrative framework which was erected by the Council of Saint-Félix was spiritually completed when Nicetas administered the *consolamentum* not only to the newly chosen bishops, which was normal, but to all those present. In the ordinary way a Cathar was consoled only once in his lifetime, unless either his own sin or that of another necessitated a reconsolation, which was a solemn ceremony undertaken only after confession, penance and preparation. On this occasion, however, it was necessary because Nicetas, as a Dragovitsan, did not admit the validity of the *consolamentum* of the *ecclesia Bulgariae* which had first proselytized the region. The effect of his mission, therefore, was not only to give a pattern of organization to the new churches of the Languedoc, but to bring about a fundamental change in their allegiance, from modified Bulgarian to absolute Dragovitsan dualism. It is generally held that his success in this respect was greater in the Languedoc than in Italy, for there is no further trace of the presence of modified dualism there until after the Albigensian crusade. In accepting that view it may be prudent to remember that the Languedoc lacks any source comparable with the *De heresi Catharorum in Lombardia*, which traces the early fissures of the Cathar communities with intimate knowledge and at an early date, and that the advice which the bishop *ultra montes* gave to the followers of Mark on two occasions after his death and the mission of Nicetas to seek a new *consolamentum* in Bulgaria suggests, if it does not prove, that modified dualism did not disappear from the Languedoc as an immediate consequence of Nicetas' work.[21] Nevertheless the *Acta* of Saint-Félix provides some reason for expecting that doctrinal unity would be more easily preserved in the Languedoc than in Italy. The disputes which followed the death of Mark of Lombardy centred not on doctrine but on personality, on the struggle for his succession and the unwillingness of the leaders of the various congregations to subordinate themselves to one of their number. This was precisely the situation which the advice of Nicetas enabled the Languedocians to avoid. The creation of separate dioceses for the distinct communities and the agreement that each was to be independent within its own boundaries avoided the need for any of them, or their leaders, to assert their autonomy by seeking a *consolamentum* from a new, and allegedly purer source, as Nicholas of the March and others did from Bosnia. The Languedocian leaders accepted this solution readily. The new congregations had presumably been formed as a result of the activity of the church of Albi, and Sicard Cellerier had been the only bishop in the region before the events recounted by the *Acta*, but he made no objection to the demand of the younger communities for their own bishops, and it was '*cum consilio et voluntate et solucione*' of Sicard that Guiraud Mercier was chosen by the men of Carcassonne and Raimund de Casalis by those of Agen.

The intimate relationship between the establishment of the Cathar churches in the Languedoc and in Italy implies that the 'introduction of two principles' to which Raymond of Toulouse referred in 1177 was a recent event, and may be among the reasons for the alacrity with which the powers of Christendom answered his call for help. The next year a papal mission was despatched to Toulouse under the leadership of the Cardinal of St Chrysogonus, Peter of Pavia, accompanied by Abbot Henry of Clairvaux, the Archbishop of Bourges and the Bishops of Poitiers and Bath, and Raymond of Turenne, a vassal of Henry II. It was clearly intimated, in other words, that Raymond would be supported not only by the papacy but, if necessary, by the temporal power of his overlords Henry II and Louis VII, who had recently made peace with each other. The situation which the party found was alarming. 'Such was the licence of the heretics', wrote the abbot of Clairvaux, 'that as we entered the city they mocked us as we travelled through the streets, making signs with their fingers and calling us impostors, hypocrites and heretics.'[22] The Cathars adopted the same tactics as they had used at Lombers. Bernard Raimundi, whom Nicetas had consecrated bishop, and Raymond de Baimac, who had been one of the commissioners chosen to settle the boundary between the dioceses of Toulouse and Carcassonne, claimed that they were being unjustly persecuted by Count Raymond, and demanded safe conduct to defend their orthodoxy before the legate. He was reluctant to grant it, but realized that he had little choice 'because if we refused them a hearing they might ascribe it to indifference on our part',[23] and it was agreed that if they appeared before him they would be allowed to return home in safety. As at Lombers they made a full profession of orthodox faith, denying the doctrine of two principles, affirming the legitimacy of matrimony, and validity of the sacraments of baptism and the eucharist regardless of the morals of the priest who conferred them. The nature of their preaching was well displayed by the assurance which was required of them that 'archbishops, bishops, priests, monks, canons, hermits, Templars and Hospitallers can be saved', that churches should be honoured, tithes and first fruits paid, and the priest obeyed in all parochial matters.[24] On this occasion, however, their assertion that they had never preached anything contrary to these worthy sentiments was hotly denied by Count Raymond and 'many other clerks and laymen who had heard them preach otherwise', and once again they refused to clear themselves of the charges by oath. They were excommunicated with bell, book and candle 'before the people, who applauded continually and booed them vigorously', and proclaimed outlaws from the lands of all faithful lords unless they should recant.

The legate and his party did not realize that in Bernard Raimundi they had confronted the Cathar bishop of Toulouse. The man whom they identified as 'the leader of the damned, the chief of the heretics in that city' was Peter Maurand, whose adherence to the new faith is indeed a striking testimony that it represented a more potent threat than any of its precursors. Maurand, 'great even among the greatest men of the city' was the head of one of the leading clans of the *bourg*, one of a group which though not new families were finding themselves at this time able to take advantage of the commercial expansion of the *bourg* to increase their wealth rapidly, dealing both in land and credit, to challenge the power of the former masters of the City.[25] His father, Bonmancip, had been active in the politics of Toulouse in the 1140s, when the power of the Count over the town was first challenged and Henry of Lausanne had found sympathizers among the wealthy burghers, and in spite of the humiliation which was about to be inflicted upon him Peter himself would take his place among the chaptermen in 1184. Whether it was for his social influence or for the skill in the exposition of heretical teaching which Henry of Clairvaux attributed to him, Maurand was singled out as an example to his fellows. He relied upon his eminence to save him first from being examined, and when that failed from being required to support his profession of orthodoxy by oath, but though the Count was anxious to deal courteously with him the legate insisted, threats were uttered, and a great public confrontation was arranged. Before the relics of the saint the old man's nerve broke, he confessed himself a heretic, and after a few days' imprisonment agreed to undergo whatever penance should be required of him. The opportunity was avidly seized:

> Before an enormous crowd Peter, now our man, was led naked and barefoot from the doorway of the church, being scourged by the bishop of Toulouse and the abbot of St Sernin until he prostrated himself at the feet of the lord legate on the steps of the altar. There, in the face of the church he abjured all heresy and pronounced a curse on all heretics and was reconciled with the sacraments of the church. All his possessions were confiscated and taken from him, and the penance was laid on him that he should depart as an exile from his native land within forty days, and spend three years at Jerusalem in the service of the poor. In the meantime he was to go round every church in Toulouse on each Lord's Day, naked and barefoot, with disciplinary scourges, to restore all the goods which he had taken from churches, to return all the interest which he had won by usury, to make amends for all the injuries that he had inflicted on the poor, and to raze to its foundations one of his castles which he had polluted with meetings of heretics.[26]

Although Henry of Clairvaux was delighted by the triumph over Peter Maurand, which would open the way to the discovery of more of his fellow believers, it is doubtful whether it had a very great effect. Peter pulled down the town house whose fortified tower was a symbol of his power, paid a heavy fine, and handed over one of his richest properties, of tithes at Valségur, to the canons of St Sernin. But he and his descendants continued to play a leading part in the city, and the permanence of his renunciation of heresy may be judged by the fact that four of his sons and their descendants were Cathars. Despite occasional losses to war and inquisition the Maurand were still both wealthy and influential when, just a century later, the royal amnesty of 1279 lifted the threat of confiscation from the descendants of those who had been convicted of heresy during the crisis.

Nicetas left the Cathars unity in the Languedoc and disunity in Italy. The diocesan structure which had been worked out under his inspiration remained the administrative framework and the two principles which he had introduced the theological foundation of what soon became known as the Albigensian heresy. In Italy the various churches continued each to go its own way, sometimes harmoniously, sometimes acrimoniously, and sometimes in direct competition; in some Lombard cities there were congregations of both Concorezzo and Desenzano, each of which regarded the other as a path to damnation. As their greatest historian has insisted, it is a gross historical error to think of Catharism as a monolithic rival to the monolith of the Roman church: 'there were various *dualist sects*, both in the east and in Lombardy, which had in common only more or less affiliated doctrinal legacies'.[27] The consequent affiliations of doctrine, ritual and organization make it possible to consider the convictions and customs of the Cathar churches as a whole, but that warning must be borne firmly in mind while we do so.

'They say that human bodies are given life partly by evil spirits which have been created by the devil, and partly by souls which have fallen from heaven. The souls do penance in the bodies, and if they are not saved in one body they enter another body and do penance in that. When penance is complete the soul is reunited with the body

and spirit which have remained in heaven.'[28] So the Cathars understood the human predicament. The theologies of the different sects
and the myths which were associated with them varied in their detailed
accounts of how the catastrophe had taken place. All agreed that its
author was Lucifer, whom the mitigated dualists regarded as the
steward of God corrupted by the four-faced monster 'which had no
beginning and lived in chaos',[29] while to the absolute dualists he was
the son of the evil principle who had entered heaven by stealth or
force; the spirits whom he took were sometimes represented as good,
sometimes bad, sometimes both, sometimes seduced by promises of
splendour and sometimes seized in battle. But the central point was
always the same. Body and soul belonged to different orders of
creation, were the work of different creators, wholly alien to each
other. The nature of their union was vividly expressed by one
Bulgarian description of how it came about, when Lucifer made a
body of clay in his own likeness, seized a good angel, and throttled
him into it to give it life. From this he took a portion to make another
body, into which he forced a second angel, to become Eve. Then he
'poured out upon her head a longing for sin, and Eve's desire was like
a glowing oven', so that Lucifer in the form of a serpent might 'sate
his lust upon her with the serpent's tail' before pouring his own
desire over the head of Adam, so that the wretched creatures, infected
by his lasciviousness, were condemned to perpetuate the work of
procreation which he had begun.[30]

The origin of the Cathar abstinence from the act and fruits of
procreation in this premise made it wholly different from Catholic
abstinence, and imposed a radically different structure upon Cathar
religious institutions. Catholic abstinence was a spiritual end in itself: the Catholic fasted or was celibate not because meat or copulation were inherently evil but because abstention signified spiritual
discipline, devotion to God, and the capacity to master the desires of
the body. Among Catholics, therefore, the distinction between those
who abstained and those who did not was one only between the
degrees of function in the Christian order and of progress in the
spiritual life; similarly if a Catholic failed to accomplish the abstention which was required of him the failure, though regrettable in
itself, did not vitiate the objective for which he had undertaken it. It

was faith that made a Christian, and the distinction between Catholic and non-Catholic was therefore that between those within and outside the community of believers whose threshold was marked by the sacrament of baptism. For the Cathar, on the other hand 'freedom from the flesh' was not a metaphorical but a literal imperative. Abstinence was the physical condition of the liberation of souls from the prisons of Lucifer. To this object faith, all important to the Catholic, was of itself irrelevant, a necessary preliminary to the battle for freedom, but not a weapon in the battle itself. Hence a Cathar was defined not by conviction but by behaviour. However clear a man's perception of truth, however profound his faith in its message, he was not a Cathar until he had disavowed the flesh, been reunited through the *consolamentum* with the soul from which his spirit had been snatched, and observed until the moment of death unfalteringly and without any slip the prohibitions which prevented him from crossing once more, and in the wrong direction, the gulf that separated the spiritual world of good from the material world of evil.

From this it followed that the position of the *credentes* of the Cathars was quite unlike that of Catholic laymen, for they were not members of the church. Their support and assistance were indispensable; the perfected Cathars often needed food and shelter (although they were not forbidden labour, and many of their communities supported themselves, for example by weaving), guidance through strange territory, concealment from their enemies and messengers to their friends, and believers assisted also with much of the business of the Cathar churches and the administration of their funds. In return they might receive material assistance from the charitable and hospital works which the *perfecti* organized and conducted, and spiritual consolation from the sermons which they preached, the blessing which they conferred on the believer when he knelt in greeting before them, and the bread which they broke and passed around when they presided at his table. But the overwhelming benefit to which the believer aspired, and to confer which the *perfecti* travelled far and wide and incurred infinite danger, was the *consolamentum*, the single act of purification which freed the believer from his flesh, reunited his spirit and his soul, and made him a Cathar.

The *consolamentum* was a solemn and elaborate ceremony, performed if possible by a number of Cathars though in necessity, which
persecution made often, it might be done by one alone. The recipient
knelt three times before the officiant, imploring him 'by the mercy of
God to do that good to me which God has done to you'; taking a copy
of the Gospels he abjured his sins and vowed himself to observance
of the rules enumerated to him; the Gospel was then placed on his
head, the hands of his initiators on his shoulders, and he joined them
all in repeating seven *Pater nosters*, in the praise of God and the plea
for mercy. Finally 'the Gospel is removed from the initiate's head,
and he is placed among the Cathars who say to him "Now you are
one of us, in this world a sheep among wolves." '[31]

The concluding words of the *consolamentum* were perhaps the
most significant, a reminder that the newly created Cathar had
become a member of a spiritual élite, separated from the rest of the
world, including the believers, by the gulf of the flesh. Matter in all
its forms was now abjured. Sexual intercourse, the eating of meat,
milk and eggs, were prohibited. Mondays, Wednesdays and Fridays
were fast days, when wine, oil, fish and shell-fish would not be
taken. Each year there were three fasts of forty days, the first coin-
ciding with Lent, the second from Whitsun to the end of July, the
third from Martinmas to Christmas, when fish and shell-fish were
forbidden throughout and wine, oil and vegetables in the first and
last weeks of the first fast and the first weeks of the other two. The
state of purity thus achieved was sustained by a monthly confession
(the *apparallamentum*) when as many Cathars as could be assembled,
in the presence of believers, recited a general formula of confession
and contrition, to be absolved and given the penance of three more
days of fasting.

A Cathar's breach of the prohibitions from the weakness of the
flesh was a much graver matter. The sins of a Catholic, however
heinous, need not damn him if they did not touch the faith in which
was his salvation, but the Catharism of a *perfectus* resided in his
purity. If he lost it he tore his spirit once more from his soul and fell
back into the material world. His *consolamentum*, with any which he
had conferred on others, was nullified and the whole process must
begin again. According to the gravity of his sin, in the judgement of

his bishop, reconsolation must be preceded by a period of 'passing over' – returning that is, to the state of purity – which might involve up to three periods of forty days on bread and water in addition to the regular fasts. Moreover in very grave cases the reconsoled Cathar was not allowed to administer the *consolamentum* again lest his inconstancy should imperil others, unless a dying man should find himself in the desperate condition of having no more reliable source of consolation available to him.

Rainier Sacchoni was confident that when he wrote in 1250 'there were not more than about four thousand Cathars in the whole world'.[32] By then the inquisitors had inflicted considerable losses on those of the Languedoc; the church of Agen was 'now almost destroyed', and to those of Toulouse, Albi and Carcassonne Rainier allotted only two hundred of his four thousand, compared with ten times as many in Lombardy. Allowing for this destruction his estimate, that of an informed and sober observer, probably indicates fairly accurately how numerous active Cathars were at the height of their influence; it may be presumed that he did not try to include those who followed the ordinary course of the believers and received the *consolamentum* on the deathbed. The Cathars, separated from ordinary men by their abjuration of the flesh and their rigorous and highly articulated regime of fasting, constituted a reservoir of holiness for their followers, combining, roughly speaking, the functions of the Catholic secular and monastic clergy. Many of them lived quietly in houses and retreats, while the work of organization and proselytization was the responsibility of comparatively few. Each church – Rainier lists sixteen, including five in the east – had a bishop, who was assisted by two 'sons', his *filius major* and *filius minor*. The *filii* were the principal link between the bishop and his scattered congregations, and were obliged to travel constantly, together or separately, to keep in touch with them. Each congregation had its own deacon, whose chief regular duty was to preside over the monthly *apparallamentum*.

The organization thus adumbrated was adapted to the dangers which threatened it. When a bishop died he was succeeded by the *filius major*, and he in turn by the *filius minor*; a new *filius minor* was chosen by an assembly of as many Cathars of the church as could be brought together. Each rank, including the deacons, could perform all the duties of the others in their absence. The missionary origin of the Cathar churches was reflected in the tradition of travel and contact among themselves which they maintained around the Mediterranean, although there is little to suggest that the northern communities, whose continued existence was attested by the bloody inquisitions of Conrad of Marburg and Robert the Bugger in 1231-3, remained in close touch with their co-religionists in the south. The relations between the Cathars of Lombardy and the Languedoc, so close since the earliest days remained so, and were reinforced by steady emigration from the *midi* to Italy under the pressure of persecution.[33] When Mark of Lombardy died in Calabria he was on his way to Bulgaria for a new *consolamentum* by the usual route, crossing the straits of Otranto; his eventual successor John the Jew and Nazarius, bishop of Concorezzo who brought the *Interrogatio Johannis* from Bulgaria towards the end of the century, would have followed the same route. When they travelled the Cathars provided themselves with introductions to fellow-believers who would give them shelter and hospitality as they moved; in this way Yves of Narbonne made his way, about 1214, through the Po valley and the March of Friuli to Aquilea, being passed from one group to another.[34] Contact therefore was maintained, and nourished the legend of the 'Black Pope' who haunted the imagination of the orthodox,[35] but travel, exposing them as it did to idle curiosity and the risk of chance discovery, was always a dangerous business for the heretic. The problem is expressed by the etiquette of visiting: 'When a Cathar or believer of one of the sects enters a strange Cathar household he says "Greetings. May we better ourselves here?" If there is anyone present who is not of their faith, or of whom they are nervous, the master of the house replies "Sit down," which indicates the presence of someone they distrust; if not, "Do as you please." '[36] Although links were maintained between the different Cathar churches stretched around the Mediterranean each of them was self-contained and autonomous, and the real strength of the Cathar movement lay in the individual congregations rather than in any bonds between them.

The life of the Cathar believer is difficult to approach. The status itself was necessarily ill-defined, covering as it might people of every degree of conviction from casual sympathy to those who had formed a settled intention to receive the *consolamentum* before they died. Of the former it may be supposed that the degree of sincerity involved in associating with Cathars and attending their services increased as it became more dangerous, while towards 1240 it became possible for the latter to make a pact, the *convenensa*, which would enable them to be consoled by the imposition of the perfect's hands alone, lest he could not reach them before they lost strength or consciousness to repeat the Lord's Prayer. Specific instances of the *convenensa* and of deathbed consolations are, naturally enough, very rare, and the number of believers there may have been accordingly impossible to estimate.

That the believers were not required to observe the prohibitions imposed on the *perfecti* and that consolation on the deathbed was held wholly to cleanse its recipient of the sins of his life, together with the powerful disquiet which the Cathar horror of procreation has usually aroused in those who do not share it, quickly made them particularly vulnerable to the lurid fantasies which heretics so regularly stimulated. The myth of ritual suicide, the *endura*, is still persistent, though there is nothing to support it beyond the remark of Rainier Sacchoni that since the very ill would sometimes instruct those taking care of them not to feed them unless they were strong enough to say the Lord's Prayer which ought to precede all refresh-ment, 'in this sense it is true that many of them kill themselves in this way';[37] thus the rigour of extreme piety might be interpreted as a mark of the most shocking depravity. In the same way insistence on the avoidance of procreation could rapidly be understood as a claim that all other sexual activity was innocent. Such assertions as those of the Cistercian apologist of the Albigensian crusade Peter of Vaux de Cernay that some Cathars held it 'impossible to sin from the waist down', or of Rainier Sacchoni that 'many of their believers, both men and women are not afraid to treat their sisters or brothers, daughters or sons, nieces or nephews or cousins as they would husband or wife'[38] are typical of the beliefs about the Cathars whose persistence through the centuries has had no difficulty in surviving the utter lack of any serious evidence to support them.

James Capelli, a Franciscan whose detestation of Cathar teachings was as strong as anybody's provides a more sober basis for the assessment of the life of their followers.[39]

They administer this imposition of hands to believers in their sect who are ill, out of which has stemmed the popular rumour that they kill them by strangulation, so that they may be martyrs or confessors. From personal knowledge we affirm this to be untrue and we urge that no one believe that they commit so shameful an act. For we know that they suppose their behaviour to be virtuous and they do many things that are in the nature of good works; in frequent prayer, in vigils, in sparsity of food and clothing, and – let me acknowledge the truth – in austerity of abstinence they surpass all other religious . . . the rumour of fornication which is said to prevail among them is most false. For it is true that once a month, either by day or by night, in order to avoid gossip by the people, men and women meet together not, as some lyingly say, for purpose of fornication, but so that they may hear preaching and make confession to their presiding official, as though from his prayer pardon for their sins would ensue. They are wrongfully wounded in popular rumour by many malicious charges of blasphemy from those who say they commit many shameful and horrid acts of which they are innocent. And, therefore, they vaunt themselves to be disciples of Christ, who said 'If they have persecuted me, they will also persecute you. . .'

Capelli was perceptive enough to see not only how rumour starts, but how it may be counter-productive, by increasing the solidarity and self-righteousness of its victims. There is no doubt that the contrast between the calm austerity of the *perfecti* and the flagrant indulgence which too often characterized the Catholic clergy was one of the most powerful instruments of their proselytization. In many ways indeed the Cathar church could appear to those who saw holiness more easily in example than in theology to justify its claim to be the church of the apostles. Its leaders venerated the Gospels, preached their message in terms, language and allegory which sounded familiar to those innocent of the doctrinal deviations behind them, and observed their precepts with conspicuous fidelity in forms which, however radically they might be justified in private, were hallowed by long centuries of Catholic ascetic spirituality. Their repeated use of the Lord's Prayer, before sitting at table, before taking up food or drink, setting out on a journey or crossing a dangerous bridge, the sobriety of their dress and demeanour, their absolute rejection of violence and abjuration of all oaths, seemed evident marks of authenticity. Their plain and dignified rituals, seemingly descended from those of the early Christians, and the simplicity of the sacramental and confessional structure enhanced the clarity of their message.[40] Even the difference between the position of their believers and that of baptized Catholics was far less evident in practice than in principle, for it was not so long since Catholics had doubted whether any but monks could be saved, and it was still conventional for many of them towards the end of their lives to renounce the world and retire to a monastery. It is a mistake, too, to imagine that because Cathar theology was rooted in contempt of the material world (a theme much in vogue among Catholic commentators on the holy life) their followers must have been conspicuously more miserable than their neighbours. Like most devotees of any cult they regarded their faith as one of liberation, and drew relief and sustenance from the knowledge that the aspects of their own natures which Catholic culture itself had taught them to distrust and fear as the engines of their damnation were not truly part of them, and might be joined in battle, and conquered.[41] Like most persecuted minorities they found comfort and pleasure, as Capelli noticed, in the strong bonds of affection between them, and Yves of Narbonne who travelled among them as a fugitive was impressed by the kindness of their welcome, the vigour of their conversation, and the excellence of their fruit and wine.

The Cathars were not unusual in their preoccupation with bodily purity. Between the third and fourth Lateran Councils (1179 and 1215) the contrast between the ideal of the apostolic life and the imperfections of a worldly clergy headed by the cumbersome and venal bureaucracy of the papal curia created, much as in the Gregorian period, an atmosphere in which the line between zeal and heresy often appeared arbitrary, dividing men and women otherwise almost indistinguishable. The immense expansion of intellectual horizons and forms of religious life in the twelfth century had multiplied the ways in which unease could be expressed. In 1177, for example, the canonist Vacarius wrote to his undergraduate contemporary Master Hugh Speroni, a consul of Piacenza to rebut, in terms far friendlier than a humbler heretic might have anticipated, Hugh's assertions that the sins of the clergy had annulled the authority of the church, and that since salvation was the reward of inner purity alone progress towards it was assisted by neither good works nor the sacraments of baptism, the eucharist and confession. The Speronists were condemned by the Council of Verona in 1184, together with the Arnoldists, who had something in common with them since they were accused of reviving the doctrines of Arnold of Brescia, and the Passagians, who drew their inspiration from the Old Testament instead of the New, and wanted to revive the observances of the Mosaic law, including ritual circumcision.[42] In 1209 ten followers of another intellectual, the Parisian master Amalric of Bène, were burned for claiming to be so imbued with the Holy Spirit that they had lost both the capacity to sin and the need for the sacraments of the church; their doctrine seems to have been derived from the neo-platonism of Eriugena, which had encouraged them to believe themselves participants in the divine essence.[43]

Much greater popularity was achieved by another sect which Lucius III anathematized in 1184, the Lombard *Humiliati*.[44] As their nickname implies they aspired to a humility of life which fate had not imposed upon them. For the most part literate, and including many from the nobility, both men and women, they bound themselves 'to be poor and live with the poor', adopting the rule which was no less real to them because it would have seemed ridiculous to those whom they wished to emulate, that they would not eat more than twice a day or indulge in excessive finery of dress. They sought, as others had done before them, to live the common life without fleeing the world and bound themselves in austerity, prayer, fellowship and manual labour while continuing to live with their families. They had been condemned not for any aberration of doctrine but because they persisted in preaching without canonical authority, and when they appealed to Innocent III in 1199 the investigation which he ordered led to their institution in three orders, the Tertiaries who continued to live under vows in the world, and two enclosed orders of men and women: the structure anticipated that which would soon be adopted by the Franciscans and later by the Dominicans. They were allowed to preach provided that they eschewed theological questions: that they appear, on the whole, to have done so tells a good deal of the nature of their movement. Its emphasis was not doctrinal, but ethical and social. Its members sought not simply the abstract ideal of apostolic poverty, but actually to be like the poor around them, and licence to communicate their message was the only point upon which they felt the need to defy authority if need be. They were distinguished by no unusual teaching but by a way of life simple, regular and fraternal, and their success was great in just the places where the Cathars prospered: they had early communities in Como, Pavia, Piacenza, Brescia, Bergamo, Verona and especially Milan, the 'capital of heresy' where Jacques of Vitry estimated in 1216 that they had one hundred and fifty convents, and more family groups than he could begin to count.

Part of the appeal of the *Humiliati* was the same as that of the Béguines, for whom Marie d'Oignies obtained a papal licence in 1210, and whose desire for an ordered and holy life in the world had been anticipated by the admirers of Lambert le Bègue. In another aspect they had something in common with the Waldensians or Poor Men of Lyons who were also condemned by the Council of Verona, though they did not deviate from orthodox doctrine, because they insisted on preaching and who were destined to become, after the Cathars, the most detested heretics of the age and the only ones who succeeded in founding a church which survives to this day.

The Waldensian movement began with a conversion of classical splendour. One day in 1173, or thereabouts, a usurer of Lyons named Valdès heard a street performer tell the story of the death of St Alexis, a chestnut of contemporary popular piety, and was overcome by the sense of his need for salvation. A schoolmaster whom he consulted, doubtless complimenting himself on the aptness of his reflection, quoted Christ's words, 'Go sell what thou hast and give to the poor and thou shalt have treasure in heaven. And come follow me.'[45] Valdès took him literally. When he got home he offered his wife her choice between his cash and the revenues of his lands, and though taken aback she retained enough judgement to prefer the latter; with the cash he returned what had been wrongly acquired, settled dowries on his two daughters to secure their admission to Fontevrault, and distributed the rest to the poor. Thus began a career of preaching which lasted for some thirty years, and the nuances of the story are worth dwelling upon. Valdès was a usurer at a time when cash, becoming for the first time the commonest visible sign of wealth, was therefore also being identified as the source of worldly evil.[46] He belonged to a class which prospered at the expense both of a declining patriciate which borrowed to maintain the pre-eminence that income from land no longer guaranteed, and of the poor. At the time when accident precipitated a conversion which was obviously the result of a more prolonged unease with his way of life a famine was abroad whose unusual severity is attested not only by the comments of the chronicler but by the fact that the relief which Valdès provided was needed as early as Whitsun, when he began a thrice-weekly distribution of bread and soup that lasted until his money ran out at the beginning of August. Finally, when he explained his actions to his fellow citizens, who naturally enough thought he had gone mad, he said 'I know that many of you disapprove of my having acted so publicly: I have done so both for my sake and for yours; for my sake because anybody who sees me with money in the future will be able to say that I am mad. . .' Those words betoken a certain desperation, the self-consciousness of a man who had felt himself torn by the prosperity which he had earned at the expense of public disapprobation – usury was now becoming a term of abuse often equated with heresy – from which he could only redeem himself by renouncing it as publicly. It is not often that the pressures which make a convert are so clearly acknowledged.

With such a beginning it was inevitable that Valdès should show an evangelical talent, and within a few years he had been joined by others who renounced their property, gave no thought to the morrow, lived on charity and 'gradually began to inveigh against their own sins and those of others'. At the Lateran Council of 1179 their manner of life was applauded by the Pope, and they were assured of the church's blessing so long as they did not take it upon themselves to preach. It is not clear for how long they restrained themselves. A year or two later the legate Henry of Clairvaux took the opportunity of a visit to Lyons to demand a profession of orthodoxy from

Valdès,[47] and obtained it without difficulty, but by 1182 it seems that discretion was exhausted, for the Waldensians were excommunicated and expelled from Lyons and the sentence was confirmed at Verona because the prohibition on preaching had been violated.

After their expulsion from the church the Waldensians spread rapidly into the *midi* and Lombardy, and devoted themselves especially to preaching against the heresy of the Cathars, to whom indeed they presented a far more formidable challenge than the regular clergy or Cistercian missions had been able to mount. Their appearance and demeanour were very similar to those of the *perfecti*, and offered the same visible example of the apostolic ideal: 'they go about two by two, barefoot, clad in woollen garments, owning nothing, holding all things in common like the Apostles, naked following a naked Christ'.[48] There were among them men of histrionic skill and evangelical talent as well as dedication, and some of them were beneficiaries of the policy of Innocent III, already applied to the *Humiliati*, of trying to recoup some of the loss which too rigid a suspicion of new enthusiasm had cost the church; in 1208 and 1210 groups of French and Lombard Waldensians, under the leadership respectively of Durand of Huesca and Bernard Prim were received back into the church, given a rule, and permitted to carry on the war against dualism as the societies of Poor Catholics and Poor Lombards, in many ways the direct fore-runners of the Dominican friars.[49]

It is possible that the division from which that development among the Waldensians arose was one manifestation of disputes for succession which followed the death of Valdès himself, probably in 1205, and which also hastened the differences which began to appear between the Poor Men of Lyons and of Lombardy; the most important was probably that while the Poor Men of Lyons interpreted their vow of absolute poverty so strictly as to refuse all manual labour the Lombards, influenced by the dignity which the apostolic ideal had accorded it in their cities, did not. Unsurprisingly, since they struggled unremittingly against its most potent enemy, the attitude of the Waldensians to the church which had rejected them became bitter, but their convictions remained simple and their teachings theologically moderate. A dislike of elaboration was expressed in their refusal to venerate the cross or sacred images, to bow to the altar or to observe the fasts of the church, and in their detestation of oaths. Both groups accepted the validity of Catholic baptism and the mass, which the Men of Lyons thought might be celebrated by any Christian, good or bad, priest or laymen, while the Lombards held it valid only if the officiant was in a state of grace, and the French also accorded authority to the writings of the fathers of the church 'when it suits them to do so'. Both therefore preached an apostolic Christianity which, supported by their lives of simplicity and dedication, can hardly have appeared pernicious to their simple hearers, and gave the greater force to their contempt for both worldly and ecclesiastical hierarchy and their absolute denial of the authority of the Roman church, which they said had been annulled when Silvester I accepted temporal possessions from the Emperor Constantine.[50]

Though their theology was radical the attitudes and precepts of the Cathars were of a piece with the religious climate of the time. The idealization of bodily purity, the rejection of wealth, the devotion to the Gospels, the abhorrence of oaths, the abjuration of violence and of power based on it, the hatred of the Roman church and the conviction that its structure of ecclesiastical authority represented and originated in the betrayal of true Christian teaching, were all shared with the Waldensians, to various degrees, with other heresies, and even (except the last) with groups for which the church could find an honoured place, the *Humiliati*, the Béguines, the Poor Catholics and Poor Lombards, the early Franciscans. It is hardly necessary to stress how these attitudes were nourished not only by the weaknesses of the church and the force of the apostolic idea, but by revulsion against city life, and especially money-making and the violation which it involved of both moral values and human relations. In these aspects the Cathars like the other enthusiastic movements of the late twelfth century plainly inherited impulses and aspirations which had appeared with increasing insistence for well over a century. Their ability to secure a following and to entrench themselves as ubiquitously and tenaciously as they did, however, depended not only on the existence of a congenial moral climate but on the inability of their opponents to obstruct them. The motives of Raymond V in appealing for help against the Cathars of Toulouse in 1177 were not only religious. In the preceding two years the citizens of the city had secured some signal triumphs in their perpetual struggle to rid themselves of the control of the Count and his officials. The twelve chapter-men who formerly assisted the comital Vicar in his judicial business had constituted themselves into a body which explicitly represented both City and Bourg and adopted the vague but politically resonant title of Consuls. They bound themselves by oath conscientiously to deal with 'matters of common interest to the City and Suburb' brought before them, and when they gave judgement in a case of a kind which had customarily been reserved to the Count or his representative they added that henceforth their judgement should be followed in similar cases. In some sense, therefore, they had transferred the power of legislation from the Count to the community, and taken, as their historian remarks, 'a major step towards making Toulouse a true consulate on the Italian model'.[51] The humiliation of Peter Maurand, the head of one of the clans certainly most prominent in these developments, consequently had real political significance, and the destruction of his fortified house in the *bourg* proclaimed not only the dangers of dabbling in heresy, but the reassertion of comital authority.

It is more than coincidence that Catharism established itself in Toulouse during these years of political change. Heresy often found a lodging in fissures which had been opened by other forces. The Cathars made two attempts to proselytize Orvieto, before and some time shortly after 1176, without much success; on each occasion they were detected by the bishop and expelled without apparent difficulty.[52] But in 1199 Orvieto's long-standing dispute with the papacy about which had the right of jurisdiction over the small town of Acquapendente came to a head, and Orvieto was placed under interdict and the bishop withdrawn to Rome. The Cathars moved in again, and this time they were successful, not only in that the absence of ecclesiastical authority enabled them to meet and preach openly, but in securing converts enough among both nobles and people to engage in street battles with the Catholics over a prolonged period, and to make it impossible for a papal *podesta* sent to root them out to use direct force until their rashness in arranging his martyrdom produced a reaction against them. In one form or another the story was a common one; whether in the Languedoc where the Count laboured without much success to diminish the strength of his internal rivals while he looked over his shoulder at the growing ambitions of the Aragonese, Angevin and Capetian houses, or in Lombardy and Tuscany where the communes were perfecting their institutions and establishing control over their *contados* under the feet of the lumbering giants Empire and Papacy, the 1170s were years when the Cathars who made their way to these regions found that the stresses on the ordinary fabric of authority and society left them many cracks in which they might shelter.

It was not only in the city of Toulouse that Count Raymond V lacked authority. Power in the Languedoc was quite remarkably diffused. Lordship was divided between a multiplicity of claimants at every level; feudal homage and service, the sinews of contemporary government, had barely marked the surface of noble society here; administration was rudimentary, and the church which in other regions provided a firm buttress of secular authority in the Languedoc shared its fragmentation and feebleness. Raymond himself was a vassal of the king of France for his county of Toulouse, and of the Emperor for the marquisate of Provence which constituted the eastern part of his lands; the Angevin kings who ruled Aquitaine did not renounce their claim to the lordship of Toulouse until Richard I exchanged it for acknowledgement of that of the Agenais in 1196. The kings of Aragon controlled Roussillon and, until it was bought from them in 1204, part of the Albigeois and other lands in that region, and their overlordship was accepted by Raymond's most powerful vassals, the Counts of Foix and Comminges and the Trencavel family who were vicomtes of Albi, Béziers, Carcassonne and the Razès, and Aragon also held the County (in effect the southern portion) of Provence. Surrounded by these aggressive state-builders the rulers of the house of St Gilles walked a tightrope from which intervention always threatened to topple them, as it did in various forms on the seven occasions between 1142 and 1185 when they were at war with the vicomtes of Béziers,[53] before the papal mission of 1178, and finally and catastrophically in the Albigensian crusade.

Neither Raymond nor his recalcitrant vassals had ready access to the ordinary sources of feudal power. In the south-west of France, the classical antithesis of Normandy,[54] most of the land and the innumerable castles were held allodially not feudally, and the failure of primogeniture to develop there as it had in most of the west during the past two centuries created a labyrinthine confusion of tiny lordships. On the eve of the crusade Montreal, Mirepoix and Lombers – all notorious centres of heresy – were shared between thirty-five, thirty-six and fifty lords respectively, while the passage from one generation to another compounded the confusion so magnificently that Raymond of Dourgne could hold one half of each of three quarters of his family's lands.[55] Even where the obligations of vassalage existed they could not be effectively enforced in such conditions, and the multiplicity of rival lords and pauper knights produced a scourge which the Lateran Council of 1179 thought as serious as heresy in the *routiers*, mercenary soldiers who availed themselves voraciously of the opportunities for pillage and depredation which reward their kind. Henry of Clairvaux, who was largely responsible for the interest of the Lateran Council, saw the consequences of this situation on his way home from Toulouse, when he passed through Albi to free its bishop from the prisons of Roger of Béziers, and found 'a great cess-pit of evil, with all the scum of heresy flowing into it'. One of his successors as legate, Abbot Arnold-Amaury of Citeaux, estimated in 1211 that the region boasted five hundred heretical lords who owed no allegiance to the Count of Toulouse.[56]

The impotence of the church which had been so harshly revealed at the Council of Lombers was in part, of course, a direct result of the absence of the secular power upon which it would have relied elsewhere. It had also suffered indirectly, since the impoverishment of the aristocracy by partible inheritance both reduced the opportunity of large donations of land, and increased the pressures which led to the alienation of those lands it had. In the tenth and early eleventh centuries ecclesiastical office had been universally and systematically exploited for the support of the minor nobility,[57] and

although the monastic (especially Cluniac) and Gregorian reforms
had secured here as elsewhere a considerable restitution of revenues
and a somewhat greater degree of delicacy in the disposition of
benefices, the church was much less wealthy and less active than it
was in the north, its lands and tithes always at risk of expropriation.

It remained true that, especially by comparison with the secular
nobility around it, the church had considerable wealth. But if the
benefices at its disposal had been richer it might have been able to
secure clergy of a quality more capable of opposing the heretics than
the agricultural labourers who were often presented to them, and to
initiate and support the houses of canons who could bring its
services more widely and more reliably to the populations of the
growing villages and towns. Here was another example of the old
bogey of reform, that though poverty might be good for the souls of
the clergy it was bad for the government of the church.[58] The
reputation which the prelates of the *midi* gained for exceptional
worldliness and avarice was certainly swollen by some of their
personal characters, but it is also attributable in some degree to a
genuine need to labour for the protection and augmentation of their
revenues, as well as to the disappointment of those whom they
frustrated in the process. Especially in the towns, where new wealth
was to be found and squabbled over, the lordship which involved the
Archbishop of Narbonne and the Bishops of Albi and Béziers,
among others, in prolonged litigation did nothing to enhance their
reputation for spiritual leadership. The confusion of diocesan
organization was perhaps even more damaging. That the western
Languedoc was divided between the jurisdiction of four archbishops,
and the Count's Provençal lands of two, largely deprived them of
the benefits of the flow of councils and synods which elsewhere had
carried the work of reform forward, erratically but in sum impres-
sively, throughout the preceding century, and largely explains why a
united reaction to heresy could not easily be mounted without the
external stimulus of a papal legation.[59]

The position of Peter Maurand as a leading member of both
the victorious groups in 1175–6, the Cathars and the families of the
bourg which led the consular movement, raises the temptation to go
beyond the recognition that both benefited from the weakness of

comital authority and consider whether there was a more positive connection between them, and the heresy should be understood as the ideology of a rising political force. Such a proposition should be treated with scepticism. Religious enthusiasm is at least as likely to distract its votaries from political affairs as to excite radical sentiment, and though the contempt of Catharism for human institutions in general may have encouraged any tendency there was to question them there is nothing in it to suggest that it might lead to the advocacy of positive alternatives. More seriously, it does not appear that Peter Maurand was a wholly typical Cathar. There were many heretics among the artisans and small tradesmen of Toulouse, and many too among the patrician families of the City which also provided the most enthusiastic members of the White Confraternity which Bishop Fulk organized against heresy and usury after 1206. These were families whose economic position was threatened by falling land values, and both they and the poor might blame their misfortunes upon the accumulators of new wealth, the great merchants and moneylenders of the *bourg*. Antagonism to usury, therefore, could be conveniently expressed under cover of zeal against housing, but in fact although there were exceptions like the Maurand the newly rich families preferred for the most part to be unobtrusively conventional in religion, often generous benefactors of the church and of the hospitals and charitable institutions which were founded in abundance at this time.[60]

The heads of the great noble families, including Raymond VI of Toulouse himself and such of his most powerful vassals as Raymond Roger Trencavel and Raymond Roger of Foix were regularly accused of sheltering and supporting heretics, and of having formed the intention of receiving the *consolamentum* before their deaths.[61] It was, of course, a convenient view for those who might have designs upon their lands to hold, and it is certainly the case that in general they showed little disposition towards persecution, and were undisturbed by the presence of *perfecti* at their courts and of believers among their followers and in their families; Raymond Roger of Foix, for example, would not make the gestures of respect towards the perfected which would have shown him a believer, but both his wife Philippa and his sister Esclarmonde received the *consolamentum* and were regarded as leading members of the heretical community. Among the lesser nobility, whose battles with the church over land and revenues were less celebrated but not less tenacious than those of the greatest lords, there is rather more solid ground for thinking that a positive enthusiasm for heresy was widespread; it was the knights whom the bishop of Albi had warned against supporting the heretics at Lombers, and in whose *castra* Henry of Lausanne had his greatest success.[62] Of the poor in the countryside as in the town little that is positive can be said; there is striking evidence of the survival of pre-christian cults among the peasantry of the Albigensian region, in the form of underground chambers and tunnels which were still in use in the twelfth century, and which the inquisitors may have regarded as the sanctuaries of Cathars, but none that such a connection if it was made was valid.[63] Beyond the general observation, which will be more closely considered below, that on the whole the mass of the populace was influenced by the appearance of sanctity rather than the message which it clothed, there is nothing which permits a sustained assessment of the impact of the heresies on the greatest part of the population.

The immense vitality of the society of communal Italy, with its extremely rapid growth of wealth and population and its constant physical and social mobility, provided a milieu in which the heretics could hardly help succeeding. It was rare indeed for any authority, Pope or Emperor, bishop or *podesta*, to hold power securely enough or effectively enough to sustain an attack on them. While Lucius III and Frederick I met at Verona in 1184 to celebrate their reconciliation and proclaim their united determination to extirpate heresy from Christendom the Cathars of the city continued their nocturnal services as usual, and in 1207 Innocent III could resort to no weapon more expeditious than patient negotiation to persuade the people of Piacenza to take back the bishop and clergy whom they had expelled three years earlier.[64] The great thing for the Cathars in Italy was that their enemy always had an enemy who would protect them for whatever reasons of his own, whether it was a noble avenging himself on the enemies of his family, an Ezzelino da Romano or an Oberto Palavicino forbidding the inquisition access to great stretches of Ghibelline-controlled territory for years on end, or the *podesta* of Genoa, in 1221, telling a papal envoy who wanted to inspect the statutes of the city and see that anti-heretical legislation had been implemented to mind his own business.[65]

In the half century or so after the conversion of Mark of Lombardy the Cathars found converts and protectors in every city of any size, and often expected to preach their sermons and conduct their schools perfectly openly, and publicly to advertise the houses where travelling perfects and believers would find hospitality. If action were taken against them it was easy to take refuge in some noble supporter's castle in the *contado*, or move to a neighbouring city where things for the moment were easier, and they could always return before long: after the murder of the papal *podesta* Peter Parenzo at Orvieto there was a popular reaction, more than two hundred nobles were charged with complicity in the deed, and the heretics were driven from the town, but they remained entrenched, influential there throughout the century; they led an assault on the monastery of St Ufficio in 1239, and the inquisition condemned eighty members of Orvietan noble families in 1269.[66]

The first Cathars, Mark, Joseph and John the Jew, were humble men, a grave-digger, a smith and a weaver, and travelling artisans and petty merchants and pedlars were the primary agents of dissemination, partly because these were occupations that might support and disguise the itinerant evangelist. Most of the Cathar bishoprics were associated with villages of the *contado* rather than with the cities themselves – Concorezzo in the *contado* of Milan, Desenzano of Verona, Bagnolo of Mantua – but since the inquisitors rarely looked beyond the city walls there is nothing to indicate what success the heretics had with the rural population.[67] In the cities they penetrated every class including the highest. The biographer of St Peter Martyr was right when he complained that they were 'not only numerous but strong in secular power':[68] Viterbo elected a believer as chamberlain and two others as consuls as early as 1205, and several *podestas* are known to have been believers, including the one who presided over the beating up of the inquisitor Roland of Cremona at Piacenza in 1233. Their success was so universal and the society of the cities so fluid, so marked by overlapping of class,

family, function and wealth, that it is difficult to generalize about
their support. Certainly it was widespread among the traditional
artisan and small trading groups, and in some places among notaries,
but it was the nobles who were presented as the supporters of heresy
par excellence. The sixty who were burned at Verona in 1233 were
typical in containing members of almost every noble family; ten
years later they could claim members in all the great Florentine
families, and the story was repeated wherever the inquisitors went:
at Orvieto it was said that the words noble and heretic were synonymous.[69]

The rhetoric of the inquisitors as well as the interconnections
between all the privileged groups makes it hazardous to lean heavily
on the constant appearance of noble involvement with heresy, and,
as in Toulouse it was also the nobles who often took the lead in the
companies and confraternities of Jesus Christ, the Blessed Virgin or
the Holy Spirit which were organized everywhere to be vigilant
against the heretics and usurers, sodomites or whatever other group
it was thought appropriate to connect with them.[70] That point,
however, permits the tentative suggestion that, as in Toulouse, the
chief beneficiaries of change, merchants and money-lenders, often of
newer stock, appear less conspicuously in the records of dissent than
those whose wealth and influence they were overtaking. If it is
difficult to relate enthusiasm for heresy closely to membership of one
class rather than another it would be naïve to attempt to relate it to
causes. Ghibelline lords often protected the Cathars but anti-
imperialist Milan was the acknowledged capital of heresy. Difference
of religious affiliation could easily join and reinforce divisions which
it had not created, and become a means of expressing other hostili-
ties: the nobles of Brescia when accused of persecuting Catholics in
1225 replied indignantly that they had been divided into factions for
years, and had defended their towers not as heretics but 'as members
of their party'.[71]

Both in the Languedoc and in Lombardy the extreme diffusion of
governmental power and the rapidity of social change created
conditions ideal for the establishment of heretical sects. In neither
can Catharism be said to have caused political or social conflict, nor

can its adherents be identified with those who most wished to alter the established order. On the contrary, if there is a suggestion of any such correlation it is the opposite, that Catharism, like the orthodox enthusiasm of the friars and the vigilantes, appealed most to those who had reason to be dissatisfied with the results of change, either spiritually because they saw accepted moral values eroded by the love of money, or socially because they found their own traditional status and influence eroded by the money-makers. It is therefore worth observing that in spite of its theological radicalism (which in fact began to be blunted by some Cathar theologians in the thirteenth century, as when the Concorezzan Desiderius taught that Christ's miracles were real, and that he was incarnated and resurrected in a body of true flesh, or when the Albanensian John of Lugio accepted the truth of the whole Bible, though he held that it recorded events in another world[72]) established Catharism was in some ways a comparatively conservative religion. The charismatic force and fervour of Cathar preachers cannot now be compared with that of their Waldensian and orthodox opponents, but it can hardly have exceeded it. More important, although Catharism emphasized total bodily purity for the *perfecti*, the route which it offered to salvation was not the agonized inner search for the divine, the spiritual athleticism and lonely personal endeavour of the evangelist strain of contemporary orthodoxy and the older heresies, but the exact and impersonal observance of prescribed ritual and regulation. In considering why it was the Cathars who brought the heretical challenge to the Roman church to its highest pitch, and what was the nature of that challenge, therefore, it would be unwise to assume that it succeeded because it offered the most radical alternative.

Part Three | *Ramparts Against These Savage Beasts*

Chapter IX | *Elucidations and Reactions*

The first problem which the discovery of heresy among the unlearned presented was intellectual. No comprehension and no response were possible without the help of some analysis of what it was and where it came from. When Ralph Glaber attributed the 'madness' of Vilgard of Ravenna and Leutard of Vertus to the operation of dreams he adopted a familiar explanation of the inexplicable vagaries of human conduct. As Marc Bloch remarked, 'no psychoanalyst has ever examined dreams more closely than the monks of the tenth or eleventh century'[1]; dreams were the instruments through which God communicated his designs to man and Satan plotted to seduce him. Bishop Gerard of Cambrai pointed to a more precise and therefore more satisfactory source of comprehension when he used St Paul's prophecy of the last times as the basis of his interrogation in 1025, and inaugurated the long tradition of assuming that the two aberrations which it specified, of forbidding to marry and abstaining from meats, would characterize clandestine sectaries. Most of the heretics of the eleventh century were not formidable enough to require a more elaborate analysis than St Paul provided. Action was taken to speak louder than words, and their examination concluded by putting them to some concrete test of their obedience to the church, whether they would abjure their heresy at Monforte, endorse a confession of faith at Arras, kill a chicken at Goslar. A readiness to suppose that these heretics were the same as others who had troubled the church in the past was intimated by Adhémar of Chabannes when he called them 'Manichees', as by Anselm of Liège who said that Mani was their heresiarch and compared Henry III's treatment of them with Maximus' of the Priscillianists, and by Wazo who found them 'guilty of the Arian sacrilege'.

The names of the great heresiarchs of antiquity conjured both the destructive power of heresy to shatter the unity of the church – to rend the garment of Christ, as William the Monk put it – and the majesty and authority of the fathers who had joined and defeated it in battle. Their invocation against modern heresies did not imply any systematic comparison of the new tenets with the old, nor any but the most general presumption that the one was descended from the other. To be most readily countered a heresy was best shown to be both new and old, to embody doctrines and precepts that were unsanctioned by the traditional interpretation of the scriptures, and at the same time to be already condemned by the immense storehouse of patristic thought which constituted the principal bulwark of orthodoxy.[2] Wazo demonstrated the technique clearly when, amplifying his point that 'the heresy of the people you write about is clear and was discussed of old by the fathers of the church', he described as Arian the Manichaean condemnation of the eating of meat, and then rebutted it by discussing the interpretation of the commandment 'thou shalt not kill', which was not the Manichaean justification of that position, but the one which had been adopted by the people with whom he was in fact concerned. Wazo was a learned man, perfectly capable of distinguishing the tenets of one heresy from another if it had been relevant to his purpose, and no doubt he would have done if he had been confronted by a learned heresy. All that was needed on this occasion was a general demonstration that the Bishop of Châlons ought to take action against the *idiotae et infacundi* who were holding secret meetings in his diocese, and a broad indication of the lines upon which their teachings could be most effectively refuted.

The persistent assumption of eleventh-century observers that heretics held doctrines more elaborate than they admitted, notably the denial of matrimony and the mass, indicates that they drew upon a preconceived model of heresy more consistently than their occasional use of patristic labels suggests. Its principal components, however, were derived from St Paul's prophecy rather than from Arianism or Manichaeism, and also owed much to the coherence of orthodoxy itself, since it was easy to suppose that what so patently stood together would also fall together. Guibert of Nogent was the first to go beyond name-dropping to the categorical assertion that a new heresy was the same as that of Mani, and his analysis did not become general until much later, after Eckbert of Schönau had used Augustine's writings to arrive at a systematic understanding of the teachings of the Cathars whom he had met; it had not occurred to Eberwin of Steinfeld, St Bernard or the canons of Liège in 1145 to do so. The existence of the generalized assumption that the new heresies were revivals of the old makes it easy to underestimate Eckbert's achievement. In his time there was still a good deal of confusion as to the nature of the enemy, illustrated for example by St Bernard's complaint that the heretics of whom Eberwin had written to him had no proper heresiarch after whom their sect could be called, and by the fact that the formula of abjuration which was required from Peter Maurand had been devised for the wholly different heresy of Berengar of Tours more than a century since, while the one which was presented to the Waldensians a few years later was only slightly adapted from a very ancient formula which Gerbert of Aurillac had been asked to subscribe when he was consecrated as archbishop of Rheims in 991.[3] Eckbert's use of the Manichaean model differed from that of Guibert and his other predecessors in one important way. He really was writing about a new heresy, and one which was in many ways genuinely susceptible to the analysis which he applied. Catharism had much in common with Manichaeism, although the similarities were the result not, as he thought, of direct descent but of common exposure to widespread religious traditions and recurring social conditions. If his model misled him in some details, of which the most important was his belief in the presence of absolute dualism, it also enabled him to arrive at a clear understanding of the nature of the new heresy which was confirmed in its essentials by the much later and more sub-stantially grounded discoveries of the inquisitors. Even so only Anselm of Alessandria among his successors felt like him that a historical as well as a doctrinal affiliation was worth stating at any length, and though Cathars were quite often referred to as Manichees it was used much less commonly from the 1170s than *Patarini*, which was treated as synonymous both with *Cathari*, the only universal term, and *Publicani* which still appeared occasionally. That from the same period *Ariani* also came to refer specifically to the Cathars expresses a good deal about the implications of all these appellations.[4] The Manichees like the Cathars denied the incarna-tion of Christ, while the Arians held that he had succeeded God the Father in time: from the orthodox point of view, therefore, both seemed to belittle Christ and hence to be equally dangerous enemies of the Christian faith. As the Cathars became pre-eminent among its modern antagonists it seemed appropriate to call them by the names of their most sinister predecessors, less to point to a historical des-cent or an identity of doctrine than to make clear the scale and seriousness of the threat which they offered.

When William the Monk rebuked Henry of Lausanne for attacking confession to priests, in the only sustained passage of personal invective in the debate, he used these words:

> You too are a leper, scarred by heresy, excluded from communion by the judgement of the priest, according to the law, bare-headed with ragged clothing, your body covered by an infected and filthy garment; it befits you to shout unceasingly that you are a leper, a heretic and unclean, and must live alone outside the camp, that is to say outside the church.[5]

The physical image was a compelling one, for the heretical preachers with their haggard and tattered appearance and their voices hoarse with passion must have borne a striking resemblance to the lepers who wandered through the countryside in growing numbers in

Henry's time, the objects of increasing fear. It was also more than an image, and more than an example of the conventional exegesis of the sanitary prescriptions of Leviticus as an allegory of spiritual infirmity. For the early middle ages a metaphor widely used by the fathers had become a firm identification. The Donation of Constantine, forged towards the end of the eighth century, began with a description of his conversion to Christianity and his recovery from leprosy at the intercession of Pope Silvester I, the two events in reality one.[6] When Rhabanus Maurus classified disease and vice a little later according to the imbalances of the humours from which both resulted, he said flatly that 'lepers are heretics blaspheming against Jesus Christ'. In the twelfth century the language of leprosy and its symptoms were applied to heresy with great regularity: Guibert said that the people of Soissons burned Clement and Everard *quorum ne propagaretur carcinus*, Jonas of Cambrai was 'a putrid member of the body of Christ' – the phrase was taken by Gratian from St Jerome[7] – the Council of Tours said that the new heresy spread *more cancri*, and Raymond of Toulouse in his letter of 1177 that *haec putrida tabes praevaluit*: the *tabes* were leprous sores, and when they became putrid, according to the prevailing diagnosis, death was inevitable.

This language, used in almost every account of popular heresy in the twelfth century, provided the key to a systematic understanding of what heresy was and how it worked. Heresy was a *pestis*, which was defined by Isidore of Seville as 'an infection which when it catches one man quickly spreads to many', transmitted so rapidly because the poisoned breath of its carrier polluted the air and thence found its way to the *viscera* of the next victim; thus Henry left Le Mans 'to infect other regions with his viper's breath', Raymond V said that the heresy of the Cathars had penetrated the *viscera* of Toulouse, and Rainer Sacchoni linked the mode of its transmission to its original source when he spoke of 'the poison which they drink from the mouth of the ancient serpent'. In addition to these the heresies of Tanchelm, Peter of Bruys, Eon de l'étoile, the *Publicani* at Arras, Oxford and Rheims, the Cathars at Orvieto, are all described as a *pestis*: the idea is invoked with far greater regularity than any association with ancient heresies. Leprosy, a term which covered any malady that showed itself by scabs, ulcers and tumours on the skin, including erysipelas, elephantiasis and syphilis, was increasingly believed at this time to be extremely contagious, and it was held to be congenital and sexually transmitted, and to make its victim exceptionally libidinous. Thus the diagnosis would explain why heresy ran in families, and was consistent with the orgiastic behaviour which tradition attributed to heretics. Tanchelm and Henry were accused of converting women by sleeping with them, Peter the Venerable was worried about the *dogmatis semina* of Peter of Bruys, and Henry, the heretics found at Liège in 1145 and the *Publicani* at Oxford were all accused of spreading the *virus*, which Isidore defines as seminal fluid, of their heresy.

The identification of heresy with leprosy is an index of the growing fear of both. Leprosy was not unknown in the early middle ages. The earliest law codes had prescribed the segregation of lepers, but it was certainly not universally enforced. At the beginning of the twelfth century lepers might still be found living freely among the uninfected, but there was a growing determination to confine them to the leper houses which were founded in enormous numbers (though many were general infirmaries and charitable institutions) and to the leper villages which proliferated even more universally. Legal disabilities, especially in relation to inheritance and landholding became more severe until by the middle of the thirteenth century, if not sooner, the leper was treated as being legally dead. Present knowledge of medieval leprosy is insufficient to determine whether this rising hostility was caused by a real increase of leprosy, or of other diseases which were confused with it, or whether it owed more to less objective stimulants. But the course of reaction to heresy ran parallel. In the eleventh century the language of disease was used of it only by Ralph Glaber and Paul of St Père of Chartres in his account of the clerks of Orléans, and to him it was probably suggested by the same patristic source which informed him that their secret meetings were enlivened by orgies and summonings of the devil: in this too he was unusual, for though the doctrinal aberrations of the eleventh-century heretics were commonly exaggerated they were not accused of lewd or scandalous behaviour. Tanchelm and Henry of Lausanne, with their ferocious appearance and demeanour suggestive of madness, their capacity to inflame the humours of large crowds, especially of the poor, and to disseminate their error with mysterious rapidity, aroused more deep-seated anxiety, as did the earliest Catharism which appeared unpredictably and travelled far and wide – just like leprosy, said Eckbert of Schönau. When the establishment of the Cathar churches and of the inquisition gave a greater reality to the enemy and a more substantial knowledge of its nature the image became less important, but the same associations lingered. If it was the forbidding of marriage which directly caused the heretics to be suspected of lurid sexual aberration, and the name of the Cathars, like that of the lepers, to become synonomous with buggery, and societies to be founded for the suppression of heresy and sodomy in the thirteenth century, the diagnosis of leprosy reinforced it. The same complex of ideas embraced other groups which were the object of increasing social disfavour. The remarkable capacity to anticipate the nastier prejudices of his age which made Guibert of Nogent allege that Clement of Bucy and his followers were both Manichees and carriers of plague also made him one of the first to report that Jews sold themselves to the Devil with the libation of seed and used the powers which they obtained from him to poison Christians, and the Lateran Council of 1215 made Jews wear identifying dress (as lepers had to do). Usurers like sodomites were inaccurately linked with heretics by the associations which were enthusiastically multiplied for the suppression of both. The elevation of the ideal of apostolic, or voluntary, poverty was similarly accompanied by an increasing nervousness of those who were poor in fact, who were invariably though not always accurately supposed to be the chief disciples of the heretics, and one writ of Henry II used *leprosi* as a synonym for beggars and vagabonds.

This tangled nightmare of association and assumption was part of the background against which the authorities of church and state worked out their response to the growing problem of heresy. It was only one of the forces which seemed to threaten the security of Christian society, but just as the fearful always exaggerated the coherence of the threat which the heretics themselves presented the web of common attitudes and responses to other sources of anxiety shows how, both consciously and subconsciously, they also tended to assume that all their enemies were in reality the same one. One measure of the growing horror of leprosy was the way in which for a Hugh of Lincoln or a St Francis the care of lepers, a willingness to touch them, to wash their wounds and kiss their sores was an unmistakable attribute of sanctity, and like them Robert of Arbrissel had shown, by his devotion to the poor, to lepers and to preaching, that the physical and moral aspects of these infirmities were indissolubly linked, redemption of their bodily and mental ills a single mission. The implications of the identification for heresy are best displayed in William of Newburgh's account of the *publicani* who came to England.[8] He told, it will be recalled, a balanced and factually scrupulous story, whose exactness reveals, for example, that the accused did not subscribe to the docetist heresy. Yet it uses the language of disease more completely than any other source. England had remained free, until now, of the *pestis* which infected so many lands, the *Publicani* came to England 'in order to propagate the infection', they met with little success but those who did succumb 'were so deeply infected by the disease' as to become resistant to all correction, the bishops denounced them 'lest the seed (*virus*) of the heresy should be spread more widely', and thanks to the severity of the treatment 'the kingdom of England was cleansed of the infection'. The nature of the treatment is equally interesting: the heretics were driven from the city, all men were forbidden to assist them, and they died in the winter's cold, and the houses in which they had lived were dragged outside the city and burned, as the belongings of lepers would be lest they harboured the infection.[9]

By canonical definition heresy must be openly avowed and stubbornly defended to deserve the name, and its detection therefore posed no difficulty in principle. The charges with which the bishops of the eleventh and early twelfth centuries dealt were invariably of propagating, not simply of holding, heretical opinions. In many cases, and especially those where the heresy in question began by attacking the corruption of the clergy, its discovery presented no problems and there is no difficulty in discerning how it came to the knowledge of the bishop concerned. As the fear of heresy increased, however, an ambivalence which had always been present in the modes by which heretics came to trial became more pronounced, and the transition from accusatory to inquisitorial procedures which had been completed by the later decades of the twelfth century was hastened. There was an inherent contradiction between the requirement of open avowal and biblical predictions that the heretics of the last times would act in secret, which was reflected, for example, in the accusation of Roger II of Châlons that those of whom he complained to Wazo of Liège both conducted secret meetings and propagated their doctrines openly. Nevertheless for the first century or more the canon predominated over the prophecy. The clerks of Orléans were uniquely unfortunate in being infiltrated by the enthusiastic Aréfast, a layman acting on his own initiative and without the knowledge of the diocesan, although he had the approval of the king of France and the precentor of Chartres. That such a tactic was necessary proves that the clerks did not attempt public proselytization. In this they differed from their contemporaries and successors who were charged with heresy. There were differences of degree: the community at Monforte came to Archbishop Aribert's attention by rumour, and are not said to have attempted to preach to the populace at large until after they had been arrested, while evangelistic fervour accompanied by the maximum of publicity was inseparable from the career of a Tanchelm or a Henry from its outset, but until their time some circumstantial justification at least accompanied each charge of propagating error. The first victims of the pure spirit of Grundyism were perhaps the group found at Liège in 1135, for until then it is unusual even for a very short account to contain no suggestion of public evangelism. The case of the Cathars who were burned at Cologne in 1163 is clearer: they 'came to Cologne from Flanders, and stayed secretly in a barn near the city. But when they did not go to church on Sunday they were found out by their neighbours. . .'[10] The *Publicani* of Rheims were similarly unfortunate in owing their discovery not to any obtrusive enthusiasm on their own part but to the reluctance of one of their followers to be seduced by Gervase of Tilbury, and though William of Newburgh respected convention in accusing those who came to England of propagating their faith the single old woman whom they converted is so modest a trophy as to suggest that it was really the 'enquiries' of 'certain curious men' which he mentions that led to their discovery, and that their ill fortune had its origins in neighbourly curiosity.

The growth of popular vigilance accompanied, and may have been stimulated by, an increasing readiness of the church to counter the threat of heresy with all the weapons at its command.[11] If there had been no doubt in theory since ancient times that some kinds of heresy at least, and particularly that of the Manichees, might be visited by the death penalty, it had in practice ceased to be a problem to such an extent that the canonical collection of Burchard of Worms, composed between 1008 and 1012, did not concern itself with the punishment of heresy at all, and its resurgence in the following decades was met by a considerable degree of uncertainty. Certainly it was the bishop's duty to deal with heresy in his diocese, but how he should do so was not clear. If an accusation reached him he would investigate it by examining the accused about their beliefs, but not until the twelfth century, and then irregularly, are witnesses described as having been produced to attest this activity. If the heresy was admitted but not recanted the bishop's responsibility was in effect ended. He had the option of handing the convicted heretic over to the secular power for punishment, but he was not categorically instructed to use it until the Council of Rheims in 1157. Before that an aggressive lay authority like Robert I in 1022, the *majores* of Milan in 1028 or Henry III in 1052 might step in and assume the right of punishment, and if the bishop, like Aribert, did not approve of the sentence he did not contest the right to determine it. In the absence of such intervention excommunication and expulsion from the diocese were the most general resorts, though the Archbishop of Utrecht imprisoned Tanchelm, and Lisiard of Soissons held Clement and Everard of Bucy while he sought further advice. In 1144 the canons of Liège – the diocese of Wazo, who had so strongly deprecated the use of physical coercion against heretics – dispersed those whom they had rescued from a mob intent on burning them in various religious houses while they sent one to Rome for examination and awaited a papal ruling.

Until this time Wazo's view that the church had no business with blood on its hands, even indirectly, continued to govern ecclesiastical reaction to heresy, although it could scarcely continue to be felt for long after the pontificates of Alexander II, Gregory VII and Urban II that bloodshed was invariably obnoxious in the sight of God. The understandable regret of St Norbert's biographer that no prince or magistrate would dare to kill Tanchelm was a lesser sign of changing attitudes than Peter the Venerable's urging of the recipients of his treatise against the Petrobrusians that though conversion was preferable to coercion they should not hesitate to invoke the help of secular princes if persuasion failed, or St Bernard's remark of the perpetrators of the burnings of Cologne in 1143 which the local clergy had tried to prevent that 'we must applaud their zeal though we cannot approve their action'.[12] In 1148 the Council of Rheims handed the followers of Eon de l'étoile to the secular arm and they were burned on the first occasion on which it must be presumed, though it is not recorded, that the action was endorsed by the deliberate approval of the church as a whole, and although when Arnold of Brescia was executed by Barbarossa a few years later with papal approval the charge was not heresy but rebellion, there is no question that in reality he was a victim of the substitution of physical for spiritual power which he had devoted himself so strenuously to opposing.

The executions of the Eonites and Arnold of Brescia mark a watershed in the church's attitude the more decisively because they did not break new legal ground. The Councils held by Leo IX at Rheims in 1048 and by Victor II at Toulouse in 1056 had called for heretics and their supporters to be excommunicated, the Council of Montpellier in 1062 demanded that the secular princes should use their powers, and the Council of Toulouse in 1119, presided over by Calixtus II, made it explicit that excommunication should be followed by punishment by the secular arm in a canon which was repeated by the Lateran Council of 1139. In fact, however, this course had been followed on no occasion since Aribert of Milan had done so in 1025, while as we have just noted there were several occasions during that period when ecclesiastical authorities found themselves in possession of convicted heretics and unsure what to do with them. The incident which makes the point most strikingly, since it concerns so notorious a heretic, is that of the Council of Pisa in 1135 which condemned

Henry of Lausanne but handed him over not to the secular arm but to a monastery. There is too little information on these decisions to allow profitable speculation on the reasoning which lay behind them; it may be that the difference lay in some expression of repentance which Geoffrey of Auxerre hints that Henry had made, and which the Eonites and Arnold certainly refused, while the Eonites had also committed violent assault upon monasteries and religious. Nevertheless the contrasting treatments do signify a change in the atmosphere in which the decisions were made, and point to a distinct hardening of attitudes during the 1140s; if the function of coercion was still *correctionis vel admonitionis cause* there was at the least a diminishing reluctance to abandon condemned heretics to whatever fate the princes should think appropriate.

Another long step was taken by the Council of Rheims in 1157.[13] It was now ordered that suspected adherents of the *secta Manichaeorum* who were described in such bitter terms should be arrested by whoever might discover them, that their assertions should be tested by the ordeal by hot iron, by the extraction of a confession or by the testimony of witnesses, and that their *majores* should be sentenced to perpetual imprisonment if not to graver punishment while the followers, if released, were to be branded on the forehead and cheek.

The reference to the *majores*, whose functions had been clearly described by the canons of Liège in 1145, makes this look very much like a response to the Cathar missionaries who were active in the north by now, and the change in treatment which was envisaged was important. Not only were harsher punishments and a more severe form of the ordeal than had generally been employed in such cases prescribed, but the function of the bishop was changed. Formerly he had investigated reports of heresy which reached him; now he was to be the recipient of the accused themselves, who might be captured on the initiative of curious or malicious laymen, well on the way to the position of the inquisitors whose business was to search out heresy on the premise that any failure on the part of the heretics to advertise their presence only confirmed the danger which was represented by their secrecy. It was because of the secrecy that the Council of Tours in 1163 ordered bishops and priests to forbid Catholics to assist or even communicate with those who were 'known to be followers of this heresy'. When at the instruction of the papal legate to Toulouse in 1178 'the bishop and certain of the clergy, the consuls of the city and some other faithful men who had not been touched by any rumour of heresy were made to give us in writing the names of everyone they knew who had been or might in the future become members or accomplices of the heresy, and to leave out nobody at all for love or money' the inquisitorial procedure was to all intents and purposes complete.

In the course of this evolution the greatest enthusiasm for repression had come not from the bishops and local clergy but from secular magnates and, after the reform, the papacy. The general reasons for mounting papal interest are clear enough. This was an obvious theatre for the exercise of the leadership of the western church whose assertion was both the premise and the principal consequence of the papal reform, itself forged in the battle against the *simoniaca haeresis*, and it became increasingly the appropriate level of response as heresy became less a local problem: the Pope could scarcely be content with the bishop's standard remedy of driving the heretic into the next diocese. The area in which papal policy evolved, long before the appearance of the Cathars, was the Languedoc. The vacuum of secular authority left by the disintegration of the Carolingian monarchy had exposed the church to the depredations of ambitious feudatories even more in that region than elsewhere and as early as the middle of the tenth century it turned habitually to the papacy for support, calling successfully for the condemnation of usurpations and the defence of churchmen against their recalcitrant neighbours. When Henry of Clairvaux went to Albi in 1178 to deliver the bishop from the cellars of Roger of Béziers he followed precedent, for the bishop of Limoges had owed his liberty to papal intervention a century and a half before. This link between the papacy and the Languedoc was greatly strengthened by the presence of Cluny, which developed its order there from the middle of the tenth century, depending heavily on papal support and grants of immunity from episcopal jurisdiction, and in return propagating respect for St Peter and his vicar.[14] The appearance of popular heresy in the eleventh century allowed the Capetians and the Emperor to show that they would protect the church against it. The Duke of Aquitaine had undertaken the same role when he summoned the Council of Charroux in 1020 to call upon the bishops and abbots to act against the heretics, but neither his nor any other power in the region was effective. When the Councils of Toulouse in 1056 and 1119 and of Montpellier in 1062 declared heretics excommunicate and summoned the secular power to act against them, therefore, the popes were not only forging the weapons of the future, but observing the traditional policy of their predecessors in lending the authority of their office to support the church in the Languedoc against its oppressors. Peter the Venerable's writing against Peter of Bruys may also be seen as an expression of the responsibility which his order had long exercised in the Languedoc, and his retirement from the lists in favour of St Bernard as one acknowledgement that Cîteaux had now taken over some of the functions which Cluny had once performed as the protector of the faith and the proponent of papal leadership in the church.

St Bernard's mission, which did so much to pioneer the paths of coercion, also represented therefore the continuation of an older tradition by which the papal and monastic leaders of the western church endeavoured to compensate in this region for the deficiencies of the lay authority. Hence Bernard was particularly anxious to deprive Henry and his followers of the support of secular notables, and his secretary reported as his main achievements the agreement which he secured in Toulouse that Henry's associates would be denied access to the courts and assisted *neque in convivio neque in commercio*, and the partially successful attempt to undermine the acceptance which the heretic had won from the knights of the countryside. As the canon of the Council of Toulouse in 1119 had been reiterated for the whole church at the Lateran in 1139 so Bernard's concern was picked up and given legal form at Rheims in 1148 when it was ordained that no succour must be given to the heresiarchs of Gascony and Provence 'or elsewhere' and their disciples, on pain of anathema for individual offenders and interdict for their lands.

The process was repeated thirty years later by Bernard's successor in both his capacities, Henry of Clairvaux. The mission of 1178 had further developed the methods of inquisition to attack the patrons of heresy in Toulouse, and at Béziers had been shocked to realize its strength in the countryside. Henry of Clairvaux inspired the legislation of the third Lateran Council in the following year which denounced the insolence of the heretics, their protectors and the mercenaries, insisted that there should be no dealings of any kind with them, and proclaimed as the penalties of persistence not only excommunication but the dissolution of feudal bonds and liability to the confiscation of lands and goods. Where Bernard had been disappointed in his hope that the *midi* might become the object of a 'great work of preaching' Henry was not. The Council pronounced heresy in the region the fitting goal of a crusade and granted indulgences and the spiritual protection of the Holy See to those who would go there to defend the faith. In 1181 the eloquence of Henry of Clairvaux was rewarded by the recruitment of an army which, as legate, he led to the Languedoc to lay siege to the castle of Lavaur and secure the delivery to him of Raymond de Baimac and Bernard Raimundi, the Cathar leaders who had defied the mission of 1178 under the protection of the safe conduct which Peter of St Chrysogonus had granted so unwillingly.[15] It was a taste of what would come when the Count of Toulouse could no longer maintain his precarious balance between the pertinacity of his subjects, the rapacity of his neighbours and the zeal of the papacy.

The experience won in the Languedoc was distilled into a final solution at Verona in 1184.[16] There, under the joint patronage of Pope and Emperor, the decree *Ad abolendam* unveiled the counter to the menace of heresy. An exhaustive list of heresies, headed by that of the Cathars, was condemned and to their number added in general terms all who dared to preach without the authority of the Holy See or the bishop, whose beliefs departed from the Roman tradition, whose bishop had excommunicated them as heretics, and all who protected heretics. Bishops and archbishops were commanded either in person or through a competent deputy to visit once or twice a year every parish where the presence of heresy was suspected, and in each to place three or more reputable people on oath to denounce all those whom they knew or suspected to be heretics:

refusal of the oath would itself be incriminating. Those who were identified by this means were to be examined and required to abjure heresy on pain of anathema; among the guilty the opportunity of renunciation would be offered to clerks, but laymen were immediately to be handed to the secular arm for punishment. Holders of secular office, counts, barons, consuls or *podestas* who failed in their duty would be excommunicated in their turn, deposed and deprived of the attributes of personal freedom, their right to plead in court, to give evidence, to hold public office; towns which sheltered heretics would be subjected to commercial boycott and deprived of their episcopal see if they had one; the fiefs of heretics and their suspected supporters were declared forfeit and their lands placed under interdict; and for the glory of God and the suppression of heresy this decree was to be published by bishops and archbishops on every feast day and solemn occasion, on pain of three years' suspension from their office.

The origins of these penalties and procedures were various and sometimes ancient, but their combination and application reflected the experience of successive attempts to counter heresy in the Languedoc, not so much because it was especially prone to infection as because the special responsibility which the papacy had long felt towards it made it the place where the problems of heresy were first confronted and, in the vacuum of secular authority, most recalcitrant. The same factors which made it a haven for heretics in the second half of the twelfth century also made it a laboratory of repression, then and for a long time to come.

The formation of papal policy and the evolution of inquisitorial procedures have long been stressed, but another technique for the trial of heretics, that by ordeal, was more widely used than has always been recognized. In its most notorious forms it was confined to comparatively few cases when Dominic William was made to say a mass and Clement of Bucy and the *Publicani* of Vézelay were subjected to the ordeal by water. To these should be added, however, other occasions on which the two prime characteristics of trial by ordeal appear, the submission of the accused to a test which involved the invocation of divine judgement, and the public character of the trial. Thus, before the men of Arras were examined by Bishop Gerard they were confined for three days beforehand and the bishop ordered the monks and clerks to fast on the day before the examination; these were the ordinary preliminaries to the appeal to divine judgement, so that when at the end of their examination the accused were required to make a solemn oath that they abjured what had been condemned and believed what had been pronounced orthodox, and to sign a confession of faith with their cross, their trial was given the character of ordeal, as was that of Ramihrdus when he was required to affirm his attestation of orthodoxy by hearing a mass, and of Peter Maurand when 'the relics of the saints were produced and a solemn chant sung before he was to affirm the truth of his denials on them, in the presence of a great crowd of clerics and laymen'.

These tests were imposed on every occasion on which those charged with heresy were examined in public and denied the charge, and on no occasion when they were examined only in the presence of clerics and holders of secular office, as for example at Orléans, Monforte, Oxford and Rheims. In short there were two forms of trial, those which involved the community at large and those which did not, and the latter included every occasion when secular magnates controlled the proceedings. There were also two occasions when the examination was public and the heretics confessed and defended their convictions, at Cologne in 1143 and Liège in 1144. Each time the crowd burned the heretics in spite of the efforts of the clergy to protect them.[17]

Churchmen opposed trial by ordeal on the grounds that it was barbarous, irrational, and blasphemous. No doubt it was, but it had another aspect. Contrary to what is often supposed, the ordeal did not supply an unambiguous verdict. When the bandages had been removed after three days there would be scope for argument whether or not the wound had healed cleanly. At Vézelay 'one of [the heretics] was judged by everybody to be saved by the water, though there were some afterwards who cast doubt on the verdict. . .' The argument is unrecorded, but easily imagined: had the man been correctly bound and weighted? did he have to sink like a stone to be 'received' by the water, or could he float beneath the surface? *all* of him beneath? for how long must he sink or float? – and so on. When Dominic William escaped unscathed after perjuring himself at the mass to be killed shortly afterwards when taken in adultery, had he been condemned by his ordeal or not? It was in this area of doubt, in the need for the ordeal to be interpreted, it has been well shown, that its value as a social institution lay.[18] It was intended to test not the truth of the facts alleged, but the character of the witness to them, an appeal in effect to divine oath-helping. During its lengthy preliminaries, the process itself and the appraisal of its result the community, far from passively awaiting divine judgement, provided itself with the opportunity of prolonged and painstaking considera- tion of the case, while the attribution of the judgement to God permitted its acceptance by all.

In this light, popular attacks on heretics reveal a tension between two jurisdictions. It was shown most clearly at Soissons, where the local consensus was clearly established: 'Clement was thrown into the vat and floated like a stick. [Nobody was prepared to argue about *that*.] At this sight the whole church was filled with unbounded joy. . .' When Bishop Lisiard, whose view of the procedure was perhaps indicated by his having asked Guibert of Nogent to examine the accused in private beforehand, set out to ask his fellow bishops what he should do next he was in effect appealing to an alien jurisdic- tion and the united community vindicated its traditional procedure. When Ramihrdus expressed orthodox views on doctrine he satisfied the clerks, but when he refused the mass on the ground that the clerks themselves were corrupt he appeared to the bishop's servants to confess his guilt on the real issue, that of personalities, and to admit that the divine judgement would not support him: they acted accordingly. When the public nature of the interrogations at Cologne and Liège placed them by implication in the same juridical frame- work the confessions rendered ordeal unnecessary and the hesitation of the clerks to act provoked the same response.

What trial by ordeal tested was not whether the accused had infringed the laws of church and state but what action the community wished to take in the light of what was believed about his character and actions. That is why it was attacked by those who struggled, no doubt for the most enlightened reasons, to impose their universal law. Although it had worked out well for the church in these cases it was potentially a very hazardous process in relation to popular heresy, since it offered the prospect of escape even to an avowed heretic if he commanded public sympathy: the more dangerous he was to the church the less probably would he be convicted. If it cannot be discerned whether any such force sustained Dominic William when he braved his thunderbolt it is worth recalling that Albero of Mercke, whose critic testified that he was held in great affection and respect by his parishioners, offered to undergo the ordeal – the offer seems not to have been accepted – and that the *publicani* at Vézelay had been put to it at their own request: they were condemned, but perhaps less certainly than they would have been if the prelates had proceeded unaided. These appeals suggest not an anachronistically sophisticated or cynical appraisal of the process but an instinct to prefer long-established communal procedure to the cold and remote judgement of the clerks. Hence while it might be in the church's interest to urge the laity to lay charges against those suspected of heresy it could hardly be so, in the long run, to encourage public participation in the trial. A failure to make that distinction probably explains the prescription of the ordeal by the Council of Rheims in 1157, an aberration of papal policy which was not repeated, and was brought to an end when the Fourth Lateran Council forbade the performance of the ceremony of purification which was the ordeal's indispensable preliminary. Innocent III could hardly say, as William Rufus did when a group of Kentishmen blandly insisted that the hands of some Saxons accused of theft had positively benefited from the application of the heated iron, 'Is God a just judge? Damn whoever thinks it! He will answer for this by my just judgement and not by God's, which can be folded this way and that as anyone wants it.'[19] Nevertheless the dissemination of popular heresy was a singularly pertinent reminder of the urgency of placing the power of judgement securely in reliably orthodox hands.

Under papal leadership the church evolved a coherent counter to the threat of popular heresy in the same decades when the Cathars, who would realize that threat most persistently and ubiquitously, appeared, settled, and organized their congregations in western Europe. The coincidence was largely accidental. The reaction, both in analysis and in devising means to undo the successes of the heretics, to deter their patrons, root out their adherents, and secure their conviction, was formed in part by the church's own long history and heritage, and partly by its immediate experience of two quite distinct, though overlapping, phases of western heresy, those of the native anti-clerical preachers and the Cathars, neither of which owed anything directly to the other. That the discontinuity of heresy was not clearly recognized certainly did not hinder, and very probably assisted, the continuity of response.

Chapter X | *The Challenge of Dissent*

The history and teachings of the heresies which we have rehearsed tell a tale of fragmentation. In different places and circumstances they appeared ostensibly for different reasons. Eventually a few succeeded in evolving doctrine and organization which could be sustained over a wide area of Europe, and from generation to generation, but most of them were the work of personal leaders, and faded and withered when their inspiration passed on to another place, or another life. Although society did not wholly fail to recognize this discontinuity it treated heresy as a single enemy, and secular and ecclesiastical potentates settled to the task of decapitation confident that all the heads belonged to one monster. The monster had being, in the form of a concept of heresy whose essential unity was not diminished by the diversity of its manifestations, but it remains to consider a question which would have appealed to the schoolmen, whether it also had reality outside the perceptions of its observers, and did in fact confront church and society with any general challenge.

The variety of the heresies and the circumstances of their appearance itself excludes some of the more obvious possibilities. It need not be laboured further that they were not descendants, survivals or revivals of Manichaeism or of any other ancient heresy or cult. By the time any significant influence from outside contemporary western Europe materialized, in the middle of the twelfth century, a native tradition of dissent was firmly established, and if the Bogomil missionaries passed their theology and organization to some of its votaries to give birth to Catharism others continued from time to time to part ways with the church in pursuit of ideals which owed nothing to any alien source. The interpretation which regards the heresies as that part of the continuing crusade for reform of the church and religious life whose enthusiasm exceeded its discretion has much more to commend it. Reformers and heretics, moved by the same indignations, the same impatience and frustration, the same ideal of apostolic purity and of the disentanglement of the church and its mission from the ties of worldly corruption, were undeniably 'protagonists on the same stage' and the welcome that the Cathars received is partly attributable to their having provided a 'philosophical superstructure' which might give form and structure to dissent already both endemic and articulate.[1]

The recognition of that truth has contributed immeasurably to the understanding of these movements; it is not too much to say that it has made them intelligible. Yet in doing so it poses another and intractable question. That a few heretics are not explicable in these terms is no obstacle: it is not too much to concede that any society may produce individuals like the clerks of Orléans or Eon whose motives and convictions remain beyond the reach of systematic inquiry. On the whole the picture of religious enthusiasm in the twelfth century and of its eleventh-century antecedents is one of great coherence in respect of the ideals and personalities of its leaders, the models and principles which inspired them, and the criticisms of contemporary institutions which they made in consequence. The ever deeper and ever more bitter rift which appeared between the orthodox and the heretical is therefore a greater puzzle than is altogether accounted for by the general tendency of enthusiasts and reformers to take themselves and their differences of emphasis too seriously. That Robert of Arbrissel, Bernard of Clairvaux and Francis of Assisi were revered as heroes of the church whose faithful fell over themselves to provide for their followers, while Henry of Lausanne, Arnold of Brescia and Valdès were reviled as the emissaries of Anti-Christ and their disciples hounded and hunted to be visited with increasingly savage penalties, argues either a singular arbitrariness on the part of the church or the existence of some source of division more profound than the niceties of religious doctrine.

Part of the answer, of course, is that for the Christian niceties of doctrine were important, that Christianity 'has always been concerned with right belief as well as right conduct, [that] the Christians' interest in abstract truth led them to try to define it in a system of orthodoxy, and since no definition of truth ever goes unchallenged, the inevitable companion of orthodoxy is dissent',[2] and that those who believed themselves charged with securing the salvation of other men felt compelled to prevent the dissemination of heterodox teachings by whatever means were available. Yet that reflection, doubtless impeccable *sub specie aeternitatis*, does not assist greatly in the explanation of temporal change. Both the incidence of disagreement over theological questions and the nature of reaction to it did change sharply during this period, and what was at stake was not only doctrinal orthodoxy. On the one hand, while the subjects of this book were treated with growing severity the schoolmen who were at least as prolific of heterodox ideas and might have been thought more influential were subjected to less rigorous constraints and less harshly punished when they exceeded them. Equally on the other hand, as we have seen in the cases of Ramihrdus, of Arnold, of Lambert le Bègue for example, it was not necessary to be a heretic to be treated as one both by popular audiences and by the disposers of established authority. Heresy was only an approximate criterion of dissent, and does not wholly explain either its incidence or its reception.

The heterogeneity which excludes the characterization of dissent as the dissemination of particular doctrines also prevents it from being regarded as the prerogative of a particular class. The association of the spread of heresy with the revival of commercial and urban life has a limited significance. That it travelled along the trade routes, which were after all the obvious places to travel, only illustrates its general character as one of the accompaniments of an expanding civilization in which men and with them ideas moved farther and more frequently than they had done formerly. There is no evidence of any notable incidence of heresy among merchants, and if itinerant artisans were more often described as such than other kinds of men it was as probably because the nature of the trade suited their fugitive faith as the other way round. Heresy appeared in the cities because journeys ended in cities, the natural places for those expelled from their diocese or driven by persecution from their homeland to seek shelter, support and an audience. The city was where population was most concentrated, social ties most fluid or most lacking, where grievance and distress could mount most suddenly, and where authority, especially ecclesiastical authority, was most often hampered by conflict; it was therefore where the possibility of attracting a following and holding it together was greatest. To that extent the rise of the towns clearly, and indispensably, assisted that of the heresies, even though they held no particular attraction for the prosperous merchants and bankers who for the most part, while they quarrelled vigorously with the bishops over taxation and government lavished their wealth with the equal vigour of new aspirants to respectability upon 'the innumerable religious foundations with which the cities abounded, the pious and charitable confraternities which were so numerous there'.[3]

The report of Heribert of Périgueux that 'many have joined the sect, including nobles who have relinquished their property as well as clerks, monks, priests and nuns' is as precise a comment as any on the social composition of heresy's following. The habitual description of the heresiarchs as appealing to the rabble, preaching in the gutters, calling the poor around them, may have a tincture of truth but it is purely conventional in character. Among the followers of Ariald, Ramihrdus, Tanchelm and Henry the most clearly identifiable are small tradesmen and artisans, but the Patarenes also numbered notaries, and they, like Henry and Arnold, had knights and clerks among their supporters, and the Cathars enjoyed the patronage of noble families in the Languedoc and in many Italian cities.

The conclusion of the preceding chapters, in short, is that there were circumstances in which heresy might appeal to members of every social group, and that none of them predominated sufficiently to allow an interpretation of it as the ideology of any class. It was not, or not simply, a revolt of the urban poor against nascent capitalism, of the rural poor against the elaboration of seignorial control and exploitation, of women against the growing domination of men, or laymen against the growing domination of churchmen, or of a rising bourgeoisie against ecclesiastical control of their activities and communities.[4] It would be a mistake however, in reaction against such over-general judgements, which have often been inspired by *a priori* expectation more than historical investigation, to abandon out of hand the search for a social explanation. Fixed as their thoughts undoubtedly were upon the next world heretics were not immune to the influence of this one, and they did not die to maintain views which had no meaning in their lives; they did not draw their notions of truth and reality exclusively from the contemplation of the supernatural or even from the study of the scriptures with perceptions and judgements uncontaminated by their daily experience. Heresy was not the reverse side of some other coin, the desire for ascetic purity or political freedom, the resentment of taxation or work in an artisan's shop, but it does not follow that because none of these was always present with it they had no great significance if they were. On the contrary the surviving evidence shows a bewildering variety of such associations because they existed, and shows them irregularly because they were irregular. The threat of heresy, like the power of Catholicism, rested not on the foundation of one force but on the capacity to ally itself with many.

Among those forces, however, one is very frequently suggested by such indications as there are of the kind of people who found heresy attractive. They included members of every class, but at every level the beneficiaries of change are conspicuously less well represented than its victims. The banker Nazarius helped the Patarenes in Milan and Peter Maurand was a leading Cathar in Toulouse, but they were not typical of their class. One reason for that lies in the popular enthusiasm which greeted the conviction and public humiliation of Maurand, which we need not suppose to have been actuated in every case by an unmixed zeal for the vindication of Catholic truth, and in the identification which Valdès made of his religious conversion with the abandonment of his class and way of life. In the cities the heresies found most support among those at whose expense such men as these advanced in wealth, status and power, the small traders and artisans on one side, and the older patrician families on the other. Among the landed aristocracy the indications are similar. The vavassours of Milan were threatened by the archbishops' consolidation of fiefs in the hands of the *capitanei* who were their leading champions, the Roman knights and their brothers in orders were being squeezed from influence by the greater nobles and papal functionaries in the 1140s, the knights and nobles of the countryside around Toulouse and the Albigeois, constantly impoverished by partible inheritance, were gradually deprived by the slow course of reform of their accustomed compensation through the alienation of church lands and rents and the disposition of ecclesiastical office. This does not dispatch whole classes into the category of potential heretics, for social change did not affect all their members in the same way. As elder sons gained at the expense of younger with the spread of primogeniture, churchmen at the expense of laymen with the recovery of tithes or the ending of alienation, commercial incomes on those derived from land rents, the creation and distribution of wealth could create new differences and tensions between those who belonged to the same classes, as they were generally conceived, and even the same families. As Andrew of Sturmi remarked of the Patarenes and the experience of the Cathars would often show, heresy also could be vertically rather than horizontally divisive. We do not endorse any hypothesis of class conflict in remarking that among those most ready to think that there was something wrong with the church were many whose daily experience suggested to them that there was something wrong with the world.

The occasional connection between the appearance of religious dissent and the outbreak of struggle for communal liberty is a case in point. There would be no justification for postulating a close relationship between the two. Most of the communes achieved their creation without any suggestion that freedom from the bishop's temporal lordship implied rejection of his spiritual authority, and heresy could and did find a hearing where there was no civic strife. In fact an exact coincidence was rare. Ramihrdus preached in Cambrai at the time of a communal rising there, the mission to Toulouse in 1145 was followed closely by, and that of 1178 followed closely upon a crisis in the city's relationship with the Count, and Arnold of Brescia was deeply involved in, though he did not in any sense initiate, the Roman revolution. In the last two cases, however, the significance of the heresy was exaggerated by the authorities to strengthen their hand in reasserting political control, and in the last three the chief discernible connection between revolt and dissent was that the one diminished authority's capacity to prevent the preaching of the other. The more common pattern, of Milan, Liège, Le Mans, Vézelay and many others, was for heresy to appear not at the same time, but in the same places where there was conflict between urban communities and their secular or ecclesiastical lords because, as Henry's experience at Le Mans had shown, the two forms of rebellion fed on the same resentments and frustrations.

The case of an episcopal city in the early twelfth century is instructive. After its two archdeacons had been successively elected to the vacant bishopric by different parties among the clergy, and confirmation was refused them because one was a man of violence and the other a notorious lecher, the choice fell upon a royal treasurer, not in priestly orders, from whose ill-gotten gains the clergy hoped to benefit; his election was vigorously opposed by many of the reform-minded, led by the famous and respected master of the cathedral school, and was vindicated by bribery at the papal court; the bishop later refused to excommunicate his brother and other members of the chapter for the murder, in the cathedral, of his most outspoken lay critic. To this is added the embroidery of almost every character in the story by lurid and circumstantial tales of vice and extortion, and that it was the bishop's habit to augment his income by giving judgement in his court, on charges often trumped up by his officers for the purpose, to whoever offered him the largest bribe, and that he used his right of minting to debase the coinage at great profit to himself, and misery to his subjects. Would not a Henry or a Tanchelm, still more an Arnold of Brescia, have expected a warm welcome in such a place for his denunciation of clerical corruption? The conditions are described not by the fervent imagination of an anti-clerical historian, but by an abbot who was closely involved in the events: this is a partial summary of Guibert of Nogent's famous description of the prelude to the communal rising at Laon in 1112.[5] Its value in the search for the roots of heresy is in the reminder that similar causes may have different consequences, and similar grievances find different expression.

The first quality of the man who aroused popular passion and devotion was that he was an outsider.[6] He might have begun to preach in his own parish, but he achieved success, or notoriety, when he moved to another diocese or from the *contado* to the city. His dress and demeanour advertised his separateness, whether like a Robert of Arbrissel or a Henry he donned the tattered garments and animal skins of the hermit or affected grandeur with gold thread in his hair and clothes like Tanchelm, or princely trappings like Eon. In some at least, Ariald, Arnold, the Cathar missionaries, the detachment from the ties and pressures of ordinary life that brought corruption with them was proclaimed as it was by the saints and hermits in conspicuous personal purity, a quality which the chroniclers were always anxious to deny them. By showing themselves set apart from ordinary men in these ways the preachers stimulated the dramatic interest which made the people of Le Mans 'long for [Henry's] meetings all day and every day', and advertised their readiness to bear the burdens of their hearers upon their own shoulders, like the hermit Roger of Huntingdon whose 'compassion on the afflicted and their wretchedness was so great that he could not have borne their miseries more hardly if they had been inflicted on himself'.[7] Moreover dissociation from humanity implied association with divinity, and made a man more able to assist in the resolution of conflict where those directly involved were paralysed by their own interest or suspected interest, or their habitual deference to man or custom. At Le Mans Henry had done far more than preach heresy: he had provided a channel through which the leaderless community could endeavour to dispute the political and economic subjection in which they were held by the clerks and he swept aside the burgeoning convention of dowry and the new and harsher view of what constituted a consanguineous marriage to relieve distress, poverty and pain no less potent because now uncountable. Leutard, Tanchelm and Peter of Bruys gave poor men who were told that God demanded fees for new and more rigorously enforced services of the church not only a pecuniary dispensation, but the relief of knowing what was the right thing to do, and Arnold of Brescia lent an eloquent voice and a clear head to those in Rome who kept seeing the rewards of their revolution about to be snatched from them by a rapprochement between pope and nobility.

The expression of collective sentiment implies its existence, which cannot be taken for granted in time of movement. One of the persistent motifs of those taken in heresy was resistance to the disruption of human ties and accustomed relations which came with change. In 1025 the men of Arras stated it as their objective 'to abandon the world, to restrain the appetites of the flesh, to earn our food by the labour of our own hands, to do no injury to anyone, to extend charity to everyone of our own faith'. They equated injury to others not only with the indulgence of fleshly appetite but with living at other people's expense, which they saw as directly opposed to neighbourly charity. In the same way when Gerard of Monforte expressed his community's rejection of property he stressed the positive aspect of poverty, as sharing rather than as renunciation, by saying that 'we hold our possessions in common with all men'; Lambert le Bègue criticized the fashion of pilgrimage as one which gave a spurious respectability to those who could afford the journey because they had profited at others' expense or at best encouraged them to neglect the needs of their dependants, and Valdès marked his new life by renouncing his wealth and making restitution to those whom he had wronged in acquiring it. A particular form of this resistance to the creation of new barriers between men, either by malpractice or by progress, was that of the priests who sought closer association with their flocks through dissociation from their colleagues: the impulse which led the young clerks at Le Mans to prepare a platform for Henry and sit weeping at his feet while he denounced the sins of their order, or Albero of Mercke and Lambert to devote themselves to their parishioners as eagerly as they decried the defects and abuses of their brother priests, shared something of the sentiment if not the opinion of those who renounced the concept of ordination altogether.

The corollary of that sense of alienation between people was the tendency which was picked out again and again as a most sinister habit of heretics, that of forming conventicles meeting together by private arrangement not, as their enemies supposed, to conduct orgies, but to express their fellowship in prayer and religious exercises like singing the metrical translation of the Acts which Lambert made for his pious women or studying the scriptures with which, from the men of Arras to the old lady who defended the virgin of Rheims, they displayed so unnerving a familiarity. The propensity of the Cathars to teach their followers to read was regarded with deep distrust, and since the skill was traditionally confined to the clerical class it easily became further evidence to support the suspicion that they invoked the assistance of magical powers. So Heribert added to his tales of how the heretics worshipped the devil and were helped by him to escape from the most secure and vigilantly guarded prisons the information that 'nobody is so stupid that if he joins them he will not become literate within eight days'.[8]

To become associated with a heretical sect, therefore, was to do much more than endorse heretical doctrines. It was to accept a new solidarity, often in conscious rejection of the forces which had disrupted the old, and with it the ties of loyalty, acceptance of a common rule of life, and by implication a communal interpretation of it, which could give role and purpose to those deprived by geographical or social mobility of the familiar structures of community and kin. The affinity with the search for new forms of association which marked especially the town life of the twelfth century was sometimes betrayed in the vocabulary of the heretics. The Cathars, like the townsmen of southern France, called their leaders *bons hommes* and each attained the status by accepting the most solemn ties of obligation. When Tanchelm's associate Manasses gathered a dozen companions in a fraternity – inevitably it was alleged for the most blasphemous purposes – it was called a Guild. Hence the activity of a heretic could become the focus of simple and powerful emotions, loneliness, the need of protection, the desire to work for a common end, which might be widely felt and yet require external leadership or inspiration to precipitate their expression and resolution. The strength of the commitment which could result is horrifically attested by one quality that heretics had which puzzled and worried honest men. 'The amazing thing', Eberwin wrote to St Bernard, 'was that they entered and endured the torment of the flames not merely courageously but joyfully. I wish I were with you, holy father, to hear you explain how such great fortitude comes to these tools of the devil in their heresy as is seldom found among the truly religious in the faith of Christ'. Part of the answer was that the heresy gave a place in the world and among their fellows to those who otherwise lacked it. This may be one reason why women, and especially widows and young girls like those whose insistence on martyrdom so distressed observers at Cologne in 1163 and Rheims a decade later, were so often among their most prominent and tenacious disciples.

The developing theme of the heresies of the early twelfth century, that the corruption of the clergy had annulled its authority so that each man must assume responsibility for his own salvation, was well adapted to the needs of those to whom it was offered. A faith which jettisoned the services of the intercessionary priesthood and abandoned the supports of the sacramental and penitential structures matched the spiritual condition of those who found themselves alone before the hostile forces of famine, disease, extortion and exploitation to their worldly state, and in doing so offered them some framework in which they might hope to deal with it. The personal role of the heresiarch offered a positive substitute for the lost consolations of ritual. To attack the priests, to assert that their power had deserted them because they were not fit to have it, was to issue a challenge. Holy power did not simply disappear when its holders were deposed. When Henry was described as a man who would not bow his neck to *human* obedience or Tanchelm said that he was not less divine than Christ, words which may not have been intended to express more than scepticism of the church's claims raised wider questions in the minds of their hearers. Eugenius III and his cardinals knew that Eon's conviction that he was *dominus noster* referred to in the mass was absurd, but there were many to share it, and some to believe profoundly enough in Eon's access to the super-natural to go to the stake confident that, though dead, he would cause the ground to swallow them before the flames could reach them.

It was around the question of access to spiritual power that the final battle between the church and the heresiarchs raged. The assertions that the soiled priest could not perform the mass – because, said Albero of Mercke, in his presence the altar was surrounded by evil spirits instead of angels – that prayer could be offered and would be heard by God in fields or taverns and not only in churches, that the music of the church, meant to drive demons away according to Peter the Venerable, was a mere irritant in God's ears, that relics and crosses were no more than empty symbols, prayers and benefactions for the dead a waste of time and money, burial in holy ground a foolish imposition, amounted to a compre-hensive rejection of the idea that the church was the house of God, the priests its custodians and the guardians of its powers. The preachers, set apart from human imperfection by dress and demean-our, denounced the pretenders with thunderous eloquence, and proved their point with the most foolhardy daring, as Tanchelm did when he pronounced his nuptials with the Virgin, and Dominic William when he survived the ordeal of the mass.

As usual the career of Henry of Lausanne demonstrates the issues best. When Bishop Hildebert returned from Rome to Le Mans he confronted Henry and by examining him on the offices and services of the church proved him, to the satisfaction of the clerks at least, an impostor and a charlatan. Yet he did not discredit him, for though he drove him from the city 'the people had become so devoted to Henry that even now his memory can scarcely be expunged, or their love for him drawn from their hearts'. In the early 1130s, as no doubt on other occasions, Henry was confronted, seemingly in public debate, by the monk William, who demolished his teachings from the point of view of orthodox theology with a comprehensive and accurate rebuttal: there is nothing to suggest that in doing so he diminished Henry's influence. Hildebert and William fought valiantly and well, but they fought the wrong battle. Henry's power did not depend on popular conviction of the accuracy of his knowledge of the church and its teachings, or the soundness of his doctrines. St Bernard did not repeat their mistake.

When Bernard's secretary described his victory to the monks of Clairvaux he did not rehearse the arguments by which the teachings of the heretic were rebutted.[9] His concern was with the means by which Bernard demonstrated comprehensively to the people of the Languedoc that he had better access than Henry to the springs of divine support. Like Henry he was an outsider, a man of striking appearance set apart from ordinary mortals by his life and behaviour, a preacher of surpassing skill. He used his powers to the full in the succession of miracles which Geoffrey recounts. Beginning at Bordeaux by bringing an end to the battle between bishop and chapter which had caused the town to be under interdict for several years, to great popular discontent – a feat which Geoffrey says 'deserves to be called a miracle' – he proceeded to Bergerac where he performed cures upon a nobleman on the one hand, and a man destitute through illness on the other; at Cahors he relieved one of the bishop's servants of blindness and another of a long-standing fever. At Toulouse, which he approached with the prayer 'Lord, they are seeking a sign and we can make no progress without one' he showed how his potency excelled that of the local clergy in the most convincing manner possible, by curing their most skilful doctor, a canon named John, of a wasting disease which he had failed to cure himself, and disposed of a generous selection of withered hands and cases of blindness among the poor. That he could dispel the powers of evil as well as summon those of good he showed by exorcising a woman who felt herself unable to eat because she was possessed by a devil, and he proceeded through the countryside where Henry's most stubborn support was to be found distributing healing as he went, restoring a dozen or so withered hands and at Verfeil curing the infant son of a leading heretic. How could Henry compete with that?

The value of these achievements to the mission was proved at Albi, where it reached its climax. Three days before Bernard the legate who accompanied him, Alberic of Ostia, had reached the city, to be greeted with jeers and catcalls and find less than thirty people at his mass. St Bernard had a different reception. News of the miracles had preceded him, he was welcomed by an enthusiastic crowd, and when he preached next day the church was overflowing. He would have none of their devotion: his moment had come.

> I have come to sow, but I find the field already sown with wicked seed. But you are a reasonable field. You are, after all, God's field. I will show you both seeds, and you can decide which to choose.

Now, and only now, did the abbot embark upon the systematic refutation of Henry's doctrine, and when he had finished,

> he asked them which they would choose. The whole people began to execrate and decry the wickedness of the heretic, and joyfully to receive the word of God and the Catholic faith. 'Repent' said the abbot, 'each of you is contaminated. Return to the unity of the church. So that we can know which of you has repented and received the word of life, raise your right hand to heaven as a sign of Catholic unity.' All of them raised their right hands in exultation, and so he brought his sermon to an end.

St Bernard recognized that he did not succeed in extirpating heresy from the Languedoc, but he did bring an end to popular support for Henry who now 'found the roads so well blocked and the footpaths so carefully watched that he was safe hardly anywhere, and was captured and brought to the bishop in chains'. Unlike Hildebert and William, Bernard played the heretic at his own game, and won: the rules deserve examination.

The miracles which Bernard performed were neither fables nor conjuring tricks. The conditions that Geoffrey described in his patients would now be described as psychosomatic: the withered hand, for example, is a common symptom of hysteria, which can also produce blindness, and whose incidence is exacerbated by malnutrition. Exorcism is a technique for persuading the sufferer to identify the source of trouble with some concrete object – in one of these cases the diabolic presence was represented by a stone – which under the influence of the healer can be isolated and expelled from the body. Moreover, the miracle, like the verdict of the ordeal, had to be recognized. It was, in effect, a judgement upon the capacity of the would-be miracle worker to focus the conviction and hope of his supplicants, and thus to enable them to triumph over their disabilities. Like the verdict of the ordeal also, it was a process which might take time, as the community mulled over the evidence that had been put to it to reach its decision about the location of the holy power: Geoffrey remarked that it was a sign of Bernard's humility that 'the sick are always cured after his departure'. But Bernard did not neglect the human skills which would support his credibility. The affair at Bordeaux is the clearest instance of mediation in hitherto irreducible conflict, but the blindness of the bishop's servant at Cahors had been caused by a blow on the head, presumably in a quarrel, and if Canon John at Toulouse had been moved out of the monastery and lodged in the town 'because of his smell and his weakness' it is fair to suspect that his brothers might have put up with those afflictions if they had liked him enough. In Toulouse also Bernard was careful to undermine Henry's influence with the knights, securing promises that he would not be supported in future and that those who stuck by him would meet the displeasure of the community. Finally, there and in the villages he used Henry's unwillingness to confront him in debate as evidence of the heretic's unworthiness: he would not appear to defend his cause, and with it those who had committed themselves to it.

The patient work of diplomacy and negotiation was, of course, no different in kind from that which had enabled Henry to consolidate his position at Le Mans by offering solutions to the grievances of the citizens. This was the practical test of a man's claim to exercise influence in the community, and St Bernard's miracles were the popular endorsement of his assertion that the teachings of the true church were better able than its adversary's to assist the relief of distress and the solution of tribulations which had appeared insoluble.

The pre-Gregorian world enjoyed a secure understanding of the nature and location of the holy. It resided not in men but in places, objects and rituals under the custody of a priesthood whose value resided not in the ephemeral acknowledgement of personal virtue, but in the general recognition that it held the keys. The monastery, the shrine and relics of the saint, the altar itself, were the temples of spiritual power around which the rhythms of daily life might be organized and regulated.[10] In religion as in law tradition is a sound arbiter of unchanging problems, and so long as the world which moved around the priest did not change his private qualities were irrelevant to his capacity to perform his public duties, because his office and his rituals themselves embodied ancient wisdom and skills. But new questions require new answers, and new answers cannot immediately be authenticated by tradition. Their source must be scrutinized afresh. When Hildebrand proclaimed that he stood for truth and not for custom he spoke with the voice of an age whose needs had changed, in whose perplexities custom no longer offered a certain guide, and men were cast instead upon the more elusive and complex quest. In consequence he threw a dazzling light upon the inner lives of his clergy just at the moment when the endless work of canalizing communal sentiment and resolving humdrum tension and grievance which assured their standing and influence was assuming infinite variety, and when they stood most in need of the spiritual authority which enabled them to perform their tasks.

This fact was not equally important everywhere. 'What the priest cannot achieve by preaching and teaching, that the royal power does or commands by fear of punishment' wrote Hugh of Fleury.[11] Conversely, especially between the brief promise of Charlemagne's reign and the discovery of government as an active art in the twelfth century, royalty in most of Europe rested less on the power to punish than on the aura of mystery which consecration threw around a king, 'the deficiencies in human resources were supplied by the power of the saints',[12] and the maintenance of peace, the first condition of political authority, lay heavily in the hands of the church and depended precariously upon its spiritual power. But where, as in England, peace and order were secured by self-confident village communities and a close network of secular lordship subject to the restraint of a sophisticated monarchy, in part supplanted and in part supplemented by the pragmatic and flexible if brutal institutional precocity of the Norman kings, the parish priests never had to bear so broad a burden as that which identified their spiritual authority with their ability to perform a multifarious range of social functions, and the necessity of conferring those powers upon others when the priests were deprived of their eminence did not arise.

Where the pace of change was greater and its reverberations less surely contained by the institutional framework, the connection which the reformers made between the personal life of the priest and his right to his office had grave consequences. When it ceased to be accepted without question that whatever the personal appearance to the contrary, the priest as priest was a man of God he lost precisely the confidence of his detachment from the preoccupations and infirmities of ordinary men which enabled him to solve countless trivial problems, and settle innumerable petty disputes. The vacuum was filled not only by heretics, but far more often by the army of hermits, preachers and wandering monks whose rivalry with the secular clergy reflected a struggle for temporal influence as well as spiritual prestige.[13] Marbod of Rennes knew well when he accused Robert of Arbrissel of undermining the church by criticizing the morals of its priests before the people that in the end the two were inseparable.

During the half-century or so after the crisis of the reform the heretics, like the prophets, competed for the power which had been thrown, as it were, upon the open market with the classical weapons of charisma. Described by their apprehensive opponents in heroic terms, as false prophets, Anti-Christs, ravening wolves in the clothing of sheep, they could arouse wherever they went the un-directed passion of those who saw in them the purity that had deserted the world, direct their force against the holders of tainted office, and win for themselves the abiding veneration which made Tanchelm's followers accept his bathwater as a sacrament and the ashes which Ramihrdus' disciples collected from his pyre the objects of adoration half a century later. This was the force which Barbarossa acknowledged when he ordered the body of Arnold of Brescia to be burned and the ashes scattered on the Tiber lest they should serve the same purpose.

The identification of spiritual authority with personal worthiness which gave the great heretical preachers their power also limited its extent. Committed as they were to a conviction of the inherent wickedness of ritual and structure, imprisoned by the force with which they articulated the grievance of their followers, identifying the very principle of organization as the source of corruption, their diagnosis of the illness itself precluded them from offering a permanent cure, or leaving their disciples any legacy more enduring than memories and ashes. The successors of Henry and Arnold, more successful and most of them anonymous, were perceived in less grandiose though not less sinister terms, as the little foxes who destroy the vines, the grubs which undermine the foundations, the poison which flowed through the bloodstream, and most insistently the leprosy which swept through the community, disfiguring or killing all whom it touched. They were preachers, but they were not primarily exponents of charismatic power. It has been wisely remarked that 'the solution to grave problems of social organization rarely comes from those who experience them, [who] inevitably can only think according to the cosmological type in which their social life is cast'.[14] That judgement is precisely in accord with the failure of the great anti-clerical preachers and the success of the Cathars. The Bogomils brought to the west a myth, a vision of man and his nature from which permanent principles of ideology and organization could be derived. The *perfecti* challenged the local power of the clergy, inserted themselves in the fissures of a changing world as effectively as their predecessors if more discreetly, but their claim to detachment from the wells of corruption was more pervasive and more permanent because it had been embodied in a ritual to pass from man to man, from place to place, and from generation to generation. Thus the respects in which Catharism was less radical as a faith (though not as a theology) than its forerunners, stopping short as it did of jettisoning the sinews of religious organization, of myth, sacrament and hierarchy, enabled it to present a more comprehensive, more sustained, and infinitely more dangerous alternative to the Roman church.

For the church also the faith in charismatic power which marked the age from Hildebrand to Bernard was necessarily transient. Since the battle between orthodoxy and heresy was in the last resort a struggle for the leadership of their respective representatives in local communities the stakes were high. They are well described by this characterization of the church's transfer of its reliance, in the second half of the twelfth century, from charismatic to bureaucratic authority:

Leadership meant lordship, and the popes descended into the
arena where lordship was to be won. It could only be won in the
fashion of every other medieval ruler, in the ceaseless petty round
of business and litigation.[15]

Here was the real challenge of dissent. When Hildebert re-entered
Le Mans he heard that Henry had pronounced upon the problems of
its people, had propounded a solution, and had collected money to
secure its implementation. As he entered the city he was met by the
cry 'we have a father, a bishop and defender greater than you. . .'
The words revealed that Henry had tapped the very spring of power
in medieval society. Lordship was the ability to be accepted as
defender, and hence to dispense judgement and secure collective
action. The persistence of the chroniclers in describing those who
flocked around the heretics as *pauperes* was not, and not meant to be,
a comment on their affluence. *Pauperes* were not those who lacked
wealth but those who lacked power, contrasted not with the *divites*
but with the *potentes* to whom they gave submission and service in
return for protection. This was the basis of every structure of
authority in the early middle ages. The appeal to the poor was an
appeal to the powerless, and their readiness to confer the rights of
leadership upon those who could win their confidence constituted a
direct and fundamental threat to the men who were accustomed to
exercise them.[16] This is why the critical difference between a Henry
of Lausanne and a Robert of Arbrissel lay in the licence: the one who
preached with the approval of the church acquired spiritual and
social power with the consent of, and within the limits acceptable to,
constituted authority. In consequence the moment when heresy
was born was often, as with the Waldensians, the moment when it
was required that preaching should be abandoned, or conducted
only with the permission of the diocesan.[17] Refusal was in effect a
declaration of rebellion.

For these reasons the true nature of popular heresy was demonstrated far more clearly by its relations with secular than with
ecclesiastical authority. In seeking a correlation between the
incidence of heresy and other phenomena one alone holds. It
appeared sometimes among the poor, sometimes among the rich,
sometimes in the backward regions if more often in the progressive,

sometimes where the reform of the church was advanced and sometimes where it was retarded. It always flourished where political authority was diffused, and never where its concentration was greatest. After Robert I's vigorous and ruthless action in 1022 the Capetian demesne remained remarkably untouched by the heresies which pullulated around it, Henry II was no less decisive on the only occasion when it appeared, rather pathetically, in England, and Normandy too was largely immune. There are only the most shadowy reports of the presence of heretics in the Norman kingdom of Sicily, where the abundant presence of alternative religious currents, Greek and Moslem, might have been expected to stimulate it, and Frederick I and Frederick II were always ready to cooperate with the Popes in harsh legislation and rapid action against heresy, though in nothing else. The secular princes were always ahead of the clerks in the race to coercion for the excellent reason that while they were less inhibited about shedding blood, their power was no less directly at risk.

At the end of the day all power was local power. 'How is the king to control thousands of thousands,' asked Walter Map, 'when we poor lords can hardly control the few men that we have?'[18] The achievements which made twelfth-century Europe that which we recognize as the mother of our own were predominantly those of organization and centralization, the creation by popes and kings of legal and administrative systems which gave substance to their claims to universal jurisdiction by transmitting their will to the point of its application and seeing it observed. To do so they had to subordinate ancient habits of thought and action, to restrict or annul old privileges like those of private warfare and justice, and trial by ordeal. At the same time change brought needs which they had not foreseen and generated institutions which they had not initiated. In that process power was conferred upon those who seemed able to exercise it for the resolution of pressing problems by their skill in persuasion and mediation, and their ability to win acceptance as men of competence, vision and integrity. Since religion was often the most potent expression of group solidarity and the most acceptable instrument for resolving tensions and dislocations within the group, the struggle thus precipitated between local enterprise and the prerogative of distant lordship was often conducted in religious terms. For the same reason the church must be pitted against the centrifugal tendencies of social diversification and disruption, and society could not abandon the ideal of religious uniformity until such time as it should become confident that its institutions could preserve its fabric by other means.

Resistance to central authority was therefore compounded of opposite elements, of the recalcitrance of those who, without the conscious aid of programme or ideology, resolutely preferred to walk their ancient paths, and of the turbulent improvisation of those who felt the need of new tools for new tasks. Much of this force could be accommodated by granting the substance of the demands in return for the reaffirmation of traditional obedience, and coming to terms with the burgesses who wanted municipal law and administration to suit their circumstances, the vassals who insisted on a more regular place in the councils of their lords, the holy men who could pursue their mission through the agency of new religious orders. Hence, paradoxically, by its suspicion of the embrace of national and international sovereignty the conservative instinct to hold to accustomed ways and cherish old ideals within the horizons of small communities joined with the spirit of innovation to inaugurate the tradition of change by the concession of established authority. There was no place, and only one remedy, for those who persisted in looking to the foundations of power without making obeisance to its apex, and stubbornly refused to exchange their freedom to do so for a charter of liberties.

| *Appendix*
(*by Bernard Hamilton*) | *The Cathar Council*
of Saint-Félix |

The unique source for the Cathar Council of Saint-Félix is the text printed by Besse in 1660, which claims to reproduce the copy made in 1232 of an original document of 1167.[1] It has been the subject of much controversy and M. Yves Dossat even claimed that Besse forged it.[2] This view is untenable because it is clear from Besse's work that he misunderstood Catharism,[3] whereas the information in this document accords completely with discoveries made by scholars in the post-war period.[4] There can be no reasonable doubt that Besse printed a genuine thirteenth-century text, but it presents certain problems.[5]

First, when was it transcribed? The statement that the copy was made for Peter Isarn on 14 Monday 1232[6] is clearly incorrect, since Peter Isarn, Cathar bishop of Carcassonne, was executed in 1226[7] and 14 August was not a Monday in 1232. 14 August, however, was a Monday in 1223. Peter Isarn had then recently become bishop, Crusader occupation of his diocese had virtually ended and it is likely that he wished to re-organize his church and needed an authoritative account of its origins and of the extent of his jurisdiction.[8] Internal evidence suggests that he obtained the text from which the copy was made from the Cathars of Toulouse,[9] which may indicate that his own archive had been destroyed during the Crusade. It therefore seems probable that Besse printed MCCXXXII instead of MCCXXIII in his edition.[10] This emendation is preferable to Dondaine's hypothesis that Monday 14 August relates to the events of 1167 and not to the rest of the dating formula of which it forms part. This is implausible, and does not agree with the rest of the evidence.[11]

Besse only published extracts from the document.[12] Moreover, it is not a unity, but is made up of parts of three independent sources: an account of the Council of Saint-Félix, a sermon preached by Pope Niquinta, and a charter defining diocesan boundaries. This fact has been obscured by commentators who have treated the text as a connected narrative: Besse called it a 'charter of Niquinta',[13] while Dondaine refers to it as *'le procès verbal d'une assemblée d'hérétiques'*,[14] whereas it is clearly neither of these things.

The second problem is whether the Papa Niquinta who presided at Saint-Félix is the same person as Papa Nicetas from Constantinople who introduced absolute dualism in Lombardy. The Italian sources are concerned solely with the origins of Cathar schisms in Lombardy and shed no light on this problem[15] but the names used by Niquinta to describe the dualist churches of the east in the Saint-Félix account show that he also came from Byzantium. Although this does not prove conclusively that Nicetas and Niquinta are identical, the similarity of their names and of their activity suggests that they were the same person. The strange form, Niquinta, used in the Saint-Félix account, probably results from copyists' errors in the various stages of transmission.

The evidence of place-names in the sermon is as follows: Niquinta always uses a Byzantine rather than a western form where there is a choice. Thus the *Ecclesia Bulgariae* had the same form in both cases, whereas Niquinta speaks of the *Ecclesia Dalmatiae*, the Byzantine name for the western Adriatic region, not of the *Ecclesia Sclavoniae*, the common western name for that church.[16] The church of Dragovitsa, awkwardly translated by western writers as the *Ecclesia Drugunthiae* or some variant of this,[17] is called the *Ecclesia Dragometiae* by Niquinta, for as a Byzantine he knew that Dragovet was the episcopal see of the Dragovici.[18] *Ecclesia Romanae* in Besse's text is obviously a misreading of *Ecclesia Romana* and refers to the dualist church of Constantinople, New Rome, a form which no western speaker would have used.[19] Dossat is right in claiming that the *Ecclesia Melenguiae* relates to the Milingui, a Slav tribe of the Peloponnese, although his arguments against the existence of a dualist community there are not persuasive.[20] In the twelfth century the Milingui were Slav-speaking, had only relatively recently been converted to Orthodoxy and were within easy communication by sea of other dualist centres, all of which factors would have made them potentially responsive to dualist preaching.[21] Their omission from thirteenth-century lists may be a consequence of Frankish occupation of the Peloponnese.[22]

If, as this evidence suggests, it was Nicetas of Constantinople who presided at Saint-Félix, then the date of that Council must be reconsidered in the light of the Italian sources. According to Anselm of Alessandria Catharism entered Lombardy in c. 1174 and Nicetas came there soon after that, and this agrees well with the rest of the Italian evidence.[23] There must therefore be some mistake in the opening words of the Saint-Félix document, '*Anno M.C.LXVII incarnationis Dominice, in mense madii, in diebus illis. . .*' for the Council cannot have been held before Nicetas reached the west. I would suggest that the date did not form part of the original text which began at the words '*in diebus illis*'. This is a common liturgical formula used to introduce readings from the historical books of the Bible, and is used here to preface an extract from some longer work, perhaps a history of Catharism in Languedoc, which Peter Isarn had borrowed from Toulouse, and of which he incorporated part in this document. Had the date formed part of the original text the words '*in diebus illis*' would be superfluous: the date seems to have been added either by Peter Isarn, or by some later Catholic archivist.[24] Whatever its origin, the date has either been wrongly computed or wrongly transcribed, for the earliest date for Nicetas' mission is c. 1174, and the earliest datable evidence of absolute dualism in

Languedoc comes from 1177.[25] The Council must therefore have been held between those dates.

It is known from other sources that Bernard Raimond was leader of the Cathars in Toulouse, that Sicard Cellarier was Cathar bishop of Albi, and that there were Cathar dioceses at Albi, Toulouse and Carcassonne in the late twelfth century.[26] Only three details in the account of the Council are controversial.

First there is the mention of the *Ecclesia Aranensis*. If this reading is correct it must refer to the Val d'Aran in Comminges, which, as Dossat rightly says, is nowhere else recorded as a Cathar diocese.[27] That the reading is incorrect is clear from the third part of the document, an extract from a charter fixing the boundaries of the Cathar dioceses of Toulouse and Carcassonne. These were to follow the boundaries of Catholic dioceses, probably because they were familiar to everybody, and their southern limits are defined thus: '*sicut alii episcopati dividuntur ab exitu Redensis usque ad Leridam sicut pergit apud Tolosam. . .*' Lerida is in Aragon, and the charter states that the two Cathar bishops shall have jurisdiction over part of northern Spain as well as part of southern France. The words '*sicut pergit apud Tolosam*' make no sense in this context and are obviously a copyist's error for *sicut . . . Tortosam*'. The line from Lerida to Tortosa, near the mouth of the Ebro, was intended to mark the southern boundary of the Cathar diocese of Carcassonne.[28] From this it is clear that the Val d'Aran formed part of the Cathar diocese of Toulouse, and it therefore follows that *Aranensis* should, as Mlle Thouzellier suggests, be amended to *Agenensis*, which is known to have been a Cathar diocese.[29]

The second problem in the Saint-Félix account is the statement that Nicetas consecrated Mark of Lombardy at the Council. The Italian sources agree that Nicetas was Mark's consecrator, but do not say where the ceremony took place. Mr Moore is probably right in affirming that the consecration took place in Italy before the Council was held, and that the southern French account is mistaken about this.[30]

The third problem concerns the re-consecration of the bishop of the northern French Cathars by Nicetas. This church had been moderate dualist before this time and was so again in the thirteenth century.[31] This does not exclude the possibility that their bishop was converted to absolute dualism, although it is also possible that the church of northern France soon reverted to its earlier moderate dualist allegiance. I think that the bishop *ultra montes*, who after the death of Bishop Mark advised the Cathars of Lombardy to send their new bishop to the moderate dualist church of Bulgaria for consecration, may have been the northern French bishop, who had had oversight of the Cathars of Lombardy before Nicetas came, but Mr Moore does not agree with this and no conclusive decision can be reached about it.[32]

To sum up, I would suggest that the Saint-Félix document is an abbreviated version of copies made in 1223 for the Cathar bishop of Carcassonne of parts of three documents in the possession of the church of Toulouse. The frequent copying and re-arrangement of material which this transmission must necessarily have entailed is likely to have produced the large number of major errors which are found in Besse's text.

Abbreviations

The following abbreviations are used throughout the Notes

AFP	*Archivum Fratrum Praedicatorum*
Anselm	A. Dondaine, 'La hiérarchie cathare en Italie: II, Le *Tractatus de hereticis* d'Anselme d'Alexandrie O.P.' *AFP* xx (1950), 234–324
BIHR	*Bulletin of the Institute of Historical Research*
Börst	A. Börst, *Die Katharer* (Stuttgart, 1953)
Bouquet	*Recueil des historiens de Gaule et de la France*
C de F	*Cahiers de Fanjeaux* (Toulouse, since 1966)
De heresi	A. Dondaine, 'La hiérarchie cathare en Italie: I, Le *De heresi catharorum*' *AFP* xix (1949), 280–312
EHR	*English Historical Review*
Lea	H. C. Lea, *A History of the Inquisition of the Middle Ages* (London, 1888; repr. New York, 1955)
Le Goff	J. Le Goff (ed.), *Hérésies et sociétés dans l'Europe pré-industrielle* (Paris and The Hague, 1968)
L'eremitismo in occidente	. . . *nei secoli xi e xii, Pubblicazioni dell' Università Cattolica del Sacro Cuore. Miscellanea del Centro di studi medioevali* IV, (Milan, 1965)
MA	*Le Moyen Age*

Maisonneuve	H. Maisonneuve, *Etudes sur l'origine de l'inquisition* (2nd edn., Paris, 1960)
MGH:SS	*Monumenta Germaniae Historica: Scriptores*
MGH:SRG	*Monumenta Germaniae Historica: Scriptores rerum Germanicarum in Usum scholarum*
Manselli (1953)	R. Manselli, 'Il monaco Enrico e la sua eresia', *Bulletino dell' istituto storico italiano per il medio evo* lxv
(1963)	*L'eresia del male* (Naples, 1963)
Mansi	J.D. Mansi, *Sacrorum conciliorum nova et amplissima collectio*
Mundy (1954)	J. H. Mundy, *Liberty and Political Power in Toulouse 1050–1230* (New York, 1954)
(1973)	*Europe in the High Middle Ages* (London, 1973)
Obolensky	D. Obolensky, *The Bogomils* (Cambridge, 1948 repr. Twickenham, 1972)
P & P	*Past and Present*
PL	J. P. Migne, *Patrologia Latina*
Rainier Sacchoni	*Summa . . . de Catharis et Pauperibus de Lugduno* ed. A. Dondaine, *Le* liber de duobus principiis (Rome, 1939), pp. 64–78
RH	*Revue historique*
RHE	*Revue d'histoire ecclésiastique*
RS	*Rolls Series*
RSCI	*Rivista di storia della chiesa in Italia*
Runciman	S. Runciman, *The Medieval Manichee* (Cambridge, 1947)
Russell	J. B. Russell, *Dissent and Reform in the Early Middle Ages* (Los Angeles, 1965)
Southern	R. W. Southern, *Western Society and the Church in the Middle Ages* (London, 1970)
Thouzellier (1966)	C. Thouzellier, *Catharisme et valdéisme en Languedoc à la fin du xiie et au début du xiiie siècle* (Paris, 1966)
(1969)	*Hérésies et hérétiques. Storia e letteratura* 116 (Rome, 1969)
TRHS	*Transactions of the Royal Historical Society*
Wakefield and Evans	W. L. Wakefield and A. P. Evans, *Heresies of the High Middle Ages* (New York and London, 1969)

Full details of other works are given on their first citation.

Comprehensive and up-to-date bibliographies are provided by H. Grundmann, *Bibliographie zur Ketzergeschichte des Mittelalters*, 1900–66 (Rome, 1967) also printed in Le Goff (pp. 407–74) and in the notes of M. D. Lambert, *Medieval Heresy* (London, 1977). W. L. Wakefield and A. P. Evans, *Heresies of the High Middle Ages* and R. I. Moore, *The Birth of Popular Heresy* (London, 1975) contain translations of the principal sources discussed in the foregoing pages and extensive bibliographical information.

Notes

Chapter I INTRODUCTORY (*pages 1–20*)

1. M. L. W. Laistner, *Thought and Letters in Western Europe* A.D. 500 to 900 (2nd edn London, 1957) pp. 310–14; it is not clear what office Amalarius held

2. This comment is modified for the eleventh century by the work of Cracco, and Taviani cited below, Chap. II notes 2 and 29, but conversely the heresies to which their comments are most applicable were held by *literati*, and not strictly popular in character (c.f. pp. 23–35 above)

3. J. B. Russell (1965, *passim*) argued that 'medieval dissidence began in the eighth, not the eleventh century'. Among the few specific cases which he adduced, however, most were, like Amalarius, churchmen arguing with other churchmen; only Aldebert, condemned at Soissons in 744 and Rome in 745, and Theuda of Mainz and Burgund of Bordeaux a century later, seem in any sense to have appealed to popular opinion against ecclesiastical authority, and no weight can be attached to general denunciations of heretical tendencies or opinions in the absence of circumstantial evidence that they were actually held or disseminated. I therefore remain unpersuaded that there is a case to answer against my conventional decision to open this account at the end of the tenth century

4. Lynn T. White jnr, 'The Life of the Silent Majority' in R. S. Hoyt (ed.) *Life and Thought in the Early Middle Ages* (Minneapolis, 1967) offers an

interesting attempt to approach the religious mentality of the Dark-Age peasant; cf. G. Duby, *The Early Growth of the European Economy* (London, 1974) pp. 48–57, 162–8, Southern pp. 28–33

5. *MGH:SS* IV, 138

6. By Steven Runciman (Cambridge, 1947)

7. *Acta Synodi Atrebatensis, PL* 142, col. 1271

8. Respectively *ibid.* cols. 1271, 1271–2, 1311–12, 1271–1311, 1269–70

9. Dondaine *RSCI* VI (1952) p. 62 considered this tantamount to a rejection of the Old Testament, and hence a point which these men had in common with the Bogomils – but they did not say so: see below, Chap II n. 20

10. cf. Ilarino da Milano 'L'eresia popolare del secolo XI nell' Europa occidentale', *Studi Gregoriani* ed. G. B. Borino, ii (1947), 44–6 who accounts in this way for the disavowal of heresy which was required of Gerbert of Aurillac before his coronation as Archbishop of Rheims

11. Irish monks were common in northern Europe at this time, and allowed to follow their own rites; St Gerard, Bishop of Toul 963–94, founded a monastery in his diocese for some of them to share with Greek exiles with whom they had many ascetic customs in common: P. McNulty and B. Hamilton, 'Orientale lumen et magistra latinitas', *Le Millénaire du Mont Athos, 963–1963, Études et Mélanges* I (Chevetogne, 1963), 199–200

12. See pp. 35–8, 71–2 and especially 185–94

13. Russell, pp. 24–7

14. P. Brown, *Augustine of Hippo* (London, 1967) p. 312

15. J. M. Noiroux, 'Les deux premiers documents concernant l'hérésie aux Pays-Bas', *RHE* xlix (1954), 842–55, makes a strong case for Roger I, Bishop of Châlons 1008–42; J. B. Russell, 'A propos du synode d'Arras', *ibid.* lvii (1962), 66–87, shows that it is possible that Reginard of Liège (1025–36) is not absolutely excluded by chronological considerations alone, but he remains the less likely candidate

16. I can see no support in the text for Russell's assertion (1965, p. 22) that they were tortured; for a different interpretation of the preliminaries to the investigation see p. 259

Chapter II THE AWAKENING OF EUROPE (*pages 23–45*)

1. G. Luzzatto, *An Economic History of Italy* (London, 1961) p. 47

2. *Historiarum libri . . . quinque*, Bouquet X, 23, 'studio artis Grammaticae magis assiduus'. On the other hand H. Taviani, 'Naissance d'une hérésie en Italie du nord au xie. siècle', *Annales* 29 (1974), 1241–2, points to episcopal schools in the tenth century at Bergamo, Pavia and Brescia; as she remarks, it is difficult to be sure what was studied at them: see also H. E. J. Cowdrey, 'Anselm of Besate and some North Italian Scholars of the Eleventh Century', *Journal of Ecclesiastical History* 23 (1972), 115–24

3. *Vita Odonis* I, 12, *PL* 133, 41–9

4. R. L. Poole, *Illustrations of the History of Medieval Thought and Learning*, (New York, 1960 edn) p. 71; Cowdrey, *loc. cit.* pp. 119–20

5. *Gesta Synodi Aurelianensis*, Bouquet X, 536–9, upon which the following account is based; the version of Ralph Glaber, *ibid.* pp. 35–8, agrees in the essentials of the story

6. A. Dondaine, 'L'origine de l'hérésie médiévale', *RSCI* (1952) p. 69. That the canons of Orléans were Bogomils, or Cathars, was taken for granted by most commentators from Lea (1887, 1955 edn, p. 108) to Runciman (1947, p. 117)

7. I owe this point, which makes the following interpretation of these heretics quite different from that which I suggested in *History* (1970), pp. 25–7, to Peter Brown

8. Poole, *op. cit.* pp. 84–5, H. R. Trevor-Roper, *The European Witch-Craze of the 16th and 17th Centuries* (Harmondsworth, 1967) pp. 11–23; N. Cohn, *Europe's Inner Demons* (London, 1975) pp. 1–74

9. Adhemar, *MGH:SS* IV, 143; John of Fleury, Bouquet X 498; Ralph Glaber, *ibid.* p. 38 gives the number as thirteen

10. *MGH:SS* IV, 138

11. Landulf Senior, *Historia Mediolanensis*, *MGH:SS* VIII, 65–6

12. McNulty and Hamilton, 'Orientale lumen' (cited above Chap. I n. 11), 181–216

13. See pp. 147–9

14. C. Violante, *La societa milanese nell'età precommunale* (Bari, 1953) pp. 178–179; c.f. Y. Dossat, 'Les cathares d'après l'inquisition', *C de F* 3 (1968), 85–7

15. Rainier Sacchoni p. 68

16. Taviani, *loc. cit.* 1228–42

17. *ibid.* pp. 1246–7

18. Bouquet X, 23

19. *Gesta episcoporum . . . Leodiensis*, *MGH:SS* VII, 226–8

20. P. Riché, 'Recherches sur l'instruction des laiques', *Cahiers de Civilisation Médiévale* 5 (1962), 180–81. In the tenth century Notker Teutonicus made a vernacular translation of the Psalms (P. Wolff, *The Awakening of Europe*, Harmondsworth, 1968 p. 168) and in the twelfth Lambert le Bègue made one of the Acts, and said that a 'Flemish master' had also translated parts of the Bible (p. 191). Enthusiasm for the New Testament did not necessarily imply rejection of the Old, upon whose precept the heretics reported to Wazo based their refusal to eat meat; Gerard of Monforte said that he and his followers read in both Old and New Testaments every day

21. R. Morghen, 'Problèmes sur l'origine de l'hérésie au moyen-âge', *RH* ccxxxvi (1966), 10

22. Bouquet X, 23; McNulty and Hamilton, *loc. cit.* p. 202

23. Noiroux, *RHE* xlix (1954), 853

24. See above, p. 19

25. See pp. 63–71. The suggestion of H. E. J. Cowdrey, 'The Papacy, the Patarenes and the Church of Milan', *TRHS* 5th Series 18 (1968), 32 n. 2, that

Landulf Senior attempted to link the Patarenes with heresy by deriving their name from the Greek *Catharos* is, however, open to the objection that no western heretics were referred to as Cathars until the middle of the next century: see pp. 175–6; G. Cracco, 'Pataria: *opus* e *nomen*', *RSCI* xxviii (1974), 357–87 provides a full discussion of the name and its implications

26. *Rustici* in this context is, of course, a synonym of *illiterati* or *idiotae* and does not mean, as is sometimes supposed, that those referred to were countrymen; examples are noted by Riché, *loc. cit.* p. 181n.

27. J. B. Russell, 'Interpretations of the Origins of Medieval Heresy', *Mediaeval Studies* 25 (1963), 26–53, offers an extensive survey of opinion on this point. The case against Bogomil influence in the eleventh century of R. Morghen, *Medioevo cristiano* (Bari, 1953) pp. 212–86, frequently restated, e.g. in 'Il cosidetto neo-manicheismo occidentale nel sec. xi', *Oriente ed Occidente nel medio evo*, Accademia dei Lincei, Fondazione Volta Convegno 12, Rome 1957, pp. 84–104, and *RH* cccxxxvi (1966), 1–16, and given important support by H. C. Puech, 'Catharisme médiévale et bogomilisme', *Oriente ed occidente*, pp. 56–83, is now generally accepted despite the objections of Dondaine *RSCI* (1952). I have examined the debate in detail in *History* lv (1970); see also J. Musy, 'Mouvements populaires et hérésies au xie. siècle en France', *RH* ccliii (1975), 33–76

28. cf. Dondaine (1952), 60–1

29. G. Cracco, 'Riforma ed eresia in momenti della cultura Europea tra x e xi secolo', *Riv. di storia e letteratura religiosa* vii (1971), 411–77

30. *ibid.* p. 457

31. J. Lestocquoy, *Les villes de Flandres et d'Italie sous le gouvernement des patriciens* (Paris, 1952) pp. 20–1

32. cf. B. H. Rosenwein and L. K. Little, 'Social Meaning in the Monastic and Mendicant Spiritualities', *P & P* 63 (1974), 4–32

Chapter III THE CRISIS OF REFORM (*pages* 46–81)

1. R. W. Southern, *St. Anselm and his Biographer* (Cambridge, 1963) p. 28; Damiani, *PL* 144 col. 380. cf. N. Hunt, *Cluny under St. Hugh* (London, 1967) pp. 99–109

2. Ep. 110, *PL* 182 col. 253

3. Manselli, ed. (1953) p. 61

4. cf. *Letters of Peter the Venerable*, Ep. I, 28, ed. G. Constable (Cambridge, Mass. 1967) I, 71–2

5. G. Duby, *La société aux xie. et xiie. siècles dans la région mâconnaise* (Paris, 1953) p. 11

6. On the hermits of Craon see especially *Vita Bernardi*, *PL* 172 col. 1380–3, *Vita Roberti*, *PL* 162, col. 1047–50, J. B. Mahn, *L'ordre cistercien et son gouvernement* (Paris, 1945) pp. 29–33; they have received much attention in recent years in discussion of various aspects of the reform movements, e.g. in the

important papers of Génicot, Meersseman, Becquet and Delaruelle in *L'eremitismo in occidente*

7. C. Dereine, 'La spiritualité apostolique des premiers fondateurs d'Affligem' *RHE* liv (1959), 41–65

8. C. H. Talbot ed., *The Life of Christina of Markyate* (Oxford, 1959) p. 80; J. Leclerq, 'Pierre le Vénérable et l'érémitisme clunisien', in G. Constable and J. Kritzek (eds.) *Petrus Venerabilis* (Rome, 1956) pp. 99–120

9. *MGH:SS* V, 452–3

10. cited by K. Leyser, 'The Polemics of the Papal Revolution', in B. Smalley (ed.) *Trends in Medieval Political Thought* (Oxford, 1965) p. 42

11. K. F. Morrison, *Tradition and Authority in the Western Church* 300–1140 (Princeton, 1969) pp. 312–7

12. *Epistolae vagantes*, ed. H. E. J. Cowdrey (Oxford, 1972) pp. 22–4; *ibid.* p. 14; *Registrum*, ed. E. Caspar, *MGH Epistolae* II, IV. 10, p. 309; *ibid.* I, 15, pp. 23–4

13. The following account relies principally on: H. E. J. Cowdrey, 'Archbishop Aribert II of Milan', *History* li (1966), 1–15; 'The Papacy, the Patarenes and the Church of Milan', *TRHS* 5th series 18 (1968), 25–48; G. Cracco, 'Pataria: *opus* e *nomen*', *RSCI* xxviii (1974), 357–87; Y. Renouard, *Les villes d'Italie de la fin du xe. siècle au début du xive. siècle*, ed. P. Brauenstein (Paris, 1969) pp. 375–98; C. Violante, 'I laici nel movimento patarino' in his *Studi sulla cristianita medievale* (Milan, 1972) pp. 145–246

14. Cowdrey, 'Papacy, Patarenes' p. 26

15. Violante, *loc. cit.* p. 160

16. Cracco, *loc. cit.* pp. 357–62

17. Cowdrey, *loc. cit.* pp. 31–2

18. Violante, *loc. cit.* pp. 164–71; on the moneyers see also R. S. Lopez, 'An Aristocracy of Money in the Early Middle Ages' *Speculum* xxviii (1953), 1–45

19. Cracco, *loc. cit.* pp. 362–71

20. Landolf Senior cited by Cowdrey, *loc. cit.* p. 35

21. cf. D. C. Douglas, *The Norman Achievement* (London, 1969) pp. 101–2, where it is noted that Bohemond of Antioch's tomb described him (with singular infelicity) as an Athlete of Christ.

22. Cracco, *loc. cit.* pp. 372–4, 379–86

23. *Enarrationes in Psalmos* X, v, quoted by the Canons of Utrecht in the letter against Tanchelm cited below n. 27

24. *Epistolae vagantes*, p. 142. The text is not wholly clear; I agree with the comments of E. John in *EHR* lxxxix (1974), 655–6, and would go further, thinking that the phrase *permittas per manus impositionem* does imply a reordination by Bishop Altmann of Passau, to whom the letter is addressed, and not the original ordination by the unnamed simoniac bishop

25. *Chron. S. Andreae Cameracensium*, *MGH:SS* VII, 543

26. *Registrum*, pp. 331–4

27. *Acta Sanctorum* June I, 830–2, the letter of the canons of Utrecht, is the principal source; for a full list and discussion see Russell (1965) pp. 265–9

28. That this was the object of the mission was the view of H. Pirenne, 'Tanchelin et le projet de démembrement du diocèse d'Utrecht vers 1100', *Académie royale de Belgique, Bull. de la classe des lettres*, ser. 5, xiii (1927); it has been contested by J. M. de Smet, 'De monnik Tanchelm en de Utrechtse bisschopszetel in 1112–14', *Scrinium Lovaniense, Mélanges historiques Etienne van Cauwenbergh* (Louvain, 1961), which I have not seen, summarized by Russell, *loc. cit.* The fact of the visit to Rome is not in dispute

29. *Vita Norberti* (B), *MGH:SS* XII, 691; the source is late, but the story is by no means implausible or unparalleled

30. Canons of Utrecht, *loc. cit.*

31. Russell (1965) pp. 268–9, discusses de Smet's argument on this point

32. *Gesta Treverorum, MGH:SS* VIII, 193–4

33. *PL* 156, cols. 951–3

34. see pp. 27–8 and n.

35. see Morris, '*Judicium Dei*' cited below, Chap. IX, n. 18, p. 96.

36. *Continuation of Sigebert of Gembloux, MGH:SS* VI, 389, 390; William of Newburgh, *Historia rerum Anglicarum: Chronicles of the Reign of Stephen*, etc. ed. R. Howlett (*RS* London, 1885), 60–4

37. 'Some quite ordinary perception, such as an advertisement in the newspaper, or a talk over the radio, has an unexpected meaning for the patient . . . he feels called upon to be a reformer, to spread the doctrines of a religious or political sect, to proclaim his mission as a new Messiah . . .' E. Slater and M. Roth, *Clinical Psychiatry* (3rd edn London, 1969) p. 290

38. *Annales Rodenses, MGH: SS* XVI, 711

39. Duby, *La société . . . mâconnaise*, pp. 285–90

40. Duby, *loc. cit.*, p. 287

41. E. de Moreau, *Histoire de l'église en Belgique* (2nd edn, Brussels, 1953–7), III, 361–6

42. Ordericus Vitalis, *Historia ecclesiastica* viii. 26, ed. M. Chibnall IV (Oxford, 1973), 312–14, quoted by G. Constable, *Monastic Tithes* (Cambridge, 1964) p. 138

43. Constable, *loc. cit.*, p. 143

44. e.g. Councils of Clermont 1096 (Mansi, XX col. 816), Toulouse 1119 (*ibid.* XXI col. 234), Lateran 1139 (col. 531), Rheims 1148 (col. 717), etc.

45. These developments are well – and more sympathetically – discussed by C. N. L. Brooke, *Europe in the Central Middle Ages* (London, 1964) pp. 345–50

46. Roger of Hoveden, *Chronica*, ed. Stubbs, (*RS* London, 1867), ii, 157

47. C. Violante, 'Hérésies urbaines et hérésies rurales en Italie du xie. au xiiie. siècle' in Le Goff, pp. 171–95

48. N. Cohn, *The Pursuit of the Millennium* (3rd edn. London, 1970) pp. 57–60

49. Compare, for example, Violante, 'I laici nel movimento patarino' pp. 164–71 with G. Rudé, *Paris and London in the 18th Century* (London, 1974) p. 21

and *passim*, and N. Z. Davis, 'Religious Riot in Sixteenth-century France', *P & P* 59 (1973), 53, with further references

50. I. S. Robinson, 'Gregory VII and the Soldiers of Christ', *History* lviii (1973), 169–72

51. G. Duby, 'Les jeunes dans la société aristocratique dans la France du Nord-Ouest au xiie. siècle', *Annales* 19 (1964), 835–46, Cracco, 'Pataria', p. 359

52. cf. M. Douglas, *Natural Symbols* (2nd edn London, 1973), pp. 176–88

53. cf. N. Z. Davis, *art. cit.*, pp. 55–65 and pp. 259–60

Chapter IV THE RELIGIOUS ALTERNATIVE:
HENRY OF LAUSANNE AND PETER OF BRUYS (*pages 82–114*)

1. Ep. 241, *PL* 182 col. 435

2. *Gesta Pontificum Cenomannensium*, Bouquet XII, 547–51, which is the only source for Henry at Le Mans. E. Magnou, 'Note critique sur les sources de l'histoire de Henri l'hérétique jusqu'à son départ du Mans', Actes du 87e. Congrès des sociétés savantes, Poitiers 1962, in *Bulletin philologique et historique* (1965), 539–47, argued that the arrangement of the *Gesta* is confused at this point, and that Henry's appearance at Le Mans should be associated with a journey of Hildebert to Rome in 1100. There is nothing implausible in his having made a second visit to Rome in 1116, however, whereas the lengthening of Henry's career as a heretical preacher from thirty to forty-five years – and there is no possibility of doubt that it was the same man whom St Bernard pursued in the Languedoc – does seem to strain probability. The interpretation of his views which is set out here would not be affected by the change: I agree with Mlle Magnou that Henry was opposed to clerical abuse, though not, for the reasons expounded in the rest of this chapter, that it follows that he was also a Gregorian

3. *PL* 172, col. 1399; on the association between the eremitical life and preaching see G. G. Meersseman, 'Eremitismo e predicazione itinerante dei secoli xi e xii', *Eremitismo in occidente*, pp. 164–81

4. *PL* 172, col. 1397

5. Marbod, Ep. VI, *PL* 171, col. 1483, 1485

6. Meersseman, *loc. cit.* pp. 171–2

7. *PL* 172 col. 1398; Marbod, *loc cit.*, col. 1484

8. John of Salisbury, *Historia Pontificalis* ed. M. Chibnall (London, 1956) p. 3, describing his goal and that of *cronici scriptores alii ante me*.

9. Mundy (1973), p. 222

10. R. Manselli (1953) p. 55 (= 'Debate')

11. A. Esmein, *Le mariage en droit canonique* (2nd edn Paris, 1929) I, 377–92; P. Daudet, *L'établissement de la compétence de l'église en matière de divorce et de consanguinité* (Paris, 1941), 31–68, 88–109; *PL* 171, col. 1474–5

12. Duby, 'Les "jeunes" ' cited above, Chap. III n. 51; M. Bloch, 'De la cour royale à la cour de Rome: le procès des serfs de Rosny-sous-Bois', *Mélanges Historiques* (Paris, 1963) I, 542–61

13. Bouquet XII, 554

14. *PL* 185, col. 412

15. Ep. 241, *PL* 182, col. 434-6

16. *PL* 185, col. 313

17. Debate, p. 44

18. *ibid.* pp. 53, 58, 61; *Tractatus contra Petrobrusianos*, ed. J. V. Fearns, *Corpus Christianorum, Continuatio Mediaevalis* x (1968) p. 5

19. Debate, pp. 45-6

20. *ibid.* p. 47

21. *ibid.* p. 61

22. *Contra Petrobrusianos, loc. cit.*

23. Debate, p. 59

24. A. Fliche and V. Martin (eds.), *Histoire de l'église* 9.1 (Paris, 1946) pp. 91-2

25. Debate, p. 47

26. *ibid.* p. 53

27. *ibid.* p. 58

28. *ibid.* pp. 56-7

29. *ibid.* p. 47

30. Ep. 241, *PL* 182 col. 434

31. Debate, p. 45

32. *Contra Petrobrusianos*, p. 10

33. *ibid.* p. 7

34. *ibid.* p. 5, where the main teachings of Peter of Bruys are listed.

35. *ibid.* pp. 86-7

36. *ibid.* p. 162

37. Constable, *Letters of Peter the Venerable* II, 285-8; J. V. Fearns, 'Peter von Bruis und die religiöse Bewegung des 12 Jahrhunderts', *Archiv fur Kulturge-schichte* 48 (1966), 313-17. With the exception of Borst (p. 3) those who have approached the problem by way of concern with heresy rather than the writings of Peter the Venerable have usually preferred a date before 1135 for the *Tractatus*, on the ground that it does not mention the Council of Pisa. To do so it is necessary to regard Peter the Venerable's references to the treatise against heresy which he was composing between c. 1138 and 1141 as relating to a different work, now lost, of which there is no other trace. This is straining at a gnat to swallow a camel

38. *Contra Petrobrusianos*, pp. 12, 13, 5

39. *ibid.* p. 14

40. *ibid.* p. 10

41. Ep. II, 24, *PL* 171, col. 242. Against the view that letter II, 23 (col. 237-42) was addressed to Henry see P. von Moos, *Hildebert von Lavardin* (Stuttgart, 1965) p. 325

42. R. Latouche, *Etudes médiévales* (Paris, 1968) pp. 121-6, 'La commune du Mans, 1070', reprinted from *Mélanges de l'histoire du Moyen Age dédiés à la mémoire de Louis Halphen* (Paris, 1950)

43. As it was at Bordeaux, where Henry profited from a similar conflict: *PL*

185 col. 411; C. Higounet, *Histoire de Bordeaux* II (Bordeaux, 1963) pp. 98–9

44. P. Wolff, *Histoire du Languedoc* (Toulouse, 1967) pp. 151–2. The probability that the façade of the basilica was designed to rebut Peter's teaching on the crucifixion is discussed by M. Colish, 'Peter of Bruys, Henry of Lausanne and the Façade of St Gilles', *Traditio* 28 (1972), 451–60, and A. Borg, *Architectural Sculpture in Romanesque Provence* (Oxford, 1972) pp. 124–5. If my view of the relations between Peter and Henry is correct, however, these reflections should not be assumed to include the latter

45. Mundy (1954) pp. 3–40

46. *PL* 185, col. 410–16, discussed by E. Griffe, *Les débuts de l'aventure cathare en Languedoc* (Paris, 1969) pp. 21–52, and R. I. Moore, 'St. Bernard's Mission to the Languedoc in 1145', *BIHR* xlvii (1974), 1–10

Chapter V THE POLITICAL ALTERNATIVE:
ARNOLD OF BRESCIA (*pages* 115–136)

1. F. Gregorovius, *History of the City of Rome in the Middle Ages*, trans. A. Hamilton (London, 1895–1902) IV, 546

2. *Gesta Frederici I Imperatoris* (ed. G. Weitz *MGH, SRG* 46), 134; other accounts of Arnold's death are collected by G. W. Greenaway, *Arnold of Brescia* (Cambridge, 1931) pp. 218–21

3. *De nugis curialium*, ed. M R. James, *Anecdota oxoniensia* xiv (Oxford, 1914), 59–60. Otto of Freising is the only source for the tradition that Arnold was a pupil of Abelard. It is not inherently improbable, but A. R. Motte, 'Une fausse accusation contre Abélard et Arnaud de Brescia', *Revue des sciences philosophiques et théologiques* xxii (1933), 39–42, showed that Otto may have misunderstood St Bernard's reference to their association at the time of the Council of Sens

4. *Historia Pontificalis*, ed. Chibnall (= *HP*) p. 63

5. Ep. 195, *PL* 182, col. 362

6. *Gesta Frederici*, *loc. cit.*

7. *ibid.* p. 133

8. *HP, loc. cit.*

9. cf. D. E. Luscombe, *The School of Peter Abelard* (Cambridge, 1969) pp. 26–29

10. *PL* 178, col. 1056

11. *HP, loc. cit.*

12. Epp. 193, 331, 332, *PL* 182 col. 359, 536, 537

13. *HP, loc. cit.*

14. *De nugis curialium*, pp. 38–9; *HP*, pp. 19–20

15. *Gesta Frederici, loc. cit.*; that Arnold met Eberhard of Bodmen and Rudolf of Ravensberg at this time is an inference from their appearance as acceptable negotiators in the 'Wezel' letter: see p. 132 and n. 31 below

16. Ep. 196, *PL* 182, col. 363–4

17. Ep. 238, *PL* 182, col. 429

18. L. Halphen, *Etudes sur l'administration de Rome au moyen âge* (Paris, 1907) pp. 15–36

19. *ibid.* p. 29

20. P. Partner, *The Lands of St. Peter* (London, 1972) pp. 168–87

21. *ibid.* p. 180

22. R. L. Poole (ed.) *The* Historia Pontificalis *of John of Salisbury* (Oxford, 1927) pp. lxiii–lxix; P. Munz, *Frederick Barbarossa* (London, 1969) pp. 61–2

23. *HP*, p. 64

24. *De Consideratione* IV, 2, *PL* 182 col. 774, quoted by Partner, *op. cit.* pp. 185–6

25. *PL* 180, col. 1358; Greenaway, *op. cit.* pp. 123–4

26. Eugenius III to Wibald of Corvie, ed. P. Jaffé, *Bibliotheca Rerum Germanicarum* I (Berlin, 1864) pp. 537–9; the characterization of Arnold's supporters as a *rusticana turba* implies that they were poor, not 'countryfolk', as Greenaway thought (p. 143)

27. Partner, *op. cit.* pp. 178–9, 192–3; on Milan see pp. 56–7

28. Halphen, *op. cit.* pp. 38–41; Partner, p. 179, points out that the effect of these developments was increased by Innocent II's reliance on foreign clerks in the curia

29. Jaffé, *op. cit.* p. 332 ff.

30. Partner, *op. cit.* pp. 183–4

31. Jaffé, *op. cit.* pp. 539–43. Arnold's authorship of this letter was argued by K. Hampe, 'Zur Geschichte Arnolds von Brescia', *Historische Zeitschrift* 130 (1924)

32. Munz, *op. cit.* p. 87, citing the *Carmen de Gestis Frederici I Imperatoris in Lombardia* (ed. I. Schmale-Ott, *MGH, SRG* 62), 1.850. This poem, which emanated from the imperial court about ten years later, speaks with some admiration of Arnold, and does not accuse him of doctrinal error; Walter Map commented that Arnold was condemned 'uncited, undefended, and in his absence'

33. Jaffé, *op. cit.* p. 336

34. Partner, *op. cit.* pp. 219–21

Chapter VI THE PROBLEM OF EVIL (*pages* 139–67)

1. *Phaedo*, trans. W. H. D. Rouse, *Great Dialogues of Plato* (New York, 1956) p. 470

2. *AFP* 1950, p. 308

3. *Confessions*, v. 10, trans. R. S. Pine-Coffin (Harmondsworth, 1961) pp. 103–5

4. cited by G. Widengren, *Mani and Manicheism* (1961, Engl. trans. London, 1965) p. 97, on which this account of Manichean teaching is chiefly based. The political context in which Widengren would place Manicheism is subject to

severe qualification: cf. P. Brown, 'The Diffusion of Manicheism in the Roman Empire', *Journal of Roman Studies* lix (1969), 93–103

5. C. R. C. Allbery, *A Manichaean Psalm-book, Manichaean MSS in the Chester Beatty Collection* II (Stuttgart, 1938)

6. J. Ries, 'Jésus-Christ dans la religion de Mani', *Augustiniana* 14 (1964) 436–54. For Mani's Gnostic background see especially H. C. Puech, *Le Manichéisme: son fondateur, sa doctrine* (Paris, 1949)

7. S. Runciman, *The Medieval Manichee* (Cambridge, 1947), is a classic statement of this view, and the most convenient account of most of the heresies mentioned in this chapter

8. N. Cantor suggests a Neoplatonic origin of dualist theology, *Medieval History* (New York, 1963), pp. 456–57. For other theories, see Wakefield & Evans, pp. 9–12, 18–19 and notes: each such suggestion reinforces the view that the tendency to dualism was inherent in every part of the ancient heritage, cf. N. Garsoian, 'Byzantine heresy: a reinterpretation' *Dumbarton Oaks Papers*, xxv (1971), 87–113

9. Garsoian, *loc. cit.* 108ff.

10. The view that the Messalians celebrated their liberation from the flesh by deeds of the most licentious depravity, which seems to be generally accepted by modern commentators on them (with the exception of A. Vööbus, *History of Asceticism in the Syrian Orient*, II, *Early Monasticism in Mesopotamia and Syria, Corpus Scriptorum Christianorum Orientalium*, 197, *Subsidia* 17 (Louvain, 1960), II, 131–7) deserves the same scepticism that is bestowed elsewhere in these pages on the numerous similar allegations directed at enthusiastic communities. How would St Augustine's injunction, 'Dilige et fac quod vis', have been interpreted if he had been a heretic? For a sustained discussion of the problem, as valid for earlier periods as for that to which it relates, see R. E. Lerner, *The Heresy of the Free Spirit in the Later Middle Ages* (Berkeley and Los Angeles, 1972) pp. 10–34

11. D. Obolensky, *The Bogomils* (Cambridge, 1948) p. 266; this chapter leans heavily on Obolensky's work

12. The authenticity of the *Historia Manichaeorum* has been attacked by N. Garsoian, *The Paulician Heresy* (Hague, Paris, 1967) and defended with vigour by P. Lemerle, 'L'histoire des Pauliciens d'Asie mineure d'après les sources grecques', *Travaux et Mémoires*: 5 (1973), 1–135. This invaluable discussion includes a full survey of earlier work on the Paulicians

13. Obolensky, *op. cit.* p. 11ff.

14. H. C. Puech and A. Vaillant, *Le Traité contre les bogomiles de Cosmas le prêtre* (*Travaux publiés par l'Institut des études slaves* 21), Paris, 1945

15. *ibid.* pp. 55–6

16. *ibid.* p. 59

17. *ibid.* p. 69

18. *ibid.* p. 106

19. D. Obolensky, *The Byzantine Commonwealth* (London, 1971) p. 113

20. D. Angelov, *Le Bogomilisme en Bulgarie* (Fr. trans. Toulouse, 1972) pp. 24–5. The reservations on the use of the term 'feudalisation' about the tenth century are those of Obolensky, *Byz. Comm.* p. 118

21. *Le traité . . . de Cosmas* p. 86

22. *PL* 119, col. 978–1016, discussed by Obolensky, *Byz. Comm.* p. 87ff.

23. Obolensky, *Bogomils*, p. 174ff. The followers of Tzurillas were known in western Asia Minor as Phundagiagitae, but there is no reasonable doubt that they were Bogomils. J. Ivanov suggested a Bulgarian derivation for the name Tzurillas, pointing to a direct missionary connection between the two regions (*ibid.* p. 175, n. 3)

24. The *Alexiad* of Anna Comnena, trans. E. R. A. Sewter (Harmondsworth, 1969) p. 500

25. Obolensky, *op. cit.* pp. 215–16

26. Euthymius, describing a prayer-meeting, refers to 'the presiding member of the community', *ibid.* p. 182

27. Runciman, *op. cit.* p. 69

28. M. Loos, 'Le mouvement Paulicien à Byzance' II, *Byzantinoslavica* xxv (1964), 57–68

29. M. Loos, 'Certains aspects du Bogomilism Byzantin', *ibid.* xxviii (1967) 51–3; *Secret Supper* trans. Wakefield & Evans (1965) p. 458

30. Dondaine *RSCI* (1952)

31. *ibid.* p. 61

32. C. N. L. Brooke, 'Heresy and Religious Sentiment', 41 *BIHR* (1968), 120. Brooke does not commit himself to either view on this point, but stresses the elements within orthodox religious opinion which were consonant with heretical enthusiasm

33. R. Morghen, *Medioevo Cristiano* (Bari, 1953), pp. 212–36, most recently restated in *RH* cccxxxvi (1966), 1–16, and now the most widely accepted view.

34. Above, pp. 26–45 and more fully in 'The Origins of Medieval Heresy', *History* lxv (1970), 21–36

35. Russell (1965) p. 21, but Russell is not a proponent of Bogomil influence in the eleventh-century west

36. Fearns, 'Peter von Bruis' (cited above, Chap. iv. n. 37) pp. 330–2

37. H. C. Puech, 'Catharisme médiévale et Bogomilisme', *Oriente ed Occidente nel Medio Evo* (Rome, 1957), pp. 56–84 views them from the East, and with notable scepticism.

38. Obolensky, *The Bogomils*, pp. 186–7, and above p. 27. I was not aware of Paul's imitation of Justin Martyr in *History* (1970) p. 27; there is a moral in the fact that it was noticed by R. L. Poole, *Illustrations of the History of Medieval Thought and Learning* (2nd edn Oxford, 1920, reprinted New York, 1960) p. 85, who had it from Gibbon. The tradition of distortion of which these stories are examples is now expounded by N. Cohn *Europe's Inner Demons* (London, 1975)

39. G. Cracco, 'Riforma ed eresia in momenti della cultura Europea tra X e XI secolo', *Riv. di storia e letteratura religiosa* vii (1971), 441

Chapter VII THE ARRIVAL OF THE CATHARS (*pages* 168–96)

1. *PL* 182, col. 676–80

2. *Annales Brunwilarenses*, *MGH:SS* XVI, 727

3. *PL* 179, col. 137–8 J. B. Russell, 'Les Cathares de 1048–54 à Liège', *Bull. de la société d'Art et d'Histoire du diocèse de Liège*, xliv (1961) argued that this letter, addressed to 'Pope L.' was sent to Leo IX (1048–54), but his case was effectively answered by H. Silvestre, *RHE* lviii (1963), 979–80 and P. Bonenfant, 'Un clerc cathare en Lotharingie au milieu du xiie. siècle', *MA* lxix (1963), 278–9

4. Anselm, p. 308

5. H. C. Puech, 'Catharisme médiévale et Bogomilisme', *Oriente ed Occidente nel medio evo*, Accademia dei Lincei, Fondazione volta Convegno 12 (Rome, 1957) pp. 68–71

6. C. Thouzellier, 'Hérésie et croisade au xiie siècle', *RHE* xlix (1954), 855–72 and, slightly modified (1969) pp. 17–37

7. cf. P. Brown, 'The Diffusion of Manichaeism in the Roman Empire', *Journal of Roman Studies*, lix (1969), 92–103

8. Obolensky (1948) pp. 219–22; Puech, *loc. cit.* p. 78

9. Moore *BIHR* (1974) pp. 4–7; A. Borst, 'La transmission de l'hérésie au moyen-âge' in Le Goff (1969) pp. 273–7

10. Mansi XXI, col. 483

11. cf. Rainier Sacchoni, p. 68, and Lambert le Bègue (cited below, n. 40, p. 31), on the ability of the better off to evade persecution, as well as the unsuccessful attempt of those accused at Arras in 1163, p. 183 to do so.

12. Bonenfant, *loc. cit.* pp. 271–80

13. *PL* 195 col. 11–102; the date of composition is established by Borst (1953) p. 7 n. 30, and R. Manselli, 'Ecberto di Schönau e l'eresia Catara', in *Arte e Storia: Studi in onore di Leonello Vincent* (Turin, 1965) pp. 311–38, the fullest study of Eckbert and his work.

14. *PL* 195, col. 92

15. *ibid.* col. 84, 88, 13

16. *Chronica Regia Coloniensis*, *MGH*, *SRG* 18,114; Maisonneuve, pp. 111–12

17. *PL* 195, col. 16, 18

18. *ibid.*, col. 84. But where was the *schola Catharorum* from which he had returned? This may be one of the contacts with Constantinople for which evidence is adduced on pp. 180–82

19. *ibid.* col. 51–2

20. *ibid.* col. 52

21. *ibid.* col. 15, 14, 34

22. *ibid.* col. 14, 'qui perfecte sectam illorum ingressi sunt'

23. *ibid.* col. 15–16

24. *ibid.* col. 14–15

25. *ibid.* col. 26ff.

26. cf. Marbod, Ep. VI, to Robert of Arbrissel, *PL* 171, col. 1481–2, citing

Augustine and Jerome; Geoffrey of Vendome, Epp. xlvii and xlviii, *PL* 157, col. 181–2, 184–5; Bernard, *Sermones in Cantica* lxv, *PL* 183, col. 1091; Southern pp. 314–15

27. *PL* 195, col. 30–1

28. *De heresi catharorum in Lombardia*, *AFP* (1949), 310

29. *PL* 195, col. 15, 94

30. *ibid.* col. 96, 16

31. Manselli, *loc. cit.*, pp. 330–3; for Nazarius and the *Secret Supper* see Borst (1953) pp. 101–2, and Anselm of Alessandria, *AFP* (1950) pp. 311, 319

32. Bouquet, XV, pp. 790, 792, 799; William of Newburgh, *Historia rerum Anglicarum*, Chronicles of the Reigns of Stephen, etc. (London, *RS* 1884), i, 131–4; *Historia Viziliacensis monasterii*, Bouquet XII, 343–4; Ralph of Coggeshall, *Chronicon Anglicanum*, ed J. Stevenson (London, *RS* 1875) pp. 121–5

33. Above, n. 10. The use of the name *publicani* and its variants has been much discussed, e.g. by Runciman pp. 121–2, Puech *loc. cit.* pp. 59–61. It seems to have been borrowed by crusaders from the Greeks, e.g. *Gesta Francorum*, ed. R. M. T. Hill (London, 1962) pp. 20, 26, 49, 83; that author's indiscriminate use of it as a term for heretics in general (p. 20n.) is a useful caution against attributing too much precision to it. Other references in crusading sources are collected by N. Garsoian, *The Paulician Heresy* (Hague and Paris, 1967) pp. 14–17, and in western sources by Borst (1953) pp. 246–8

34. William of Newburgh, p. 133

35. See pp. 206ff.

36. *PL* 182, col. 678

37. E. Martène and U. Durand, *Amplissima Collectio* (Paris, 1724–33) IX, col. 1252–70

38. Urban's ruling was, in fact, quite consistent with Augustine's doctrine that it was 'in God's merit in giving, and my faith in receiving' that the power of the sacrament resided: see pp. 60–61. Russell's discussion of Albero's view (1965, p. 89) appears to be based on a misreading of this passage, col. 1263: it was Urban who described the sacraments of false priests, not Albero those of sinful priests, as *imagines*

39. *Serm. in cantica* lxv, *PL* 183, col. 1092

40. P. Fredericq, *Corpus documentorum inquisitionis haereticae pravitatis Neerlandicae* II, 30

41. *ibid.* pp. 10, 29

42. *ibid.* pp. 28–9

43. *ibid.* p. 21

44. Above, notes 9, 11

45. See above, pp. 45, 51–2, 71–2; Southern, pp. 319–28; E. W. McDonnell, *The Béguines and Béghards in Medieval Culture* (New Brunswick, 1954) pp. 71ff.; A. Mens, 'Les béguines et les béghards dans le cadre de la culture médiévale', *MA* lxiv (1958), 305–15

Chapter VIII THE NEW HERESY IN THE SOUTH (*pages* 197–240)

1. *PL* 181, col. 1721
2. Puech and Vaillant (ed.) pp. 74–5. A similar formula was used in the rituals of the western Cathars: Dondaine *RSCI* (1952) pp. 71–4
3. Borst, pp. 4–5, 52, and on Bernard's view of his success Moore, *BIHR* (1974) 9–10. Wakefield and Evans (p. 138) agree that 'Catharist tenets and practices seem to be revealed in this letter', but adhere to the earlier date
4. ed. H. R. Luard, *Annales Monastici* (London, *RS* 1864) I, 15
5. Mansi XXI, col. 1177
6. *PL* 185, col. 411
7. Moore (1974). Mlle Thouzellier (1969, p. 225) draws attention to the comment of Harvey of Déols (d. 1150) that there were heretics at Agen who forbade marriage and abstained from meat. Certainly it is striking that he gave as the reason for the latter that God did not create it, and if he was right in attributing that view to his *Agimnenses* it would suggest that they were theological dualists. But the context, that of an academic commentary on I Tim. 4 – Paul's prophecy of the last days – in which they are bracketed with the *Manichaei*, makes it difficult to regard this as a piece of historical reporting
8. Mansi XXII, col. 157–68
9. Anselm, p. 308
10. *ibid.* pp. 308–9
11. *ibid.* p. 309 and *De heresi*, p. 306. The two accounts are closely in harmony, but there are occasional differences: here, for example, Anselm says that it was Nicetas who 'made a bad end'
12. *De heresi*, p. 308
13. *ibid. loc. cit.*; Rainier Sacchoni, p. 77
14. See B. Hamilton, 'The Origins of the Dualist Church of Drugunthia', *Eastern Churches Review* V (1973), 115–24
15. Anselm, p. 319
16. *Annales Florentinae*, MGH:SS XIX, 224; *Vita Sancti Petri Parentinii*, *Acta Sanctorum*, May V, 86; *Vita Sancti Galdini*, *Acta Sanctorum*, April II, 591
17. Gervase of Canterbury, *Opera historica* ed. W. Stubbs (London, *RS* 1879), I, 270
18. The controversy is well summarized by P. Wolff, *Documents de l'histoire du Languedoc* (Toulouse, 1969) pp. 99–106; the participants are listed in the notes to the Appendix, pp. 313–15 below
19. In the light of Mr Hamilton's analysis I retract the view expressed in 'Nicetas, émissaire de Dragovitch, a-t-il traversé les Alpes?', *Annales du Midi* 85 (1973), 85–90, that Nicetas did not visit the Languedoc, and am grateful to Mr Hamilton for making it possible for me to use the evidence of the '*Acta*' for what follows. The other conclusions of that note, that some Bulgarian influence remained in the Languedoc at the time of the Lombard schisms (below, n. 21)

and that the appearance of absolute dualism in Toulouse was connected, at least chronologically, with the political crisis of 1175–6, are not affected

20. It may be doubted whether the Languedocian tradition represented here is right in including Mark among those reconsoled on this occasion. It would have been a natural error, but it seems more likely that Mark accepted the *consolamentum* from Nicetas in Italy immediately on being converted by him, and the Italian sources contain no hint that he consulted outside his own followers before taking the step

21. There is no way of deciding between Mr Hamilton's view that the bishop *ultra montes* was of the French church, and mine that he was from the Languedoc. In either case, however, his advice implies that Nicetas' success had been incomplete, since Robert d'Espernon as well as the bishops of the Languedoc is said to have been reconsoled by him

22. *PL* 204, col. 236

23. 'Benedict of Peterborough', *Gesta Regis Henrici Secundi*, ed. W. Stubbs (London, *RS* 1867), i, 203

24. *ibid.* pp. 203–4. The statement of the *bons hommes* at Lombers had not included a denial of the two principles

25. Mundy (1954), pp. 60–6 and 'Noblesse et hérésie. Une famille cathare: les Maurand', *Annales* 29 (1974)

26. *PL* 204, col. 239

27. *De heresi*, p. 293. Father Dondaine's 'apparenté' might not, perhaps, have been qualified so much if he had shared the view expressed above that all the Cathar churches were descendants of the Bogomils at various stages of their evolution, and had no direct descent from the Paulicians, Messalians or any other allegedly 'Manichaean' heresy of the East. Nevertheless his judgement remains unchallengeable

28. *De heresi*, pp. 309–10

29. *ibid.* p. 310

30. The *Secret Supper*, trans. Wakefield and Evans, pp. 460–61

31. Anselm, pp. 313–14

32. Rainier Sacchoni, p. 70; for a survey of recent attempts to estimate the number of Cathars in the Languedoc c. 1200 see W. L. Wakefield, *Heresy, Crusade and Inquisition in Southern France*, 1100–1250 (London, 1974), pp. 68–71

33. E. Dupré-Theseider, 'Le catharisme languedocien et l'Italie', *C de F* 3 (1968) *Cathares en Languedoc*, pp. 299–313

34. Matthew Paris, *Chronica majora* ed. H. R. Luard (London, *RS* 1872–83), iv, 270–2, trans. Wakefield and Evans, pp. 186–7

35. Runciman, pp. 96, 162, and Obolensky, p. 246. A. Soloviev was inclined to exhume the Black Pope, 'Autour des Bogomiles', *Byzantion* xxii (1952), 91–104, but his case rested on the hypothetical influence of Balasinanza, Cathar bishop of Verona in the 1220s, and an ambiguous reference from the fourteenth century

36. Anselm, pp. 316–17

37. ed. Dondaine, p. 68; cf. Y. Dossat, 'Les cathares d'après l'inquisition', *C de F* 3 (1968), pp. 85–7

38. *Histoire albigeoise*, trans. P. Guebin and H. Maisonneuve (Paris, 1951), p. 8; Rainier, ed. Dondaine, p. 66; also Anselm, p. 310; cf. Wakefield and Evans p. 694 n. 14

39. trans. Wakefield and Evans, pp. 303–8

40. B. Hamilton, *The Albigensian Crusade* (London, Historical Association, 1974) p. 9

41. Mundy (1973) p. 452, makes the same point from the other aspect, stressing the gloom which pervaded much of Catholic thought and attitudes; cf. C. N. L. Brooke, 'Heresy and Religious Sentiment: 1000–1250', *BIHR* xli (1968), esp. pp. 125–31

42. I. da Milano, *L'Eresia di Ugo Speroni nella confutazione del Maestro Vacario* (*Studi e Testi* CXV, Vatican, 1945): Wakefield and Evans, pp. 152–8, 173–8; nothing is known of the Arnoldists except that they were condemned

43. N. Cohn, *The Pursuit of the Millenium* (3rd edn London, 1972), pp. 152–6, but cf. G. Leff, *Heresy in the Later Middle Ages* (Manchester, 1967), pp. 309–10 and R. E. Lerner, *The Heresy of the Free Spirit* (Berkeley, 1972) *passim*.

44. Brenda M. Bolton, 'Innocent III's treatment of the *Humiliati*', 'Sources for the Early History of the *Humiliati*', *Studies in Church History*, ed. D. M. Baker (Cambridge), VIII (1971), XI, 1974, and 'The Poverty of the *Humiliati*', *Poverty in the Middle Ages*, ed. D. Flood, *Franziskanische Forschungen*, xxvii (1975)

45. *Chronicon universale anonymi Laudunensis, MGH:SS* xxvi, 447–9

46. cf. B. H. Rosenwein and L. K. Little, 'Social Meaning in the Monastic and Mendicant Spiritualities', *P & P* 63 (1974), 20–32, and L. K. Little, 'Pride Goes Before Avarice: Social Change and the Vices in Latin Christendom', *American Historical Review* 76 (1971), 16–49

47. A. Dondaine, 'Aux origines du valdéisme: une profession de foi de Valdes', *AFP* xvi (1946), 191–235

48. Walter Map, *De nugis curialium* ed. James, p. 62

49. Thouzellier (1966) pp. 36–48, 170–5, 215–37

50. Rainier Sacchoni, p. 78; Anselm, pp. 318, 320

51. Mundy (1954) p. 57

52. *Vita S. Petri Parentinii, Acta Sancorum* May V, 86

53. P. Belperron, *La croisade contre les albigeois et l'union du Languedoc à la France* (Paris, 1942, reprinted 1967) p. 43; see also Mundy (1954) and Hamilton (1974) *passim*

54. Marc Bloch, *Feudal Society* (Eng. trans. London, 1961) pp. 176–7

55. Belperron, *op. cit.* p. 47

56. *PL* 204, col. 240; Hamilton, *op. cit.* p. 11

57. A. R. Lewis, *The Development of Southern French and Catalan Society* 718–1050 (Austin, 1965) pp. 317–25

58. cf. Mundy (1954) pp. 80–83

59. Hamilton, *op. cit.* pp. 16–17

60. Mundy, (1954) pp. 78–9, 289–90; 'Charity and Social Work in Toulouse, 1150–1250', *Traditio* xxii (1966), 208–39

61. Wakefield (1974) pp. 71–5 offers a useful, and sceptical, summary on this point. On the related question whether there was any affiliation between Catharism and courtly poetry I agree with him that 'such arguments, on the whole, offer no more solid evidence of a connection between the poets and the heresy than that they existed at the same time in Languedoc' (p. 59); for a terse examination of one attempt to make such a link see H. Rousseau, 'L'interprétation du catharisme' and C. Thouzellier, 'Les cathares languedociens et le "nichil"' in *Annales* 24 (1969), 128–41

62. cf. E. Griffe, *Les débuts de l'aventure cathare en Languedoc* (Paris, 1969), pp. 174–208

63. J. Bordenave and M. Vialelle, *Aux racines du mouvement cathare: la mentalité réligeuse des paysans de l'Albigeois médiévale* (Toulouse, 1973). Despite its title this extremely interesting work establishes no connection, and to my mind indicates no probability of one, between the practices which it traces and the 'roots of the Cathar movement'. The suggestion that the inquisitors referred to the subterranean chambers and tunnels whose excavation the book describes, and whose use they do seem to have attacked successfully, when they spoke of the secret refuges of the Cathars in various phrases has some plausibility, though it will be remembered that it was standard rhetoric to describe heretics as skulking in cellars and places of concealment

64. C. Violante, 'Hérésies urbaines et hérésies rurales en Italie du 11e au 13e siècle' in Le Goff, p. 181; Lea II, 196–7

65. Dupré-Theseider, *loc. cit.* p. 306

66. Violante, *loc. cit.* p. 183; G. Volpe, *Movimenti religiosi e sette ereticali nella società medievale italiana* (Florence, 1922, repr. 1961) pp. 109–10

67. Violante, *loc. cit.*; Manselli (1963) p. 294

68. cited by Volpe, *op. cit.*, p. 104

69. For general discussions of the social composition of Cathar support in Italy see especially Violante, *loc. cit.*, Volpe, *op. cit.* pp. 101–13, Manselli (1963), pp. 276–95. On the meaning of 'nobles' the remarks of D. Waley, *The Italian City Republics* (London, 1969) pp. 22–4, 43–55, are highly pertinent

70. Volpe, *op. cit.* pp. 170–1; Mundy (1973) pp. 544–5

71. Volpe, *op. cit.* p. 106

72. Anselm, pp. 310–12; Rainier Sacchoni, pp. 72–6. The convergence of these thinkers with Catholicism is discussed by Borst, pp. 120–2, 162–7, and Leff, *op. cit.* pp. 445–8, though the view of the latter that modified dualism developed after absolute dualism, as part of this convergence, is untenable; its characterization as 'conservative' is, of course, my own.

Chapter IX ELUCIDATIONS AND REACTIONS (*pages 243–62*)

1. *Feudal Society* (London, 1961), p. 37

2. Y. M. J. Congar, ' "Arriana haeresis" comme désignation du néomanichéisme au xiie. siècle', *Rev. des sciences philosophiques et théologiques* xliii (1959), 449–61

3. Bernard, *Sermones in cantica* lxvi, *PL* 183, col. 1094; J. H. Mundy, 'Une famille cathare: les Maurand', *Annales* 29 (1974), 12–14; Wakefield and Evans, pp. 205, 709

4. Congar, *loc. cit.*; R. Manselli, 'Una designazione dell'eresia catara: "Arriana heresis", *Bull. del Istituto storico italiano per il medio evo* 68 (1956), 233–46; Thouzellier (1969) pp. 204–21

5. Manselli (1953), p. 60; R. I. Moore, 'Heresy as Disease', *The Concept of Heresy in the Middle Ages, Medievalia Lovanensia* IV (Louvain, 1976); S. N. Brody, *The Disease of the Soul: Leprosy in Medieval Literature* (Ithaca and London, 1974) pp. 21–106

6. Southern p. 93

7. Maisonneuve, p. 109

8. See pp. 182–3

9. It should also be remembered, however, that the destruction of dwelling places was a traditional punishment for the violation of the communal oath: P. Ourliac, *C de F* 6, pp. 383–4

10. *Chronica regia Coloniensis, MGH, SRG* 18, 114

11. Maisonneuve, pp. 29–149, R. Manselli, 'De la "persuasio" à la "coercitio" ' *C de F* 6, *Le Credo, la Morale et l'Inquisition*, pp. 175–97, and Y. Dossat, 'La répression de l'hérésie par les évêques' *ibid.* pp. 217–51, trace the development of coercion more systematically than is attempted here

12. *PL* 183, col. 1101

13. Maisonneuve, pp. 108–11

14. A. R. Lewis, *The Development of Southern French and Catalan Society,* 718–1050 (Austin, 1965) pp. 191–4, 315–36; H. E. J. Cowdrey, *The Cluniacs and the Gregorian Reform* (Oxford, 1970) pp. 96–112

15. Maisonneuve, pp. 133–5

16. *ibid.* pp. 151–5

17. cf. *ibid.* p. 112 St Bernard, *loc. cit.* appears to refer to the burnings at Cologne in 1143 when he describes the ordeal by water as a preliminary to popular action. If so, however, he had more information than Eberwin's letter contained – perhaps from its bearer?

18. P. Brown, 'Society and the Supernatural: A Medieval Change', *Daedalus* (1975) 133–55, from which the argument that follows is entirely derived. I am also indebted to C. Morris, '*Judicium Dei*', *Studies in Church History*, ed. D. Baker, xii, *Church, Society and Politics* (1975), 95–111

19. Cited by Brown, *loc. cit.* p. 140. The same point is illustrated by the story, given to me on excellent authority, of how a member of the I.R.A. was arrested in possession of a firearm, before witnesses, in County Armagh *c.* 1960. He was charged with illegal possession and acquitted by a jury of twelve Orangemen,

whose foreman explained afterwards that it was thought wrong that a respectable family should be disgraced by the folly of a young man

Chapter X THE CHALLENGE OF DISSENT (*pages* 263–83)

1. H. Grundmann, *Religiöse Bewegungen im Mittelalter* (Berlin, 1935); the quotations are from the second edition (Darmstadt, 1961) pp. 519, 26
2. Russell, p. 2
3. H. Pirenne, *Medieval Cities* (Princeton, 1925) p. 233
4. J. B. Russell, 'Interpretations of the Origins of Medieval Heresy', *Mediaeval Studies* xxv (1963), 26–53, provides a full survey of explanations which have been advanced in the past century or so, some more serious than others; the principal Marxist view is that of E. Werner, *Pauperes Christi* (Leipzig, 1956) and *Häresie und Gesellschaft im 11. Jahrhundert, Sitzungsberichte der Sachsischen Akademie der Wissenschaften zu Leipzig* (Berlin, 1975). Russell's objection that most such interpretations have over-strained the evidence (*ibid. passim*, and *Dissent and Reform* pp. 230–58) is valid, but marred by a tendency to assume that every social – or, as he puts it, 'materialist' – explanation collapses with that of class conflict, that nothing less than a complete or nearly complete correlation has significance, and that such correlations must be shown to apply not only to the popular heresies of the eleventh and twelfth centuries, but to those of the eighth, ninth and tenth centuries whose existence as a general phenomenon he has failed to demonstrate. A. P. Evans, 'Social Aspects of Medieval Heresy', *Persecution and Liberty: Essays in Honor of George Lincoln Burr* (New York, 1931) pp. 93–116 is still a most valuable discussion
5. *PL* 156, cols. 911–21
6. The discussion which follows summarizes and in some details modifies my paper 'The Cult of the Heresiarch' which will be published among the proceedings of the Fourth conference of the Commission internationale pour l'histoire écclésiastique comparée, held at Oxford in 1974; it represents an attempt to apply to these heretics Peter Brown's analysis of 'The Rise and Function of the Holy Man in Late Antiquity', *Journal of Roman Studies* 61 (1971), 80–101; cf. Janet L. Nelson, 'Society, Theodicy and the Origins of Heresy', *Schism, Heresy and Religious Protest, Studies in Church History* 9, ed. Derek Baker (Cambridge, 1972) 65–77
7. *The Life of Christina of Markyate* ed. C. H. Talbot (Oxford, 1959) p. 82; cf. H. Mayr-Harting, 'Functions of a Twelfth-Century Recluse', *History* lx (1975), 337–52
8. *PL* 181, col. 1721
9. *PL* 185, col. 410–16
10. cf. H. E. J. Cowdrey, 'The Peace and the Truce of God in the Eleventh Century', *P & P* 46 (1970), 49–56
11. cited by B. Smalley, *Trends in Medieval Political Thought* (Oxford, 1965) p. x

12. R. W. Southern, *The Making of the Middle Ages* (London, 1953) p. 137
13. L. Genicot, in *L'eremitismo in occidente*, pp. 45–69
14. Mary Douglas, *Natural Symbols* (2nd edn London, 1973) p. 187
15. Southern (1970) p. 111
16. This point has received much attention in recent years; see especially M. Mollat, 'La notion de la pauvreté au moyen âge: position de problèmes', *Rev. d'histoire de l'église en France* lii (1966), 5–23, G. Duby, 'Les pauvres des campagnes dans l'occident médiévale jusqu'au xiiie siècle', *ibid.*, 25–32. K. Bosl, '*Potens* und *Pauper*', *Festschrift für O. Brunner* (Gottingen, 1963) pp. 60–87
17. T. Manteuffel, *Naissance d'une hérésie* (Paris and The Hague, 1960) *passim*
18. *De nugis curialium* ed. M. R. James, p. 12

APPENDIX (*pages 285–9*)

1. G. Besse, *Histoire des ducs, marquis et comtes de Narbonne*, Paris 1660, pp. 483–6. The principal works referred to in this Appendix are: A. Dondaine, 'Les Actes du concile albigeois de St-Félix de Caraman', *Miscellanea Giovanni Mercati* V, *Studi e Testi* 125 (Vatican, 1946), 324–55; *De heresi*; Anselm; Y. Dossat, 'Remarques sur un prétendu évêque cathare du Val d'Aran en 1167', *Bull. phil. et hist.* (1955/6), 339–42; 'A propos du concile cathare de Saint-Félix: Les Milingues', *C de F* 3 (1968), 201–14; Fr. Sanjek, 'Le rassemblement hérétique de Saint-Félix-de-Caraman (1167) et les églises cathares au XIIe siècle', *RHE* 67, (1972), 767–99
2. Dossat, 'A propos', *passim*
3. Besse, *op. cit.* pp. 324–6. In an earlier work he wrote of the Cathars: 'Ces Hérétiques furent appellez par les Catholiques Faidits, de mesure que nous appellons ceux d'auiourd 'huy huguenots'. *Histoire des Comtes de Carcassonne*, Paris 1645, p. 124
4. 'Comme le constate le P. Dondaine ... "L'ensemble des données historiques connues par l'auteur de la *notitia* (de Saint-Félix), leur heureuse harmonie ne permet pas de penser que cette *notitia* ait été écrite au milieu du xviie siècle.' E. Griffe, 'Le Catharisme dans le diocèse de Carcassonne et le Lauragais au XIIe siècle', *C de F* 3 (1968), p. 221
5. Some, but not all, of these problems have been raised by Dossat in the articles cited in n. 1 above. The defence offered by Sanjek of the authenticity of the document does not meet all of Dossat's objections
6. 'Hoc translatum fecit translare Dominus Petrus Isarn de Antiqua Carta in potestate supra dictorum facta, q. Eccl. sic. superius scriptum est diviserunt Feria II in mense Augusti, XIV. Die, in introitu mensis, Anno M.CC.XXXII. ab incarnatione Domini. Petrus Pollanus translatavit haec, omnia rogatus ac mandatus.'
7. Cl. Devic, J. Vaissète, *Histoire générale de Languedoc*, ed. A. Molinier, Toulouse 1879–1904, VI, p. 619, which cites a record from Montpellier which is no longer extant

8. Peter Isarn is first mentioned as Bishop in the deposition which Raimond Aiffre made to the Inquisition about events in 1223, Dondaine, 'Les Actes', p. 347, n. 46. For the renewal of Cathar activity immediately the Crusaders withdrew see E. Griffe, *Le Languedoc cathare au temps de la Croisade* (1209–29), Paris 1973, pp. 208ff. I hope to show elsewhere that Peter Isarn was also faced by schism in his diocese, and that this was an additional reason for his interest in the Council of Saint-Félix

9. The document was evidently drawn up in the first instance for the Cathars of Toulouse: it stresses that it was the Church of Toulouse which brought Niquinta to Saint-Félix; that the Church of Toulouse played some part in the appointment of the first Cathar Bishop of Carcassonne; while Niquinta's sermon is said to have been preached only to the Church of Toulouse

10. It would have been comparatively easy to read X instead of I in a 400 year old manuscript

11. Dondaine translated this passage (for the Latin see n. 6 above), thus: 'Comme on l'a écrit plus haut, les arbitres divisèrent les diocèses le lundi 14 août (sous-entendu 1167) et que Pierre Pollanus en fit une copie en 1232.' 'Les Actes', p. 329. He claimed that the construction logically demanded this interpretation, but this is not so if the abbreviation q. is expanded to *qui* instead of *que*. Dossat called Dondaine's emendation of the date 'une disposition insolite', 'A propos', p. 206. In the light of the Italian evidence which he later discovered Dondaine was forced to agree that the Council could not have been held in 1167. He suggested 1172 as a possible alternative because 14 August was a Monday in that year, *AFP* XX p. 268. As is stated below, the Council must have been held in a later year when 14 August did not fall on a Monday

12. Besse refers to 'l'Acte que ie dois donner tout entier, et dont i'employe un extraict au fond de cette Histoire', *Histoire . . . de Narbonne*, p. 325

13. *Ibid.* p. 483

14. 'Les Actes', p. 324

15. These sources are the *De heresi catharorum* and Anselm's *Tractatus de Hereticis* cited in n. 1 above

16. e.g. Rainier Sacconi speaks of the *Ecclesia Sclavoniae*, p. 70. See also Sanjek, 'Le rassemblement', pp. 795–8

17. e. g. The *De heresi* p. 306 speaks of the *Ordo Drugonthie*, R. Sacchoni, p. 70 of the *Ecclesia Dugunthiae*

18. F. Dvornik, *Les Slaves, Byzance et Rome au IXᵉ siècle*, Paris 1926, p. 236

19. This would have been a simple error for a copyist or a type-setter to have made, because all the other churches in the list have genitive forms: *Dragometiae*, *Melenguiae*, *Bulgariae* and *Dalmatiae*. The emendation *Ecclesia Romaniae* suggested by Dondaine, 'Les Actes', p. 344 n. 35, and followed by Dossat, 'A propos', p. 209, and Sanjek, 'Le rassemblement', pp. 788–9, would identify this church with that of Philadelphia *in Romania* listed by Sacchoni in his *Summa* of c. 1250, p. 70. This is not satisfactory, since it would leave the Church of Constantinople out of Niquinta's list, while, as I have stated in *Eastern Churches*

Review V, 1973, pp. 122–3, there is reason to suppose that the Church of Philadelphia was only founded after the Fourth Crusade

20. Dossat, 'A propos', pp. 209–13. His opinion about the location of this church is shared by J. Duvernoy, *Le Régistre de l'Inquisition de Jacques Fournier* (Toulouse, 1965) I, p. 28. Other scholars would locate this Church near Melnik in Macedonia: Obolensky (1948) pp. 156–7; Sanjek, 'Le rassemblement', pp. 791–2

21. Dossat argues that because the Milingui had been firmly converted to Orthodoxy none of them could have lapsed into heresy, 'A propos', p. 212. If applied to Constantinople, Lombardy or Languedoc this argument would imply that dualism could not have spread in any of those regions

22. The Milingui were constantly at war with the Franks, and in 1248/9 William de Villehardouin built a series of fortresses to contain them, H. E. Lurier, *Crusaders as Conquerors. The Chronicle of Morea* (New York and London 1964) pp. 120, 158–60, In such circumstances communications between the Church of the Milingui and other dualists may have been difficult, which may account for its absence from Rainier Sacchoni's list, p. 70

23. 'Isti portaverunt heresim in Lonbardiam . . . circa tempus quo currebat Mclxxiiii.' Anselm, c. 13, p. 319. See p. 211

24. The document must later have formed part of some Catholic archive, and may have been catalogued under the year 1167. I owe this suggestion to Mr Moore

25. See p. 212

26. *Chronica magistri Rogeri de Houedene*, ed. W. Stubbs, 4 vols. (London RS 1868–71), II, pp. 150–5; William of Puylaurens, *Cronica Albigensium* c. 4, ed. J. Beyssier, Université de Paris, *Bibliothèque de la Faculté des Lettres* XVII, 1904, pp. 122–3; Borst, pp. 232–3

27. Dossat, 'Remarques', pp. 339–42. Besse understood *Aranensis* as a reference to the Val d'Aran, *Histoire . . . de Narbonne*, p. 325

28. At Saint-Félix the council of the Church of Carcassonne was led by Bernard the Catalan

29. Thouzellier (1966) pp. 13–14. cf. Sanjek, 'Le rassemblement', pp. 786–7

30. See p. 308 n. 20

31. See pp. 205–6. 'Ecclesia Franciae concordat cum Baiolensi', Rainier Sacchoni, p. 77

32. *De heresi*, pp. 306–7. See p. 308 n. 21. The argument of the Appendix is set out in full in B. Hamilton, 'The Cathar Council of Saint-Félix-de-Caraman reconsidered', to appear in *Archivum Fratrum Praedicatorum* (1978)

Index

320] *Index*

Patarenes
of Milan 40, 55–71, 77, 266–8
as a name for Cathars 211, 246
Paul, St, prophecy of the last days (1 Tim.
4) 8, 12, 14, 243, 245
Paul of St Père de Chartres, chronicler
30, 167, 248
Paulicians, the 149–51, 159, 163–4, 173,
184–5
Pavia 128
Pelagius 4, 99
perfecti see Cathars
Périgueux 91, 114, 197–8
Peter of Bruys 95, 102–7, 110, 113, 117,
166, 199–200, 248, 271, 299, 300
Peter, Tsar of Bulgaria 151–2, 155, 158
Peter Damiani 47, 60–61
Peter of Florence, Cathar bishop 207, 208
Peter the Hermit 80
Peter, clerk of Le Mans 107–8, 190
Peter Lombard 122
Peter Martyr, St 238
Peter of Pavia, Cardinal of St Chryso-
gonus 76, 215–17, 257
Peter of Sicily, chronicler 150–51
Peter of Vaux de Cernay, chronicler 224
Peter the Venerable, abbot of Cluny 93,
102–3, 110, 248, 253, 274
Tractatus contra Petrobrusianos of 102–
106, 189, 299
Petracius 206
Philippa, countess of Foix 236
Philippopolis (Plovdiv) 149, 151
Phrygia 159
Piacenza 228, 237, 238 *see also* Councils
Pierleoni, family of *see* Jordan; Anacletus
II
Pierre Polha, Cathar bishop of Carcas-
sonne 212
pilgrimage 110, 122, 154, 191–2, 194
piph(i)les see Publicani
Pisa *see* Councils
Poitiers, bishop of 215 *see also* Gilbert
de la Porrée
Poor Catholics 230, 231
Poor Lombards 230, 231
Preslav, archbishopric of 155
Priscillianists 39, 67, 244
Psellus, Michael 167
Pseudo-Dionysus 147
Publicani 182–5, 191, 246, 247–8, 250,
251–2, 254, 258–61, 305

Quierzy, synod of 2

Rainhald von Dassel, archbishop of
Cologne 187
Rainier Sacchoni, inquisitor 177, 210,
222, 224, 247
Ralph of Coggeshall, chronicler 183

Ralph Glaber, chronicler 24, 35, 38, 39,
248
Ramihrdus, priest of Cambrai 62, 79,
260, 265, 266, 269
Ratherius of Verona 34, 42, 167
Ravenna 23–4
Raymond de Baimac 216, 257
Raymond de Casalis, Cathar bishop of
Agen 213
Raymond of Dourgne 234
Raymond V, count of Toulouse 212, 215–
217, 232–4, 247, 257
Raymond of Turenne 215
Reginald, bishop of Bath 215
relics 7, 43, 110, 152, 217, 277
Remigius of Auxerre 34
Rennes, bishops of *see* Marbod
Rhabanus Maurus 247
Rheims
archbishops of *see* Henry
heresy at 183–4, 247, 259, 273 *see also*
Councils
Rheineck, Otto, count of 169
Richard I, king of England 233
Robert of Arbrissel 50, 71, 77, 84–5, 89,
250, 265, 270, 279, 281
Robert the Bugger, inquisitor 185, 223
Robert d'Espernon, Cathar bishop of
France 242, 307
Robert II, count of Flanders 63
Robert of Molesme 74–5
Robert the Pious, king 25, 29, 252, 282
Roger I, bishop of Châlons-sur-Marne
36, 293
Roger II, bishop of Châlons-sur-Marne
36–7, 40, 251
Roger II, king of Sicily 123, 131, 132
Roger, vicomte of Béziers 234, 236, 255
Roger of Huntingdon, monk of St Albans
50, 270
Roland of Cremona 238
Romanus Lecapenus, Emperor 155
Rome, city of 38, 62, 63, 84, 85, 115–36
252, 271, 274
Rosans 102
Rosny-sur-Bois, serfs of 90
Rozzo, Benedetto 58
Rudolf of Ravensburg 119, 300
Rudolph of Zahringen, bishop of Liège
192
Russell, J. B. 292, 293, 304, 305, 311
Rustico, bishop of Orvieto 211

Saint-Félix-de-Caraman, Council and acts
of 212–15, 285–9
St Germain and St Vincent, Le Mans,
church of 88
St Gilles du Gard, basilica of 102, 110,
300
St Peter's, Rome 122